Real-Resumes For Supply & Logistics Jobs

...including real resumes used to change careers
and resumes used to gain federal employment

Anne McKinney, Editor

PREP PUBLISHING

FAYETTEVILLE, NC

PREP Publishing
1110 ½ Hay Street
Fayetteville, NC 28305
(910) 483-6611

Library of Congress Cataloging-in-Publication Data

Real-resumes for supply & logistics jobs : ...including resumes used to change careers and resumes used to gain federal employment / Anne McKinney {editor}.
        p. cm. -- (Real-resumes series)
   ISBN 978-1475099942; 1475099940   (trade paper)
   1. Resumes (Employment) 2. Business logistics. I. title: Real-resumes for supply and logistics jobs. II. McKinney, Anne, 1948- III. Series.

   HF5383.R3966 2006
   650.14'2--dc22   2006053544

Printed in the United States of America

PREP Publishing *Business and Career Series:*

RESUMES AND COVER LETTERS THAT HAVE WORKED, Revised Edition

RESUMES AND COVER LETTERS THAT HAVE WORKED FOR MILITARY PROFESSIONALS

GOVERNMENT JOB APPLICATIONS AND FEDERAL RESUMES

COVER LETTERS THAT BLOW DOORS OPEN

LETTERS FOR SPECIAL SITUATIONS

RESUMES AND COVER LETTERS FOR MANAGERS

REAL-RESUMES FOR COMPUTER JOBS

REAL-RESUMES FOR MEDICAL JOBS

REAL-RESUMES FOR FINANCIAL JOBS

REAL-RESUMES FOR TEACHERS

REAL-RESUMES FOR STUDENTS

REAL-RESUMES FOR CAREER CHANGERS

REAL-RESUMES FOR SALES

REAL ESSAYS FOR COLLEGE & GRADUATE SCHOOL

REAL-RESUMES FOR AVIATION & TRAVEL JOBS

REAL-RESUMES FOR POLICE, LAW ENFORCEMENT & SECURITY JOBS

REAL-RESUMES FOR SOCIAL WORK & COUNSELING JOBS

REAL-RESUMES FOR CONSTRUCTION JOBS

REAL-RESUMES FOR MANUFACTURING JOBS

REAL-RESUMES FOR RESTAURANT, FOOD SERVICE & HOTEL JOBS

REAL-RESUMES FOR MEDIA, NEWSPAPER, BROADCASTING & PUBLIC AFFAIRS JOBS

REAL-RESUMES FOR RETAILING, MODELING, FASHION & BEAUTY JOBS

REAL-RESUMES FOR HUMAN RESOURCES & PERSONNEL JOBS

REAL-RESUMES FOR NURSING JOBS

REAL-RESUMES FOR AUTO INDUSTRY JOBS

REAL RESUMIX & OTHER RESUMES FOR FEDERAL GOVERNMENT JOBS

REAL KSAS--KNOWLEDGE, SKILLS & ABILITIES--FOR GOVERNMENT JOBS

REAL BUSINESS PLANS & MARKETING TOOLS

REAL-RESUMES FOR ADMINISTRATIVE SUPPORT, OFFICE & SECRETARIAL JOBS

REAL-RESUMES FOR FIREFIGHTING JOBS

REAL-RESUMES FOR JOBS IN NONPROFIT ORGANIZATIONS

REAL-RESUMES FOR SPORTS INDUSTRY JOBS

REAL-RESUMES FOR LEGAL & PARALEGAL JOBS

REAL-RESUMES FOR ENGINEERING JOBS

REAL-RESUMES FOR U.S. POSTAL SERVICE JOBS

REAL-RESUMES FOR REAL ESTATE & PROPERTY MANAGEMENT JOBS

REAL-RESUMES FOR SUPPLY & LOGISTICS JOBS

Judeo-Christian Ethics Series:

SECOND TIME AROUND

BACK IN TIME

WHAT THE BIBLE SAYS ABOUT...Words that can lead to success and happiness

A GENTLE BREEZE FROM GOSSAMER WINGS

BIBLE STORIES FROM THE OLD TESTAMENT

Contents

Real-Resumes For
Supply & Logistics Jobs

Anne McKinney, Editor

A WORD FROM THE EDITOR:
ABOUT THE REAL-RESUMES SERIES

Welcome to the Real-Resumes Series. The Real-Resumes Series is a series of books which have been developed based on the experiences of real job hunters and which target specialized fields or types of resumes. As the editor of the series, I have carefully selected resumes and cover letters (with names and other key data disguised, of course) which have been used successfully in real job hunts. That's what we mean by "Real-Resumes." What you see in this book are *real* resumes and cover letters which helped real people get ahead in their careers.

The Real-Resumes Series is based on the work of the country's oldest resume-preparation company known as PREP Resumes. If you would like a free information packet describing the company's resume preparation services, call 910-483-6611 or write to PREP at 1110½ Hay Street, Fayetteville, NC 28305. If you have a job hunting experience you would like to share with our staff at the Real-Resumes Series, please contact us at preppub@aol.com or visit our website at www.prep-pub.com.

The resumes and cover letters in this book are designed to be of most value to people already in a job hunt or contemplating a career change. If we could give you one word of advice about your career, here's what we would say: Manage your career and don't stumble from job to job in an incoherent pattern. Try to find work that interests you, and then identify prosperous industries which need work performed of the type you want to do. Learn early in your working life that a great resume and cover letter can blow doors open for you and help you maximize your salary.

We hope the superior samples will help you manage your current job campaign and your career so that you will find work aligned to your career interests.

As the editor of this book, I would like to give you some tips on how to make the best use of the information you will find here. Because you are considering a career change, you already understand the concept of managing your career for maximum enjoyment and self-fulfillment. The purpose of this book is to provide expert tools and advice so that you *can* manage your career. Inside these pages you will find resumes and cover letters that will help you find not just a job but the type of work you want to do.

Overview of the Book

Every resume and cover letter in this book actually worked. And most of the resumes and cover letters have common features: most are one-page, most are in the chronological format, and most resumes are accompanied by a companion cover letter. In this section you will find helpful advice about job hunting. Step One begins with a discussion of why employers prefer the one-page, chronological resume. In Step Two you are introduced to the direct approach and to the proper format for a cover letter. In Step Three you learn the 14 main reasons why job hunters are not offered the jobs they want, and you learn the six key areas employers focus on when they interview you. Step Four gives nuts-and-bolts advice on how to handle the interview, send a follow-up letter after an interview, and negotiate your salary.

The cover letter plays such a critical role in a career change. You will learn from the experts how to format your cover letters and you will see suggested language to use in particular career-change situations. It has been said that "A picture is worth a thousand words" and, for that reason, you will see numerous examples of effective cover letters used by real individuals to change fields, functions, and industries.

The most important part of the book is the Real-Resumes section. Some of the individuals whose resumes and cover letters you see spent a lengthy career in an industry they loved. Then there are resumes and cover letters of people who wanted a change but who probably wanted to remain in their industry. Many of you will be especially interested by the resumes and cover letters of individuals who knew they definitely wanted a career change but had no idea what they wanted to do next. Other resumes and cover letters show individuals who knew they wanted to change fields and had a pretty good idea of what they wanted to do next.

Whatever your field, and whatever your circumstances, you'll find resumes and cover letters that will "show you the ropes" in terms of successfully changing jobs and switching careers.

Before you proceed further, think about why you picked up this book.
- Are you dissatisfied with the type of work you are now doing?
- Would you like to change careers, change companies, or change industries?
- Are you satisfied with your industry but not with your niche or function within it?
- Do you want to transfer your skills to a new product or service?
- Even if you have excelled in your field, have you "had enough"? Would you like the stimulation of a new challenge?
- Are you aware of the importance of a great cover letter but unsure of how to write one?
- Are you preparing to launch a second career after retirement?
- Have you been downsized, or do you anticipate becoming a victim of downsizing?
- Do you need expert advice on how to plan and implement a job campaign that will open the maximum number of doors?
- Do you want to make sure you handle an interview to your maximum advantage?

Introduction:
The Art of
Changing
Jobs...
and Finding
New Careers

- Would you like to master the techniques of negotiating salary and benefits?
- Do you want to learn the secrets and shortcuts of professional resume writers?

Using the Direct Approach

As you consider the possibility of a job hunt or career change, you need to be aware that most people end up having at least three distinctly different careers in their working lifetimes, and often those careers are different from each other. Yet people usually stumble through each job campaign, unsure of what they should be doing. Whether you find yourself voluntarily or unexpectedly in a job hunt, the direct approach is the job hunting strategy most likely to yield a full-time permanent job. The direct approach is an active, take-the-initiative style of job hunting in which you choose your next employer rather than relying on responding to ads, using employment agencies, or depending on other methods of finding jobs. You will learn how to use the direct approach in this book, and you will see that an effective cover letter is a critical ingredient in using the direct approach.

The "direct approach" is the style of job hunting most likely to yield the maximum number of job interviews.

Lack of Industry Experience Not a Major Barrier to Entering New Field

"Lack of experience" is often the last reason people are not offered jobs, according to the companies who do the hiring. If you are changing careers, you will be glad to learn that experienced professionals often are selling "potential" rather than experience in a job hunt. Companies look for personal qualities that they know tend to be present in their most effective professionals, such as communication skills, initiative, persistence, organizational and time management skills, and creativity. Frequently companies are trying to discover "personality type," "talent," "ability," "aptitude," and "potential" rather than seeking actual hands-on experience, so your resume should be designed to aggressively present your accomplishments. Attitude, enthusiasm, personality, and a track record of achievements in any type of work are the primary "indicators of success" which employers are seeking, and you will see numerous examples in this book of resumes written in an all-purpose fashion so that the professional can approach various industries and companies.

The Art of Using References in a Job Hunt

You probably already know that you need to provide references during a job hunt, but you may not be sure of how and when to use references for maximum advantage. You can use references very creatively during a job hunt to call attention to your strengths and make yourself "stand out." Your references will rarely get you a job, no matter how impressive the names, but the way you use references can boost the employer's confidence in you and lead to a job offer in the least time.

Using references in a skillful fashion in your job hunt will inspire confidence in prospective employers and help you "close the sale" after interviews.

You should ask from three to five people, including people who have supervised you, if you can use them as a reference during your job hunt. You may not be able to ask your current boss since your job hunt is probably confidential.

A common question in resume preparation is: "Do I need to put my references on my resume?" No, you don't. Even if you create a references page at the same time you prepare your resume, you don't need to mail, e-mail, or fax your references page with the resume and cover letter. Usually the potential employer is not interested in references until he meets you, so the earliest you need to have references ready is at the first interview. Obviously there are exceptions to this standard rule of thumb; sometimes an ad will ask you to send references with your first response. Wait until the employer requests references before providing them.

An excellent attention-getting technique is to take to the first interview not just a page of references (giving names, addresses, and telephone numbers) but an actual letter of reference written by someone who knows you well and who preferably has supervised or employed you. A professional way to close the first interview is to thank the interviewer, shake his or her hand, and then say you'd like to give him or her a copy of a letter of reference from a previous employer. Hopefully you already made a good impression during the interview, but you'll "close the sale" in a dynamic fashion if you leave a letter praising you and your accomplishments. For that reason, it's a good idea to ask supervisors during your final weeks in a job if they will provide you with a written letter of recommendation which you can use in future job hunts. Most employers will oblige, and you will have a letter that has a useful "shelf life" of many years. Such a letter often gives the prospective employer enough confidence in his opinion of you that he may forego checking out other references and decide to offer you the job on the spot or in the next few days.

With regard to references, it's best to provide the names and addresses of people who have supervised you or observed you in a work situation.

Whom should you ask to serve as references? References should be people who have known or supervised you in a professional, academic, or work situation. References with big titles, like school superintendent or congressman, are fine, but remind busy people when you get to the interview stage that they may be contacted soon. Make sure the busy official recognizes your name and has instant positive recall of you! If you're asked to provide references on a formal company application, you can simply transcribe names from your references list. In summary, follow this rule in using references: If you've got them, flaunt them! If you've obtained well-written letters of reference, make sure you find a polite way to push those references under the nose of the interviewer so he or she can hear someone other than you describing your strengths. Your references probably won't ever get you a job, but glowing letters of reference can give you credibility and visibility that can make you stand out among candidates with similar credentials and potential!

The approach taken by this book is to (1) help you master the proven best techniques of conducting a job hunt and (2) show you how to stand out in a job hunt through your resume, cover letter, interviewing skills, as well as the way in which you present your references and follow up on interviews. Now, the best way to "get in the mood" for writing your own resume and cover letter is to select samples from the Table of Contents that interest you and then read them. A great resume is a "photograph," usually on one page, of an individual. If you wish to seek professional advice in preparing your resume, you may contact one of the professional writers at Professional Resume & Employment Publishing (PREP) for a brief free consultation by calling 1-910-483-6611.

Part One: Some Advice About Your Job Hunt

What if you don't know what you want to do?

Your job hunt will be more comfortable if you can figure out what type of work you want to do. But you are not alone if you have no idea what you want to do next! You may have knowledge and skills in certain areas but want to get into another type of work. What *The Wall Street Journal* has discovered in its research on careers is that most of us end up having at least three distinctly different careers in our working lives; it seems that, even if we really like a particular kind of activity, twenty years of doing it is enough for most of us and we want to move on to something else!

That's why we strongly believe that you need to spend some time figuring out *what interests you* rather than taking an inventory of the skills you have. You may have skills that you simply don't want to use, but if you can build your career on the things that interest you, you will be more likely to be happy and satisfied in your job. Realize, too, that interests can change over time; the activities that interest you now may not be the ones that interested you years ago. For example, some professionals may decide that they've had enough of retail sales and want a job selling another product or service, even though they have earned a reputation for being an excellent retail manager. We strongly believe that interests rather than skills should be the determining factor in deciding what types of jobs you want to apply for and what directions you explore in your job hunt. Obviously one cannot be a lawyer without a law degree or a secretary without secretarial skills; but a professional can embark on a next career as a financial consultant, property manager, plant manager, production supervisor, retail manager, or other occupation if he/she has a strong interest in that type of work and can provide a resume that clearly demonstrates past excellent performance in *any* field and *potential* to excel in another field. As you will see later in this book, "lack of exact experience" is the last reason why people are turned down for the jobs they apply for.

How can you have a resume prepared if you don't know what you want to do?

You may be wondering how you can have a resume prepared if you don't know what you want to do next. The approach to resume writing which PREP, the country's oldest resume-preparation company, has used successfully for many years is to develop an "all-purpose" resume that translates your skills, experience, and accomplishments into language employers can understand. What most people need in a job hunt is a versatile resume that will allow them to apply for numerous types of jobs. For example, you may want to apply for a job in pharmaceutical sales but you may also want to have a resume that will be versatile enough for you to apply for jobs in the construction, financial services, or automotive industries.

Based on more than 20 years of serving job hunters, we at PREP have found that your best approach to job hunting is **an all-purpose resume** and **specific cover letters tailored to specific fields** rather than using the approach of trying to create different resumes for every job. If you are remaining in your field, you may not even need more than one "all-purpose" cover letter, although the cover letter rather than the resume is the place to communicate your interest in a narrow or specific field. An all-purpose resume and cover letter that translate your experience and accomplishments into plain English are the tools that will maximize the number of doors which open for you while permitting you to "fish" in the widest range of job areas.

Figure out what interests you and you will hold the key to a successful job hunt and working career. (And be prepared for your interests to change over time!)

"Lack of exact experience" is the last reason people are turned down for the jobs for which they apply.

Your resume will provide the script for your job interview.
When you get down to it, your resume has a simple job to do: Its purpose is to blow as many doors open as possible and to make as many people as possible want to meet you. So a well-written resume that really "sells" you is a key that will create opportunities for you in a job hunt.

This statistic explains why: The typical newspaper advertisement for a job opening receives more than 245 replies. And normally only 10 or 12 will be invited to an interview.

But here's another purpose of the resume: it provides the "script" the employer uses when he interviews you. If your resume has been written in such a way that your strengths and achievements are revealed, that's what you'll end up talking about at the job interview. Since the resume will govern what you get asked about at your interviews, you can't overestimate the importance of making sure your resume makes you look and sound as good as you are.

> Your resume is the "script" for your job interviews. Make sure you put on your resume what you want to talk about or be asked about at the job interview.

So what is a "good" resume?
Very literally, your resume should motivate the person reading it to dial the phone number or e-mail the screen name you have put on the resume. When you are relocating, you should put a local phone number on your resume if your physical address is several states away; employers are more likely to dial a local telephone number than a long-distance number when they're looking for potential employees.

If you have a resume already, look at it objectively. Is it a limp, colorless "laundry list" of your job titles and duties? Or does it "paint a picture" of your skills, abilities, and accomplishments in a way that would make someone want to meet you? Can people understand what you're saying? If you are attempting to change fields or industries, can potential employers see that your skills and knowledge are transferable to other environments? For example, have you described accomplishments which reveal your problem-solving abilities or communication skills?

> The one-page resume in chronological format is the format preferred by most employers.

How long should your resume be?
One page, maybe two. Usually only people in the academic community have a resume (which they usually call a *curriculum vitae*) longer than one or two pages. Remember that your resume is almost always accompanied by a cover letter, and a potential employer does not want to read more than two or three pages about a total stranger in order to decide if he wants to meet that person! Besides, don't forget that the more you tell someone about yourself, the more opportunity you are providing for the employer to screen you out at the "first-cut" stage. A resume should be concise and exciting and designed to make the reader want to meet you in person!

Should resumes be functional or chronological?
Employers almost always prefer a chronological resume; in other words, an employer will find a resume easier to read if it is immediately apparent what your current or most recent job is, what you did before that, and so forth, in reverse chronological order. A resume that goes back in detail for the last ten years of employment will generally satisfy the employer's curiosity about your background. Employment more than ten years old can be shown even more briefly in an "Other Experience" section at the end of your "Experience" section. Remember that your intention is not to tell everything you've done but to "hit the high points" and especially impress the employer with what you learned, contributed, or accomplished in each job you describe.

Once you get your resume, what do you do with it?
You will be using your resume to answer ads, as a tool to use in talking with friends and relatives about your job search, and, most importantly, in using the "direct approach" described in this book.

When you mail, e-mail, or fax your resume, always send a "cover letter."
A "cover letter," sometimes called a "resume letter" or "letter of interest," is a letter that accompanies and introduces your resume. Your cover letter is a way of personalizing the resume by sending it to the specific person you think you might want to work for at each company. Your cover letter should contain a few highlights from your resume— just enough to make someone want to meet you. Cover letters should always be typed or word processed on a computer—never handwritten.

Never e-mail, mail, or fax your resume without a cover letter.

1. Learn the art of answering ads.
There is an "art," part of which can be learned, in using your "bestselling" resume to reply to advertisements.

Sometimes an exciting job lurks behind a boring ad that someone dictated in a hurry, so reply to any ad that interests you. Don't worry that you aren't "25 years old with an MBA" like the ad asks for. Employers will always make compromises in their requirements if they think you're the "best fit" overall.

What about ads that ask for "salary requirements?"
What if the ad you're answering asks for "salary requirements?" The first rule is to avoid committing yourself in writing at that point to a specific salary. You don't want to "lock yourself in."

There are two ways to handle the ad that asks for "salary requirements."
First, you can ignore that part of the ad and accompany your resume with a cover letter that focuses on "selling" you, your abilities, and even some of your philosophy about work or your field. You may include a sentence in your cover letter like this: "I can provide excellent personal and professional references at your request, and I would be delighted to share the private details of my salary history with you in person."

What if the ad asks for your "salary requirements?"

Second, if you feel you must give some kind of number, just state a range in your cover letter that includes your medical, dental, other benefits, and expected bonuses. You might state, for example, "My current compensation, including benefits and bonuses, is in the range of $30,000-$40,000."

Analyze the ad and "tailor" yourself to it.
When you're replying to ads, a finely tailored cover letter is an important tool in getting your resume noticed and read. On the next page is a cover letter which has been "tailored to fit" a specific ad. Notice the "art" used by PREP writers of analyzing the ad's main requirements and then writing the letter so that the person's background, work habits, and interests seem "tailor-made" to the company's needs. Use this cover letter as a model when you prepare your own reply to ads.

Date

Exact Name of Person
Title or Position
Name of Company
Address
City, State, Zip

Dear Exact Name of Person: (or Dear Sir or Madam if answering a blind ad.)

With the enclosed resume, I would like to make you aware of my interest in exploring employment opportunities with your organization and introduce you to my background and credentials related to supply chain management.

Employers are trying to identify the individual who wants the job they are filling. Don't be afraid to express your enthusiasm in the cover letter!

As you will see from my resume, I served my country with distinction and was the recipient of numerous medals and honors praising my management abilities and technical expertise related to supply management. In my most recent position as Chief of Supply Operations, I organized the provision of all types of supplies and services for hundreds of people in worldwide projects. In my previous position, I was handpicked as Supply Branch Chief and Senior Logistics Consultant. In that capacity, I provided oversight for supply management systems of 75 different organizations and led them in activities which included reducing shrinkage, improving ordering and shipping time, and resourcefully utilizing excess equipment. As the "resident expert instructor" on automated systems for supply chain management, I established a new automated system for tracking the ordering, storage, and inventory control of perishable and non-perishable items.

While becoming one of the U.S. Army's foremost experts on supply management, I gained a reputation as an individual of "unquestionable integrity and loyalty." I believe in leadership by example, and I have learned how to motivate personnel to aim for and achieve the highest professional standards. I have managed dozens of people, controlled budgets of more than $400,000, and accounted for millions of dollars in assets. I have managed the supply chain for all types of supplies including perishable and grocery products, engineering and repair parts, telecommunications items, vehicle parts and automotive equipment, as well as computers and office supplies. In every job I have held, I have made major contributions to productivity. For example, as Logistics Branch Manager for an organization supporting NATO activities, I reduced a spare parts backlog from 635 parts to less then 44 monthly while also instituting a logistical accounting system to monitor transactions.

I have received the highest evaluations of my ability to communicate effectively with others, and I have trained hundreds of individuals in automated inventory control systems and supply management.

If you can use my expertise related to shipping and receiving, expediting and dispatching, logistics and transportation, as well as supply chain management, I hope you will contact me to suggest a time when we might meet to discuss your needs.

Yours sincerely,

Noel Turpin

2. Talk to friends and relatives.

Don't be shy about telling your friends and relatives the kind of job you're looking for. Looking for the job you want involves using your network of contacts, so tell people what you're looking for. They may be able to make introductions and help set up interviews.

About 25% of all interviews are set up through "who you know," so don't ignore this approach.

3. Finally, and most importantly, use the "direct approach."

More than 50% of all job interviews are set up by the "direct approach." That means you actually mail, e-mail, or fax a resume and a cover letter to a company you think might be interesting to work for.

The "direct approach" is a strategy in which you choose your next employer.

To whom do you write?

In general, you should write directly to the *exact name* of the person who would be hiring you: say, the vice-president of marketing or data processing. If you're in doubt about to whom to address the letter, address it to the president by name and he or she will make sure it gets forwarded to the right person within the company who has hiring authority in your area.

How do you find the names of potential employers?

You're not alone if you feel that the biggest problem in your job search is finding the right names at the companies you want to contact. But you can usually figure out the names of companies you want to approach by deciding first if your job hunt is primarily geography-driven or industry-driven.

In a **geography-driven job hunt,** you could select a list of, say, 50 companies you want to contact **by location** from the lists that the U.S. Chambers of Commerce publish yearly of their "major area employers." There are hundreds of local Chambers of Commerce across America, and most of them will have an 800 number which you can find through 1-800-555-1212. If you and your family think Atlanta, Dallas, Ft. Lauderdale, and Virginia Beach might be nice places to live, for example, you could contact the Chamber of Commerce in those cities and ask how you can obtain a copy of their list of major employers. Your nearest library will have the book which lists the addresses of all chambers.

In an **industry-driven job hunt,** and if you are willing to relocate, you will be identifying the companies which you find most attractive in the industry in which you want to work. When you select a list of companies to contact **by industry,** you can find the right person to write and the address of firms by industrial category in *Standard and Poor's, Moody's,* and other excellent books in public libraries. Many Web sites also provide contact information.

Many people feel it's a good investment to actually call the company to either find out or double-check the name of the person to whom they want to send a resume and cover letter. It's important to do as much as you feasibly can to assure that the letter gets to the right person in the company.

On-line research will be the best way for many people to locate organizations to which they wish to send their resume. It is outside the scope of this book to teach Internet research skills, but librarians are often useful in this area.

What's the correct way to follow up on a resume you send?

There is a polite way to be aggressively interested in a company during your job hunt. It is ideal to end the cover letter accompanying your resume by saying, "I hope you'll welcome my call next week when I try to arrange a brief meeting at your convenience to discuss your current and future needs and how I might serve them." Keep it low key, and just ask for a "brief meeting," not an interview. Employers want people who show a determined interest in working with them, so don't be shy about following up on the resume and cover letter you've mailed.

STEP THREE: Preparing for Interviews

But a resume and cover letter by themselves can't get you the job you want. You need to "prep" yourself before the interview. Step Three in your job campaign is "Preparing for Interviews." First, let's look at interviewing from the hiring organization's point of view.

What are the biggest "turnoffs" for potential employers?

One of the ways to help yourself perform well at an interview is to look at the main reasons why organizations *don't* hire the people they interview, according to those who do the interviewing.

Notice that "lack of appropriate background" (or lack of experience) is the *last* reason for not being offered the job.

The 14 Most Common Reasons Job Hunters Are Not Offered Jobs (according to the companies who do the interviewing and hiring):

1. Low level of accomplishment
2. Poor attitude, lack of self-confidence
3. Lack of goals/objectives
4. Lack of enthusiasm
5. Lack of interest in the company's business
6. Inability to sell or express yourself
7. Unrealistic salary demands
8. Poor appearance
9. Lack of maturity, no leadership potential
10. Lack of extracurricular activities
11. Lack of preparation for the interview, no knowledge about company
12. Objecting to travel
13. Excessive interest in security and benefits
14. Inappropriate background

Department of Labor studies have proven that smart, "prepared" job hunters can increase their beginning salary while getting a job in *half* the time it normally takes. (4½ months is the average national length of a job search.) Here, from PREP, are some questions that can prepare you to find a job faster.

Are you in the "right" frame of mind?

It seems unfair that we have to look for a job just when we're lowest in morale. Don't worry *too* much if you're nervous before interviews. You're supposed to be a little nervous, especially if the job means a lot to you. But the best way to kill unnecessary

It pays to be aware of the 14 most common pitfalls for job hunters.

fears about job hunting is through 1) making sure you have a great resume and 2) preparing yourself for the interview. Here are three main areas you need to think about before each interview.

Do you know what the company does?

Don't walk into an interview giving the impression that, "If this is Tuesday, this must be General Motors."

Research the company before you go to interviews.

Find out before the interview what the company's main product or service is. Where is the company heading? Is it in a "growth" or declining industry? (Answers to these questions may influence whether or not you want to work there!)

Information about what the company does is in annual reports, in newspaper and magazine articles, and on the Internet. If you're not yet skilled at Internet research, just visit your nearest library and ask the reference librarian to guide you to printed materials on the company.

Do you know what you want to do for the company?

Before the interview, try to decide how you see yourself fitting into the company. Remember, "lack of exact background" the company wants is usually the last reason people are not offered jobs.

Understand before you go to each interview that the burden will be on you to "sell" the interviewer on why you're the best person for the job and the company.

How will you answer the critical interview questions?

Anticipate the questions you will be asked at the interview, and prepare your responses in advance.

Put yourself in the interviewer's position and think about the questions you're most likely to be asked. Here are some of the most commonly asked interview questions:

Q: *"What are your greatest strengths?"*
A: Don't say you've never thought about it! Go into an interview knowing the three main impressions you want to leave about yourself, such as "I'm hard-working, loyal, and an imaginative cost-cutter."

Q: *"What are your greatest weaknesses?"*
A: Don't confess that you're lazy or have trouble meeting deadlines! Confessing that you tend to be a "workaholic" or "tend to be a perfectionist and sometimes get frustrated when others don't share my high standards" will make your prospective employer see a "weakness" that he likes. Name a weakness that your interviewer will perceive as a strength.

Q: *"What are your long-range goals?"*
A: If you're interviewing with Microsoft, don't say you want to work for IBM in five years! Say your long-range goal is to be *with* the company, contributing to its goals and success.

Q: *"What motivates you to do your best work?"*
A: Don't get dollar signs in your eyes here! "A challenge" is not a bad answer, but it's a little cliched. Saying something like "troubleshooting" or "solving a tough problem" is more interesting and specific. Give an example if you can.

Q: "What do you know about this organization?"

A: Don't say you never heard of it until they asked you to the interview! Name an interesting, positive thing you learned about the company recently from your research. Remember, company executives can sometimes feel rather "maternal" about the company they serve. Don't get onto a negative area of the company if you can think of positive facts you can bring up. Of course, if you learned in your research that the company's sales seem to be taking a nose-dive, or that the company president is being prosecuted for taking bribes, you might politely ask your interviewer to tell you something that could help you better understand what you've been reading. Those are the kinds of company facts that can help you determine whether or not you want to work there.

Q: "Why should I hire you?"

A: "I'm unemployed and available" is the wrong answer here! Get back to your strengths and say that you believe the organization could benefit by a loyal, hard-working cost-cutter like yourself.

In conclusion, you should decide in advance, before you go to the interview, how you will answer each of these commonly asked questions. Have some practice interviews with a friend to role-play and build your confidence.

> Go to an interview prepared to tell the company why it should hire you.

STEP FOUR: Handling the Interview and Negotiating Salary

Now you're ready for Step Four: actually handling the interview successfully and effectively. Remember, the purpose of an interview is to get a job offer.

> A smile at an interview makes the employer perceive of you as intelligent!

Eight "do's" for the interview

According to leading U.S. companies, there are eight key areas in interviewing success. You can fail at an interview if you mishandle just one area.

1. Do wear appropriate clothes.

You can never go wrong by wearing a suit to an interview.

2. Do be well groomed.

Don't overlook the obvious things like having clean hair, clothes, and fingernails for the interview.

3. Do give a firm handshake.

You'll have to shake hands twice in most interviews: first, before you sit down, and second, when you leave the interview. Limp handshakes turn most people off.

4. Do smile and show a sense of humor.

Interviewers are looking for people who would be nice to work with, so don't be so somber that you don't smile. In fact, research shows that people who smile at interviews are perceived as more intelligent. So, smile!

5. Do be enthusiastic.

Employers say they are "turned off" by lifeless, unenthusiastic job hunters who show no special interest in that company. The best way to show some enthusiasm for the employer's operation is to find out about the business beforehand.

6. Do show you are flexible and adaptable.

An employer is looking for someone who can contribute to his organization in a flexible, adaptable way. No matter what skills and training you have, employers know every new employee must go through initiation and training on the company's turf. Certainly show pride in your past accomplishments in a specific, factual way ("I saved my last employer $50.00 a week by a new cost-cutting measure I developed"). But don't come across as though there's nothing about the job you couldn't easily handle.

7. Do ask intelligent questions about the employer's business.

An employer is hiring someone because of certain business needs. Show interest in those needs. Asking questions to get a better idea of the employer's needs will help you "stand out" from other candidates interviewing for the job.

8. Do "take charge" when the interviewer "falls down" on the job.

Go into every interview knowing the three or four points about yourself you want the interviewer to remember. And be prepared to take an active part in leading the discussion if the interviewer's "canned approach" does not permit you to display your "strong suit." You can't always depend on the interviewer's asking you the "right" questions so you can stress your strengths and accomplishments.

Employers are seeking people with good attitudes whom they can train and coach to do things their way.

An important "don't": Don't ask questions about salary or benefits at the first interview. Employers don't take warmly to people who look at their organization as just a place to satisfy salary and benefit needs. Don't risk making a negative impression by appearing greedy or self-serving. The place to discuss salary and benefits is normally at the second interview, and the employer will bring it up. Then you can ask questions without appearing excessively interested in what the organization can do for you.

Now...negotiating your salary

Even if an ad requests that you communicate your "salary requirement" or "salary history," you should avoid providing those numbers in your initial cover letter. You can usually say something like this: "I would be delighted to discuss the private details of my salary history with you in person."

Once you're at the interview, you must avoid even appearing *interested* in salary before you are offered the job. Make sure you've "sold" yourself before talking salary. First show you're the "best fit" for the employer and then you'll be in a stronger position from which to negotiate salary. **Never** bring up the subject of salary yourself. Employers say there's no way you can avoid looking greedy if you bring up the issue of salary and benefits before the company has identified you as its "best fit."

Don't appear excessively interested in salary and benefits at the interview.

Interviewers sometimes throw out a salary figure at the first interview to see if you'll accept it. You may not want to commit yourself if you think you will be able to negotiate a better deal later on. Get back to finding out more about the job. This lets the interviewer know you're interested primarily in the job and not the salary.

When the organization brings up salary, it may say something like this: "Well, Mary, we think you'd make a good candidate for this job. What kind of salary are we talking about?" You may not want to name a number here, either. Give the ball back to the interviewer. Act as though you hadn't given the subject of salary much thought and respond something like this: "Ah, Mr. Jones, I wonder if you'd be kind enough to tell me what salary you had in mind when you advertised the job?" Or ... "What is the range you have in mind?"

Don't worry, if the interviewer names a figure that you think is too low, you can say so without turning down the job or locking yourself into a rigid position. The point here is to negotiate for yourself as well as you can. You might reply to a number named by the interviewer that you think is low by saying something like this: "Well, Mr. Lee, the job interests me very much, and I think I'd certainly enjoy working with you. But, frankly, I was thinking of something a little higher than that." That leaves the ball in your interviewer's court again, and you haven't turned down the job either, in case it turns out that the interviewer can't increase the offer and you still want the job.

Salary negotiation can be tricky.

Last, send a follow-up letter.

Mail, e-mail, or fax a letter right after the interview telling your interviewer you enjoyed the meeting and are certain (if you are) that you are the "best fit" for the job. The people interviewing you will probably have an attitude described as either "professionally loyal" to their companies, or "maternal and proprietary" if the interviewer also owns the company. In either case, they are looking for people who want to work for *that* company in particular. The follow-up letter you send might be just the deciding factor in your favor if the employer is trying to choose between you and someone else. You will see an example of a follow-up letter on page 16.

A follow-up letter can help the employer choose between you and another qualified candidate.

A cover letter is an essential part of a job hunt or career change.

Many people are aware of the importance of having a great resume, but most people in a job hunt don't realize just how important a cover letter can be. The purpose of the cover letter, sometimes called a **"letter of interest,"** is to introduce your resume to prospective employers. The cover letter is often the critical ingredient in a job hunt because the cover letter allows you to say a lot of things that just don't "fit" on the resume. For example, you can emphasize your commitment to a new field and stress your related talents. The cover letter also gives you a chance to stress outstanding character and personal values. On the next two pages you will see examples of very effective cover letters.

A cover letter is an essential part of a career change.

Please do not attempt to implement a career change without a cover letter. A cover letter is the first impression of you, and you can influence the way an employer views you by the language and style of your letter.

Special help for those in career change

We want to emphasize again that, especially in a career change, the cover letter is very important and can help you "build a bridge" to a new career. A creative and appealing cover letter can begin the process of encouraging the potential employer to imagine you in an industry other than the one in which you have worked. As a special help to those in career change, there are resumes and cover letters included in this book which show valuable techniques and tips you should use when changing fields or industries.

**Addressing the Cover
Letter:** Get the exact
name of the person to
whom you are writing. This
makes your approach
personal.

First Paragraph: This
explains why you are
writing.

Second Paragraph: You
have a chance to talk
about whatever you feel is
your most distinguishing
feature.

Third Paragraph: You
bring up your next most
distinguishing qualities and
try to
sell yourself.

Fourth Paragraph: Here
you have another
opportunity to reveal
qualities or achievements
which will impress your
future employer.

Final Paragraph: He asks
the employer to contact
him. Make sure your
reader knows what the
"next step" is.

**Alternate Final
Paragraph:** It's more
aggressive (but not too
aggressive) to let the
employer know that you
will be calling him or her.
(You can alter the
sentence that says "I hope
you will contact me…" to
say "I hope you will
welcome my call soon…")

Date

Exact Name of Person
Title or Position
Name of Company
Address (number and street)
Address (city, state, and zip)

Dear Exact Name of Person: (or Sir or Madam if answering a blind ad.)

With the enclosed resume, I would like to express my interest in exploring employment opportunities with your organization. While serving my country in the U.S. Army, I have risen to the rank of Major while earning respect as an astute strategic planner, international diplomat, logistician, and manager.

Education in international relations and business management

In spite of numerous deployments as a military officer, I have earned a Master's degree in International Relations as well as a B.S. degree in Business Management. I have also excelled in numerous graduate-level programs sponsored by the U.S. Army which expanded my international knowledge of Asia, Africa, Europe, Latin America, and the Middle East.

Experience as an international diplomat

In my current position in Korea, I am the acknowledged expert on Civil Affairs in the Korean theater, and I have excelled as the single U.S. planner on a combined Korean-U.S. staff. Through my leadership, we modernized an outdated Civil Affairs structure as we developed the first Civil-Military operations framework for complex humanitarian emergencies. In my previous job as a Civil Affairs Officer, I managed a $13 million budget as I also served as Deputy Executive Officer of an organization with 3,981 employees. Evaluated as a "gifted, visionary leader," I personally developed a new concept which was implemented Armywide.

Extensive management and supervisory experience

I have also excelled in challenging line management positions in high-tempo environments. As a Company Commander, I served as the "chief executive officer" of the largest maintenance and maintenance supply company in the Pacific. In that capacity, I supervised 230 soldiers while managing a budget of $1.6 million. In a prior assignment as a Maintenance Officer and Logistics Planner, I performed multifunctional logistics planning for units throughout the world and earned respect for my ability to quickly analyze a problem and determine the best solution.

With a Top Secret/SCI security clearance, I can provide outstanding references at the appropriate time. Although I have been recommended for promotion to Lieutenant Colonel and strongly encouraged to remain in military service, I have decided to leave the Army and enter the civilian work force. I hope you will contact me to suggest a time when we might meet to discuss your needs and goals.

Sincerely,

James Ray Jarvis

Date

Exact Name of Person
Exact Title
Exact Name of Company
Address
City, State, Zip

Dear Exact Name of Person (or Dear Sir or Madam if answering a blind ad):

With the enclosed resume, I would like to make you aware of my interest in exploring employment opportunities with your organization. I am responding to your advertisement for a Distribution Services Manager.

Extensive logistics management skills

Promoted rapidly to the rank of Captain, I was handpicked for jobs normally held by someone of more senior rank, and I proved my ability to manage multiple complex projects simultaneously. After completing a one-year graduate-level program called the Army Logistics Management College, I was specially selected for an important logistics planning/management job. I currently develop and implement plans to support logistical operations in 25 countries including Iraq, Afghanistan, Horn of Africa, and the entire Eastern Asia area. Logistical plans that I develop support the needs of 250,000 people and, on a daily basis, I prepare and deliver PowerPoint briefings on logistical matters for VIPs such the Secretary of Defense, U.S. Senators, presidents, ambassadors, and military executives. In my prior position, I utilized my training in transportation operations, HazMat procedures, and military contracting in order to improve organizational effectiveness, reduce costs, and boost morale.

Knowledge of logistics, transportation, and hazardous materials

In previous work as a Senior Logistics Officer, I planned and coordinated logistics support for thousands of military professionals involved in activities in Nepal, Sri Lanka, Cambodia, and other places in the Pacific. Trained in HazMat, I have certified HazMat materials transported internationally by air, sea, and land. As a military officer, I have become known for integrity and reliability, and I have been entrusted with extensive purchasing authority as well as responsibility for the use of government credit cards. I have been entrusted with one of our country's highest security clearances—Top Secret.

Although I have excelled as a military officer, I have decided to explore opportunities in the civilian world where I will be able to use my vast experience in logistics and transportation management as well as my B.S. in Business Administration and Economics. I can provide outstanding references at the appropriate time, and I would enjoy an opportunity to meet with you in person to discuss your current or future needs.

Yours sincerely,

Asacia Winkle

This accomplished professional is responding to an advertisement. He analyzed the job vacancy opening very closely and he has made sure that he has tailored his letter of interest to the areas mentioned in the vacancy announcement.

Date

Exact Name of Person
Title or Position
Name of Company
Address (number and street)
Address (city, state, and zip)

Dear Exact Name:

A great follow-up letter
can motivate the
employer
to make the job offer,
and the salary offer may
be influenced by the
style and tone of your
follow-up
letter, too!

I am writing to express my appreciation for the time you spent with me on December 9, and I want to let you know that I am sincerely interested in the position of Senior Supply Manager which we discussed.

I feel confident that I could skillfully interact with your staff, and I would cheerfully relocate to Tennessee, as we discussed.

As you described to me what you are looking for in the person who fills this position, I had a sense of "déjà vu" because my current employer was in a similar position when I went to work for them. The general manager needed someone to come in and be his "right arm" and take on an increasing amount of his management responsibilities so that he could be freed up to do other things. I have played a key role in the growth and success of the organization, and my supervisor has come to depend on my sound advice as much as well as my proven ability to "cut through" huge volumes of work efficiently and accurately. Since this is one of the busiest times of the year for my employer, I feel that I could not leave during that time. I could certainly make myself available by mid-January.

It would be a pleasure to work for your organization, and I am confident that I could contribute significantly through my strong qualities of loyalty, reliability, and trustworthiness. I am confident that I could quickly learn your style and procedures, and I would welcome being trained to do things your way.

Yours sincerely,

Jacob Evangelisto

PART TWO:
Real-Resumes for Supply & Logistics Jobs

In this section, you will find resumes and cover letters of professionals seeking employment, or already employed, in the supply and logistics world. How do these individuals differ from other job hunters? Why should there be a book dedicated to people seeking jobs related to supply and logistics? Based on more than 20 years of experience in working with job hunters, this editor is convinced that resumes and cover letters which "speak the lingo" of the field you wish to enter will communicate more effectively than language which is not industry-specific. This book is designed to help people (1) who are seeking to prepare their own resumes and (2) who wish to use as models "real" resumes of individuals who have successfully launched careers in supply and logistics organizations or advanced in those organizations. You will see a wide range of experience levels reflected in the resumes in this book. Some of the resumes and cover letters were used by individuals seeking to enter the field; others were used successfully by senior professionals to advance in the field.

Newcomers to an industry sometimes have advantages over more experienced professionals. In a job hunt, junior professionals can have an advantage over their more experienced counterparts. Prospective employers often view the less experienced workers as "more trainable" and "more coachable" than their seniors. This means that the mature professional who has already excelled in a first career can, with credibility, "change careers" and transfer skills to other industries.

Newcomers to the field may have disadvantages compared to their seniors. Almost by definition, the inexperienced professional—the young person who has recently entered the job market, or the individual who has recently received respected certifications—is less tested and less experienced than senior managers, so the resume and cover letter of the inexperienced professional may often have to "sell" his or her potential to do something he or she has never done before. Lack of experience in the field she wants to enter can be a stumbling block to the junior employee, but remember that many employers believe that someone who has excelled in anything—academics, for example—can excel in many other fields.

Some advice to inexperienced professionals...
If senior professionals could give junior professionals a piece of advice about careers, here's what they would say: Manage your career and don't stumble from job to job in an incoherent pattern. Try to find work that interests you, and then identify prosperous industries which need work performed of the type you want to do. Learn early in your working life that a great resume and cover letter can blow doors open for you and help you maximize your salary.

Date

Exact Name of Person
Title or Position
Name of Company
Address
City, State, Zip

ASSISTANT SHIPMENT MANAGER

Dear Exact Name of Person: (or Dear Sir or Madam if answering a blind ad.)

I would appreciate an opportunity to talk with you soon about how I could benefit your organization through my background in logistics, project management, inventory control, and hazardous cargo operations, as well as my proven expertise in training and motivating employees.

As you will see from my resume, in my current position as an Assistant Shipment Manager, I prepare and coordinate the movement of general and hazardous cargo to both domestic and overseas locations via military and commercial carriers. I am knowledgeable of a wide range of freight documentation, paperwork, and systems, including the United Parcel Service Worldship documentation service, Government Bills of Lading, and hazardous material specifications.

Throughout my career I have gained a reputation as a "go-getter" who can be counted on to set high performance standards and guide employees to achieve their own high goals. I feel that my ability to respond to rapidly changing circumstances calmly and with control is one of my greatest strengths. I have been recognized by top-level management for my efficiency and personal accountability.

I hope you will call or write soon to suggest a time convenient for us to meet and discuss your current and future needs and how I might serve them. Thank you in advance for your time.

Sincerely,

Carol Davis

Alternate last paragraph:
I hope you will welcome my call soon to arrange a brief meeting at your convenience to discuss your current and future needs and how I might serve them. Thank you in advance for your time.

CAROL DAVIS

1110½ Hay Street, Fayetteville, NC 28305   •   preppub@aol.com   •   (910) 483-6611

OBJECTIVE

To benefit an organization that can use an enthusiastic professional and resourceful problem solver who offers a background in logistic, air transportation, project management, inventory control, and hazardous cargo operations, along with a proven ability to train employees and motivate them to achieve outstanding results.

EDUCATION

Associate's degree, Weber State University, Ogden, UT, 1997.
Completed a wide range of college-level technical and professional courses, including classes in freight and packing/preparation and movement of cargo, accounting, personnel management, and over 200 credit hours in the transportation of hazardous material.

LICENSURE

Hold Hazardous Cargo Certification

EXPERIENCE

ASSISTANT SHIPMENT MANAGER. Department of Defense, Hill AFB, UT (2005-present). Coordinate and prepare general and hazardous cargo shipments for transportation to various domestic and overseas destinations on both military and commercial carriers while also training and supervising a staff of two personnel.
- Classify property, determine carrier equipment requirements, and choose appropriate shipping mode for all cargo. Maintain computer records of all outbound shipments; compile and process all corresponding documents and paperwork.
- Assisted in procuring the United Parcel Service Worldship automatic documentation services, resulting in a departmental savings of ten work hours a week.
- Work as Joint Cargo Inspector, ensuring all hazardous cargo is safely secured.

DIRECTOR OF SHIPPING. U.S. Air Force, Iraq (2004). Refined supervisory and planning skills while accomplishing the successful coordination and movement of 1.2 million pounds of munitions to a port 500 miles away for shipment back to the United States.
- Trained, supervised, and evaluated four personnel. Coordinated the movement of hazardous and general cargo by land, air, and sea.
- Became expert at using the performance orientation packaging for hazardous cargo.

ASSISTANT DIRECTOR OF SHIPPING. U.S. Air Force, Hill AFB, UT (2000-04). Coordinated hazardous and general cargo requirements while also initiating and maintaining strict controls on the handling of sensitive and classified cargo. Managed $300,000 budget.
- Determined approximate weight of commodities to be shipped and consolidated shipments in sufficient volume to be transported under specific commercial specifications.

LOADING AND UNLOADING SPECIALIST. U.S. Air Force, Pope AFB, NC (1999-00). Gained valuable experience utilizing Government Bills of Lading (GBLs) and other documents to ensure safe and timely receipt of all locally shipped cargo and freight. Handled damaged and short shipment claims for reimbursement from commercial carriers.

SURFACE FREIGHT SPECIALIST. U.S. Air Force, Spain (1998-99). Coordinated in-bound cargo pick-up, monitored priority and classified cargo, and maintained cargo manifests; saved thousands of dollars in shipping costs by utilizing cost comparisons for overseas movement of Department of Defense cargo.

PERSONAL

Am a versatile professional who is known for my attention to detail. Was entrusted with a Secret security clearance. Can use a wide range of forklifts and other heavy equipment. Am computer proficient with software including Word, Access, and Excel.

Date

Exact Name of Person
Title or Position
Name of Company
Address
City, State, Zip

**AUTOMATED
LOGISTICAL SPECIALIST** Dear Exact Name of Person: (or Dear Sir or Madam if answering a blind ad.)

With the enclosed resume, I would like to make you aware of my inventory management know-how and of the specialized skills in automated logistics operations I have gained while serving my country in the U.S. Army.

As you will see from my resume, I am presently stationed at Fort Wainwright, AK, where I am assigned as an Automated Logistical Specialist. In a previous job, I was selected ahead of my peers to lead a four-person receiving team in the main supply support organization. Because of this organization's mission to respond on short-notice to situations anywhere in the world, I am used to working in a fast-paced environment where priorities can change rapidly.

I was singled out in 2006 to receive an Army Achievement Medal in recognition of my accomplishments, professionalism, and dedication while maintaining 1,300 lines of Authorized Stockage List (ASL) items with 100% accuracy. In this job I have also been credited with maintaining equipment availability rates at a level 11% higher than the Army standard of 75%.

If you can use a knowledgeable young professional with special skills in supply management and inventory control, I hope you will welcome my call soon when I try to arrange a brief meeting to discuss your goals and how my background might serve your needs. I can provide outstanding references at the appropriate time.

Sincerely,

Kevin Tarver

Alternate last paragraph:
If you can use a knowledgeable young professional with special skills in supply management and inventory control, I hope you will write or call me soon to suggest a time when we might meet to discuss your needs and goals and how my background might serve them. I can provide outstanding references at the appropriate time.

KEVIN TARVER

1110½ Hay Street, Fayetteville, NC 28305　·　preppub@aol.com　·　(910) 483-6611

OBJECTIVE

To contribute my knowledge of supply operations with an emphasis on automated logistics operations to an organization that can use a self-motivated young professional.

EDUCATION & TRAINING

Received U.S. Army-sponsored training which included the four-month Automated Logistics Specialist's Course, 2006, as well as airborne operations and driver training courses.

SPECIAL SKILLS

Offer **inventory management** know-how and a strong base of experience in functional areas which include the following:

loading and unloading parts and equipment　　　　　　　　　　shipping and receiving
conducting inventories　　　　　processing parts　　　　posting counts and denials
handling and sorting inventory　　　creating locations　　　operating forklifts

AUTOMATED SYSTEMS

Have become highly familiar with automated systems and equipment including:
SARSS-1 (Standard Army Retail Supply System-Interim)　　Windows XP
ULLS (Unit Level Logistics System)　　　　　　　　　　　UNIX
PLL (Prescribed Load List)　　　　　　　　　　　　　　　LOGMARS-T
TAMMS (The Army Maintenance Management System)　　　　MROCS

EXPERIENCE

Am advancing in leadership and supervisory roles while building skills in automated logistics operations with the U.S. Army:
AUTOMATED LOGISTICAL SPECIALIST. Fort Wainwright, AK (2004-present). Advanced ahead of my peers to hold the senior leadership role for a four-person receiving section in the main supply support organization of the airborne division.

- Cited for my initiative and dedication to providing timely support services, was selected for this leadership role in 2004 after earning a reputation for professionalism and job knowledge.
- Accept parts deliveries from civilian suppliers who often arrive with no notice—immediately receive, tally, and accept these shipments in addition to seeing that regularly scheduled actions were completed accurately and on time.
- Was awarded an Army Achievement Medal in recognition of accomplishments which included consistently maintaining and controlling 1,300 lines of Authorized Stockage List (ASL) items with 100% accuracy.
- Credited with achieving and maintaining availability rates at an average of 86%, consistently exceed the Army standard of 75%.
- Was singled out to brief senior executives on SARSS and MROCS system capabilities on the basis of my knowledge of those systems.
- Worked closely with ITT Industries personnel during a 45-day exercise at the National Training Center (NTC): was a receiver in the main warehouse.
- Provide high quality services for 36 individual units and three large support organizations.
- Received a Humanitarian Service Medal for my contributions during clean-up efforts following an avalanche near Girdwood in 2005.
- Handle daily activities such as establishing and maintaining stock records as well as both manual and automated accounting records.
- Verify quantities received against shipping documents and record any discrepancies.
- Prepare and maintain records on equipment usage, operation, maintenance, modification, and calibration.

PERSONAL

Am a certified affiliate of The U.S. Army Quartermaster Corps. Offer a reputation as a self-starter who can be counted on to give my best efforts, no matter how difficult the situation.

Date

Exact Name of Person
Title or Position
Name of Company
Address
City, State, Zip

**AUTOMOTIVE
MANAGEMENT
SPECIALIST and
INVENTORY
MANAGEMENT
SPECIALIST**

Dear Exact Name of Person: (or Dear Sir or Madam if answering a blind ad.)

I would appreciate an opportunity to talk with you soon about how I could contribute to your organization through my talents in production and inventory management, procurement, distribution, and customer service.

As you can see from my resume, I am working on a degree in business management that I expect to complete in 2006. I also offer proven technical skills from my experience as a material management/inventory specialist serving my country in the U.S. Air Force. Some highlights of my military tenure include the following:

- Was an Honor Graduate from Airmen Leadership School;

- Played a key role on the team that designed and implemented a comprehensive statistical process control program to meet military and automotive specifications;

- Created a task force that increased the vehicle turnout rate from 70% to 90% over a six-month period, saving the Air Force more than $1.5 million quarterly in estimated labor costs.

I offer a professional attitude and sincerely enjoy contributing to my employer's "bottom line" while ensuring customer service and a quality product. I can provide outstanding personal and professional references.

I hope you will call or write me soon to suggest a time convenient for us to meet and discuss your current and future needs and how I might best serve them. Thank you in advance for your consideration.

Sincerely yours,

Damien Roberts

DAMIEN ROBERTS

1110½ Hay Street, Fayetteville, NC 28305   •   preppub@aol.com   •   (910) 483-6611

OBJECTIVE

To contribute to an organization in the automotive industry that can use an innovative problem-solver with proven skills in inventory and production management as well as a keen sense of quality assurance and customer service.

EDUCATION & TRAINING

B.S., **Business Management**, Oklahoma City University, OK; expected in 2006
Inventory Management courses, Community College of the Air Force, Pope AFB, NC.
Material Management courses, Community College of the Air Force, Altus AFB, OK.
Was **honor graduate** (top 5%) of Airmen Leadership School, an intensive eight-week training course to develop management and leadership skills.

EXPERIENCE

MATERIAL MANAGEMENT SPECIALIST and **INVENTORY MANAGEMENT SPECIALIST.** U.S. Air Force, Altus AFB, OK (2003-present). Involved in all aspects of production and inventory management, procurement, distribution, and customer service between major distributors and U.S. Air Force in functions directed at obtaining parts for a wide variety of vehicles.

Production Management:
- Created a task force that increased the vehicle turnout rate from 70% to 90% during a six-month period, saving the Air Force more than $1.5 million quarterly in estimated labor costs. Played a key role on the team that designed and implemented a comprehensive statistical process control program to meet automotive specifications.
- Developed strategic plans and began implementation of the Total Quality System concept, resulting in significant productivity improvements.

Inventory:
- Organized quarterly inventories of approximately $40,000 of equipment, including large quantities of automotive tools and benchstock parts.
- Applied my technical knowledge in referencing automotive catalogs and listings through microfiche and the Mitchell-On-Demand Automotive Computerized Processing System.
- Streamlined inventory, identification, and tracking systems.

Procurement/Distribution:
- Assisted in the daily procurement and distribution of high-cost automotive parts through logistic support totaling $100,000-$150,000 per month.
- Supplied high priority automotive parts to our technicians from organizations worldwide through the use of today's latest technology. Conducted orientation and training sessions for new technicians on proper applications in procuring parts through "special request."
- Processed "turn-ins" to the manufacturer involving the reimbursement of warranted automotive parts. Performed daily Quality Assurance Evaluations on distributors to confirm adequate pricing of parts ordered.

Customer Service:
- Processed high-volume requests from more than 30 automotive technicians in a timely and efficient manner, which helped to improve overall customer service.
- Served as a member of an Advisory Council Board to improve customer service. Conducted end-user surveys to determine how the organization was doing in customer service.

DEPARTMENT HEAD. Wal-Mart, Oklahoma City, OK (2000-03). At this fast-paced popular retail chain, was responsible for $200,000 of inventory each quarter, for shipping and receiving merchandise, and for placement of product on the floor.

PERSONAL

Offer an extraordinary ability to pinpoint and anticipate problems before they happen. Rapidly master new software. Hold **Top Secret/SCI** security clearance. Work well under pressure.

Date

Exact Name of Person
Title or Position
Name of Company
Address
City, State, Zip

Dear Exact Name of Person: (or Dear Sir or Madam if answering a blind ad.)

With the enclosed resume, I would like to make you aware of my distinguished background and reputation for expertise in managing material, fiscal, and human resources while providing aviation operations with timely and effective supply and inventory control management support.

As you will see from my resume, I have served my country in the U.S. Navy where I advanced to hold supervisory roles in support of naval aviation operations throughout the world. For instance, in my most recent assignment I managed a $9 million budget while achieving a 99.58% utilization of funds for one recent fiscal year. While supervising 32 people, I received official evaluations which described me as the "consummate professional" and as a senior executive's "most trusted advisor on supply-related issues." I was credited with making improvements in increasing aircraft availability rates which directly impacted the number of aviation professionals who completed training.

In an earlier assignment as an Inventory Control Manager, I handled the supply operations portion of a ship overhaul project to include planning for the transition to the newly designed facilities and reorganization of all supply operations and space prior to reopening. As the resident expert on aviation supply and material management, I controlled receiving, storing, issuing, and auditing of a $5 million inventory. I have been awarded several Joint Services and U.S. Navy/Marine Corps Achievement Medals in recognition of my accomplishments, perseverance, attention to detail, and dedicated professionalism.

With excellent time management, planning, and organizational skills, I completed degree requirements for a B.S. in Aviation Management in 2006. I am familiar with automated data processing systems used to maintain documents and records of operations from the procurement and requisitioning stages on through all aspects of storage, issuing, and control. I offer a strong base of experience in proving product support for both fixed- and rotary-wing aircraft which include C-130, P-3, F-14, FA-18, A-7, and S-3.

I hope you will call or write me soon to suggest a time convenient for us to meet and discuss your current and future needs and how I might serve them. Thank you in advance for your time.

Sincerely,

Ryan Miller

RYAN MILLER

1110½ Hay Street, Fayetteville, NC 28305   •   preppub@aol.com   •   (910) 483-6611

OBJECTIVE

To offer a distinguished background of accomplishments and extensive knowledge and experience related to inventory control management to an organization that can benefit from my effectiveness in maximizing human, fiscal, and material resources.

EDUCATION & TRAINING

B.S. in Aviation Management, Norfolk State University, VA, June 2006.
Completed extensive training with an emphasis on aviation supply and maintenance material management, leadership development, program management, and financial operations.

EXPERIENCE

Built a reputation as a meticulous and detail-oriented manager with a knack for motivating and guiding others to exceed expected standards, U.S. Navy:
AVIATION SUPPLY SUPERVISOR. Norfolk, VA (2002-present). Officially evaluated as the "consummate professional" and "most trusted advisor on all supply related issues," managed a $9 million budget while being credited with implementing improvements which improved aircraft availability rates and increased the number of pilots, flight officers, and air crew members completing training by 20%.

- Achieved a 99.58% utilization of funds for fiscal year 2006 while "aggressively" managing and expediting requisitions for a 45% reduction in outstanding requests.
- Cut aircraft parts "cannibalizing" 63% which increased availability 35 percent.
- Was credited with personally revising and updating testing materials for the "aviation storekeeper" career field; these materials were then accepted for the entire east coast.
- Supervised 32 people in the U.S. Navy's largest aviation squadron while leading the Material Control Division to perfect scores during 12 consecutive inspections.
- Earned respect for my "positive and approachable demeanor" which translated to exceptional achievements in all levels of performance and inspected operational areas.

INVENTORY CONTROL MANAGER. Pearl Harbor, HI (2001-02). Recognized as the ship's aviation supply and material management expert, supervised the receipt, storage, issue, location auditing, and inventory of material valued in excess of $5 million which was located in ten separate store rooms.

- Became highly knowledgeable of cargo handling procedures while supervising the team unloading and loading materials and equipment.

SUBSTANCE ABUSE COUNSELOR AND PROGRAM MANAGER. Pearl Harbor, HI (1999-01). Reduced alcohol-related incidents 50% through an aggressive counseling and instructional program which achieved a 68% rehabilitation rate. Excelled in additional duties as a financial advisor assisting personnel with budget and financial decisions.

SUPPLY OPERATIONS SUPERVISOR. Charleston, SC (1996-99). Earned respect for my "astute management" while providing support for day-to-day operations and a wide range of special missions which received exceptional aircraft and administrative material support for a fleet air reconnaissance unit.

- Provided perfect accountability while issuing, controlling, and providing replenishment for a $4.5 million Weapons Replaceable Assembly pack up for a project in SC.

AIRCRAFT SKILLS

Offer extensive experience in providing product support for C-130, P-3, F-14, FA-18, A-7, and S-3 aircraft.

PERSONAL

Received several Joint Service and Navy/Marine Corps Achievement Medals in recognition of my accomplishments and expertise. Effective in dealing with culturally diverse teams.

Date

Exact Name of Person
Title or Position
Name of Company
Address
City, State, Zip

CHIEF OF SUPPLY OPERATIONS

Dear Exact Name of Person: (or Dear Sir or Madam if answering a blind ad.)

    With the enclosed resume, I would like to make you aware of my interest in exploring employment opportunities with your organization and introduce you to my background and credentials related to supply chain management.

    As you will see from my resume, I served my country with distinction and was the recipient of numerous medals and honors praising my management abilities and technical expertise related to supply management. In my most recent position as Chief of Supply Operations, I organized the provision of all types of supplies and services for hundreds of people in worldwide projects. In my previous position, I was handpicked as Supply Branch Chief and Senior Logistics Consultant. In that capacity, I provided oversight for supply management systems of 75 different organizations and led them in activities which included reducing shrinkage, improving ordering and shipping time, and resourcefully utilizing excess equipment. As the "resident expert instructor" on automated systems for supply chain management, I established a new automated system for tracking the ordering, storage, and inventory control of perishable and non-perishable items.

    While becoming one of the U.S. Army's foremost experts on supply management, I gained a reputation as an individual of "unquestionable integrity and loyalty." I believe in leadership by example, and I have learned how to motivate personnel to aim for and achieve the highest professional standards. I have managed dozens of people, controlled budgets of more than $400,000, and accounted for millions of dollars in assets. I have managed the supply chain for all types of supplies including perishable and grocery products, engineering and repair parts, telecommunications items, vehicle parts and automotive equipment, as well as computers and office supplies. In every job I have held, I have made major contributions to productivity. For example, as Logistics Branch Manager for an organization supporting NATO activities, I reduced a spare parts backlog from 635 parts to less then 44 monthly while also instituting a logistical accounting system to monitor transactions.

    I have received the highest evaluations of my ability to communicate effectively with others, and I have trained hundreds of individuals in automated inventory control systems and supply management.

    If you can use my expertise related to shipping and receiving, expediting and dispatching, logistics and transportation, as well as supply chain management, I hope you will contact me to suggest a time when we might meet to discuss your needs.

Yours sincerely,

Noel Turpin

NOEL TURPIN

1110½ Hay Street, Fayetteville, NC 28305 • preppub@aol.com • (910) 483-6611

OBJECTIVE

I want to contribute to an organization that can use an experienced manager who offers expertise related to shipping and receiving, expediting and logistics management, supply chain management, as well as inventory control and warehouse operations management.

EDUCATION

College: **Associates Degree in General Studies,** Central Michigan University, 2004.
Professional and Technical Training: Graduated from these professional courses taught at the highly respected U.S. Army Quartermaster School for logistics and supply managers:

Material Control and Accounting   Food Service and Grocery Supply Management
Property Book Accounting   Automated Systems Management (SAILS, SARSS)
Advanced Logistics Supervision   Retail Supply Chain Management and Re-Supply
Total Quality Management   Safety Program Implementation and Supervision

COMPUTERS

Proficient with automated systems for supply chain management.

EXPERIENCE

CHIEF OF SUPPLY OPERATIONS. U.S. Army, Fort Rucker, AL (2004-present). Was recommended for promotion to the highest enlisted rank (Sergeant Major) based on my outstanding performance in managing the supply chain supporting a 1,500-person organization involved in hundreds of special projects worldwide.
- In one project, provided transportation, maintenance, food, water, fuel, laundry, and bath support for 1,600 people working in a rugged setting in Haiti for three months.
- Supervised 15 people while providing oversight for the ordering and storage of perishable and non-perishable materials in multiple warehouses.
- Trained more than 200 personnel in operating automated inventory control systems.

SUPPLY BRANCH CHIEF & SENIOR LOGISTICS CONSULTANT. U.S. Army, Fort Riley, KS (2001-04). Was handpicked for this position which involved providing oversight for supply management systems of 75 separate organizations; inspected their internal systems and procedures and provided expert technical direction.
- Established a new automated system used to track the ordering, storage, and inventory control of perishable and non-perishable items.
- Significantly improved customer service by speeding up ordering and shipping time.
- Decreased shrinkage and waste through highly improved automated procedures.
- In one organization, led personnel in identifying and recycling more than $6 million in excess equipment; in another organization, led personnel to establish 100% accountability of $4 million in equipment and property.
- Was the "resident expert instructor" on automated systems for supply chain management.

Highlights of prior U.S. Army management and supply experience:
LOGISTICS BRANCH MANAGER. Kuwait. Received the prestigious Joint Service Commendation Medal for my leadership and technical expertise on behalf of NATO.
- Reduced a spare parts backlog from 635 parts to less than 44 monthly while coordinating logistical support for mobile and fixed communications systems.
- Instituted a logistical accounting system to monitor repair parts and supply transactions.
- Accounted for $40 million in communications equipment.
SUPPLY MANAGER. Fort Belvoir, VA. Managed a $400,000 budget and 224 line items. Supervised 24 personnel maintaining and repairing vehicles.

PERSONAL

In formal performance evaluations, was often praised for "unquestionable integrity and loyalty." Have learned how to motivate others to reach for the highest goals.

Date

Exact Name of Person
Title or Position
Name of Company
Address
City, State, Zip

Dear Exact Name of Person: (or Dear Sir or Madam if answering a blind ad.)

With the enclosed resume, I would like to make you aware of my reputation as a mature professional with high levels of initiative, the determination to achieve results, and the ability to work with others in supervisory roles or as a contributor to the success of team efforts.

As you will see from my resume, I offer a versatile background in transportation, shipping and receiving, supply, and vehicle operations. I have always been singled out for my leadership qualities and attention to detail. In my most recent job as a Courier for DSL in Italy, I contributed skills as a supervisor and training specialist and was known for my emphasis on customer service and quality control. Earlier I supervised and trained temporary employees in shipping and packing procedures and worked in a warehouse after leaving military service.

While serving in the U.S. Army, I quickly advanced to leadership and supervisory roles and was frequently singled out to train, mentor, counsel, and guide other personnel. I have operated material handling equipment, vehicles, and automated systems while excelling in high-pressure jobs that involved working under deadlines and time restraints.

If you can use a mature and dedicated individual who is accustomed to hard work and long hours, I hope you will welcome my call soon when I try to arrange a brief meeting to discuss your goals and how my background might serve your needs. I can provide outstanding references at the appropriate time.

Sincerely,

Thomas Dyment

Alternate last paragraph:
I hope you will write or call me soon to suggest a time when we might meet to discuss your needs and goals and how my background might serve them. I can provide outstanding references at the appropriate time.

THOMAS DYMENT

1110½ Hay Street, Fayetteville, NC 28305   •   preppub@aol.com   •   (910) 483-6611

OBJECTIVE

To offer excellent organizational and planning, communication, and motivational skills as well as a reputation as a professional with a background in transportation and supply.

EDUCATION & TRAINING

Completed DSL International Courier Training and Italian Language Courses, Italy, 2004, as well as military training in personnel supervision and leadership.

SPECIAL SKILLS

Quickly learn new computer programs and applications and am familiar with Windows XP, Microsoft Word, and Adobe PageMaker; proprietary logistics systems developed for the military such as SARSS and ULLS; and the DSL shipping computer.

EXPERIENCE

Adapted to the Italian way of doing business in the following track record:
COURIER, SUPERVISOR, AND TRAINING SPECIALIST. DSL, Italy (2004-present). Was known for my attention to detail while organizing my daily work load to ensure accurate route planning so that packages were delivered properly and in a timely manner.

- Earned a reputation for my customer service orientation while providing information concerning prices, services, and products.
- Pick up and deliver international express shipments while accurately completing customs paperwork and other documents required for import and export.
- Train and supervise new couriers in route planning, operation of the DSL handheld computer, and in corporate policies and procedures.

SUPERVISORY SHIPPING AND PACKING SPECIALIST. United Parcel Service, Italy (2003-04). Supervised and trained as many as six temporary employees in proper procedures in order to meet production quotas and deadlines while assuring quality control.

Refined supervisory skills while serving in the U.S. Army:
OPERATIONS SUPERVISOR. Fort Hood, TX (2001-02). Singled out for a leadership and supervisory role, was cited for my skills in seeing that personnel were thoroughly trained and ready to perform as the senior person in a 13-person section.

- Accounted for the maintenance and operation of six vehicles valued in excess of $2 million.
- Became known as an intelligent problem solver who could be counted on to provide sound, positive advice and guidance.

TRANSPORTATION OPERATIONS SUPERVISOR. Italy (2000-01). Supervised four people while overseeing operation of a tractor-trailer transfer point including activities related to cargo management, documentation, vehicle and trailer availability, and scheduling.

- Gained attention for my initiative, enthusiasm, and authoritative manner while motivating personnel to take advantage of every opportunity for training and education.

DISPATCHER and **ASSISTANT OPERATIONS SUPERVISOR.** Italy (1999-00). Supervised and trained four subordinates in addition to my main responsibilities of ensuring smooth and timely support for trailers and transportation assets throughout Europe.

MOTOR TRANSPORT OPERATOR. Italy (1999). Supervised, trained, and offered technical guidance to six junior personnel; was singled out for praise for my ability to set high standards and lead others to meet them.

PERSONAL

Earned several certificates of appreciation for exceptional customer service as well as several U.S. Army medals for professionalism. Studied Sociology and Psychology at the college level.

Date

Exact Name of Person
Title or Position
Name of Company
Address
City, State, Zip

Dear Exact Name of Person: (or Dear Sir or Madam if answering a blind ad.)

Can you use an articulate and innovative manager who offers a strong background in logistics, technical operations, and automated data processing management?

I am sending my resume in response to your Controller's position.

As a U.S. Army officer I became adept at developing plans, molding teams, and ensuring the success of organizational goals. I have managed logistics support for an organization with 500 employees, controlled multimillion-dollar inventories of sophisticated equipment, and developed cost-saving ideas for various companies.

As you will see from my resume, I have consistently been able to develop and implement innovative programs and cost-saving ideas in every position I have held. For example, in my most recent position as the Director of Logistics and Budgeting for a 500-person organization, I reduced the cost of an office automation project 29% by going outside the usual sources to find the best equipment for the money. On numerous occasions, I have taken over substandard operations and transformed them into models of efficiency.

I offer a background of adaptability and dedication to excellence which I am certain I could apply in a manner beneficial to your organization. I am especially proud of my reputation for unquestioned integrity and high moral standards.

I hope you will call or write me soon to suggest a time convenient for us to meet and discuss your current and future needs and how I might serve them. Thank you in advance for your time.

Sincerely yours,

Roderick James

RODERICK JAMES

1110½ Hay Street, Fayetteville, NC 28305   •   preppub@aol.com   •   (910) 483-6611

OBJECTIVE

To contribute my analytical, decision-making, and managerial skills to an organization that can benefit from my knowledge of logistics/budgeting and automated systems as well as my abilities in seeing plans through to completion and performing under pressure.

EXPERIENCE

DIRECTOR OF LOGISTICS AND BUDGETING. U.S. Army, Fort Polk, LA (2005-present). Was cited for providing sound advice, using informed judgment, and displaying strong decision-making skills while reducing costs and improving efficiency as the coordinator of logistics support for a 500-person organization with a $500,000 annual operating budget.
- Identified inventories of excess equipment and developed a program which reduced operating costs 10% through collecting these items at a central location.
- Located new open market sources for automated data processing systems which reduced the estimated purchase price by 29% of the price of traditional sources.
- Established the standards for hazardous waste handling with a program accepted as the model for other companies within the parent organization to follow.
- Display managerial skills and versatility overseeing successful maintenance and facilities upkeep programs as well as food service support operations.

Established the following record of accomplishments, U.S. Army, Fort Bragg, NC:
TECHNICAL OPERATIONS MANAGER. (2002-04). Rebuilt and revitalized a struggling, substandard operation into six cohesive teams of specialists within only four months.
- Developed and implemented a personnel records section database of 70,000 critical items which was then copied by three "sister" companies for its usability and effectiveness.
- Advised a chief executive on technical and operational aspects of the strict employment and transport of nuclear weapons.
- Earned the distinction as the first company in the Army to pass stringent inspections of nuclear weapons site operations/procedures and earn a new type of certification.

FIRST-LINE SUPERVISOR. (2001-02). Provided strong leadership during a period of turbulence caused by functional reorganizations and major changes during worldwide Congress-mandated personnel reductions and draw downs.
- Polished my ability to manage a staff and administrative functions in a 50-person company through my enthusiastic and energetic style of leadership. Ensured a quality maintenance program for 20 vehicles required to support a sophisticated weapons system.

TECHNICAL OPERATIONS MANAGER. (2000-01). Was promoted to a more advanced level of management based on outstanding results achieved in my first assignment as a military officer in charge of a five-person team with more than $305,000 worth of equipment.

EDUCATION & SPECIAL SKILLS & KNOWLEDGE

B.A., Political Science, Arkansas State University, AR, 1999.
- Displayed superior leadership and athletic abilities. Was football team captain.
- Offer knowledge of the DOD contracting process including the contracting for and procurement of supplies and services as well as cost estimating, budget management, planning, analysis, and factoring.
- Familiar with the latest computer technology and experienced with today's software.

PERSONAL

Known for integrity and high ethical standards, was entrusted with a Top Secret security clearance. Earned one achievement and **three** commendation awards for accomplishments.

Date

Exact Name of Person
Title or Position
Name of Company
Address
City, State, Zip

DIRECTOR OF MEDICAL LOGISTICS SUPPORT

Dear Exact Name of Person: (or Dear Sir or Madam if answering a blind ad.)

I would appreciate an opportunity to talk with you soon about how my specialized experience, training, and knowledge of medical logistics management and the health care administration field would be of benefit to your organization.

Currently holding the position as the Director of Medical Logistics Support, I am a junior military officer excelling in a role usually reserved for a senior officer. I have the honor of being the youngest and lowest-ranking officer to have ever held this critical job.

Known as a very articulate and aggressive young "hard charger," in my relatively short time in this job I have streamlined expenditures, reduced the fiscal year operating budget by $260,000, and developed an ongoing program for retrieving excess medical materiel.

As you will see from my resume, I also offer extensive computer knowledge related to the set up and operation of Windows-based computer systems. I feel certain that you would find me to be a knowledgeable, intelligent, and determined individual with very strong budget development and staff supervision abilities.

I hope you will welcome my call soon to arrange a brief meeting at your convenience to discuss your current and future needs and how I might serve them. Thank you in advance for your time.

Sincerely yours,

David Simmons

Alternate last paragraph:
I hope you will call or write soon to suggest a time convenient for us to meet and discuss your current and future needs and how I might serve them. Thank you in advance for your time.

DAVID SIMMONS

1110½ Hay Street, Fayetteville, NC 28305　•　preppub@aol.com　•　(910) 483-6611

OBJECTIVE	To benefit an organization that can use an aggressive and articulate young professional with expertise in the specialized field of medical logistics management, experience in budget forecasting and formulation, and a reputation as an "exceptional" junior military officer.
EXPERIENCE	*Advanced rapidly in this "track record" of superior performance within the Army Medical Department: provide medical materiel and services at the nation's largest military base, Schofield Barracks, HI:* **DIRECTOR OF MEDICAL LOGISTICS SUPPORT.** (2003-present). Was handpicked to hold a critical position controlling more than $1.5 million worth of medical equipment and supplies while serving as the "subject matter expert" on medical logistics matters for the 15,000-person organization.

- Have the distinction of being the youngest manager ever to have held this position, which is usually reserved for someone two levels above my current rank.
- Developed a comprehensive "ongoing" program for turning in excess medical materiel which will result in substantial savings for the government.
- Managed 321 lines of medical supplies and a $320,000 annual operating budget.
- Planned, coordinated, controlled, and managed all functional aspects in the highly specialized support program for the health care delivery system.
- Reduced the 2006 fiscal year budget by $260,000 after reorganizing expenditures.

FIRST-LINE SUPERVISOR and **MEDICAL LOGISTICS MANAGER.** (2002-03). Controlled a $2 million inventory of medical, pharmaceutical, and military equipment while supervising 25 employees including physician's assistants, paramedics, X-ray technicians, and dental assistants.

EDUCATION	**B.S., Pre-Law with a minor in Business**, Adams State College, Alamosa, CO, 2002.

- Graduated *magna cum laude* in three-and-a-half years and maintained a 3.6 GPA.
- Earned induction into Beta Kappa Alpha, a national academics honor society.
- Commanded the university's Reserve Officer Training Corps (ROTC) and was a "Distinguished Military Graduate."

TRAINING	An honor graduate of the "basic course" for medical managers, placed on the Commandant's List at the executive-level Medical Logistics Management Course. The advanced course emphasized areas including:

- various inventory management concepts—just-in-time inventory, the prime-vendor concept, and the cart-exchange system
- analysis of financial inventory accounting, quality assurance, contract administration, stock-record accounting, resource management, and staffing requirements
- the health care facilities planning process
- the process of accrediting health care facilities by the Joint Commission on the Accreditation of Health Care Organizations

COMPUTER EXPERTISE	Offer extensive knowledge in setting up, configuring, and operating various systems including Windows-based operating systems. **Software**: Windows, Adobe PageMaker and InDesign, Microsoft Excel, Microsoft Word. **Languages**: Working knowledge of structured languages
PERSONAL	Have a Secret security clearance. Am knowledgeable in the area of budget forecasting and formulation, quality control management, and contract administration.

Date

Exact Name of Person
Title or Position
Name of Company
Address
City, State, Zip

**DIRECTOR OF
OPERATIONS,
ADMINISTRATION,
AND LOGISTICS**

Dear Exact Name of Person: (or Dear Sir or Madam if answering a blind ad.)

I would appreciate an opportunity to talk with you soon about how I could contribute to your organization through the application of my talent for maximizing both human and material resources refined in a distinguished career as a military officer.

While serving my country in the U.S. Army, I have been especially effective in identifying problems or goals, directing activities so that goals are met and problems solved, and motivating employees. I offer very well-developed organizational abilities and attention to detail along with the ability to express myself verbally and in writing.

As you will see from my enclosed resume, my experience extends to include inventory control, procurement, and budgeting as well as the management of maintenance operations. One example which highlights some of my strongest areas was a 14-month project in which 72 families and $42 million worth of property were relocated from Tampa, FL, to Fort Leavenworth, KY, due to a federal-government ordered military base closure. As liaison between the Army Corps of Engineers, civilian contractors, and personnel representing Fort Leavenworth, I coordinated the minute details of arranging for this large-scale relocation. One of the final stages of this project was conducting an inventory of equipment and directing the set-up of the relocated personnel into a $32 million building.

I feel that my organizational, time management, and team-building skills combine effectively with my ability to communicate with, train, instruct, and lead people to make me a well-rounded professional with a lot to offer the right organization.

I hope you will welcome my call soon to arrange a brief meeting at your convenience to discuss your current and future needs and how I might serve them. Thank you in advance for your time.

Sincerely yours,

Charles Rock

Alternate last paragraph:
I hope you will call or write me soon to suggest a time convenient for us to meet and discuss your current and future needs and how I might serve them. Thank you in advance for your time.

CHARLES ROCK

1110½ Hay Street, Fayetteville, NC 28305 • preppub@aol.com • (910) 483-6611

OBJECTIVE

To offer a strong background of success in managing human and material resources as a military officer known for a meticulous approach to organizing, prioritizing, and overseeing operations as well as a reputation as a good listener and effective communicator.

EXPERIENCE

Advanced in jobs requiring leadership and top-notch managerial skills, U.S. Army:
DIRECTOR OF OPERATIONS, ADMINISTRATION, AND LOGISTICS. Fort Leavenworth, KS (2005-present). Implemented changes which allowed a personnel recruiting and retention school to provide a better quality of services while representing the facility to other government agencies and high-level executives.

- Supervised an 84-person staff comprised mainly of mid-level managers and controlled a $200,000 annual operating budget.
- Planned and carried out a large-scale relocation project in which 72 families and $42 million worth of equipment were transferred from Tampa, FL, to Kansas.
- Maintained an enviable record of keeping within budget for three years with a 98.4% expenditures rate and no overages.
- Implemented changes which saved approximately $3.8 million annually by reducing a management course from nine to six weeks, thereby lowering lodging/travel expenses.

GENERAL MANAGER. Tampa, FL (2004-05). Directed the professional development and performance of 32 personnel recruiters staffing eight offices within the Tampa area.

- Managed the details of training and counseling employees and seeing that each office operated to its fullest potential while controlling a $320,000 annual operating budget which included maintenance and upkeep of 21 vehicles.
- Accomplished 124% of assigned corporate goals while guiding employees to ensure that qualified young people received information on the advantages of a military career.

DIRECTOR OF PLANNING AND OPERATIONS. Italy (2002-04). Advised the senior executive in a military community while in charge of planning and managing training, security, and personnel mobilization activities; supervising 176 employees; and overseeing an $842,000 annual budget and 1,600 square kilometers of training facilities.

- Coordinated arrangements for sending more than 4,800 people to Iraq for the War on Terror. Displayed a reassuring, professional manner while handling arrangements with the family members of soldiers killed in the war.

MAINTENANCE AND SUPPLY MANAGER. Fort Bragg, NC (2000-02). Directed the daily activities of a 148-person company involved in maintaining and operating 364 vehicles as well as managing a $638,200 budget and the operation of a dining facility which served 680 people three meals a day.

- Assisted in the development of a system used for moving large amounts of ammunition: the equipment was used successfully during the War on Terror.

EDUCATION & TRAINING

M.S., Military History, University of Maryland, Italy campus, 2003.
B.S., General Education, Concentration: History and Economics, Johnson College, Overland Park, KS, 1999.
A.S., Health Services, University of District of Columbia, Washington, DC, 1994.

PERSONAL

Was entrusted with a Top Secret security clearance. Earned a Legion of Merit, three Meritorious Service, and four Commendation Medals as well as 20 letters of commendation.

TWO-PAGE RESUME

NADINE JOHNSON

1110½ Hay Street, Fayetteville, NC 28305   •   preppub@aol.com   •

(910) 483-6611

EQUIPMENT FIELDING PROJECT MANAGER

OBJECTIVE

To apply my abilities as a manager with extensive experience in maximizing human resources to an organization which can use an articulate, resourceful professional with a "track record" of accomplishments as a military officer.

SUMMARY of EXPERIENCE

Have earned a reputation as a natural leader who can be counted on to make sound decisions, maximize human resources, and handle problems in a positive and resourceful manner while attaining the rank of major in the U.S. Army.

EXPERIENCE

EQUIPMENT FIELDING PROJECT MANAGER. U.S. Army, Fort Carson, CO (2005-present). Direct all phases of a fielding project for a high-tech mobile signal communications system.

- Monitored multimillion-dollar assets in a total package which involved 3,500 technicians receiving thousands of hours of training over an 11-month period.

MANAGER FOR PLANNING, MODERNIZATION, AND RESTRUCTURING. U.S. Army, Fort Carson, CO (2003-04). Determined equipment requirements and logistics needs for the Army's busiest tactical signal communications organization as the primary point-of-contact between the military and the manufacturer.

- Was selected for attendance at the graduate-level Command and General Staff College.
- Served as the advisor remaining at Fort Carson to oversee the total scope of the project and allow project completion on schedule once the unit's personnel returned from the War on Terror.

INDUSTRIAL MANAGEMENT TRAINEE. U.S. Army, Richmond, VA (2002-03). Was selected to participate in the one-year cooperative Training With Industry Program, which was designed to give military officers an opportunity to work with defense contractors and other major business firms to observe business practices in the civilian sector.

- Gained valuable experience in the Mobile Subscriber Equipment Division (MSED) which was directly applied in my next two military assignments.
- Was a valued member of a team applying Total Quality Management (TQM) practices while designing innovative manufacturing processes that became the new industry standard; the team received the prestigious Malcolm Baldridge Award for excellence.

GENERAL MANAGER. U.S. Army, Germany (2000-01). Managed a geographically dispersed 215-person company providing telephone service and technical support for television, AM radio, and FM radio services for military personnel as well as employees of government agencies operating in the area.

- Turned a company with serious morale problems into a productive team within only six months of taking over as manager.
- Served as the Information Systems Manager for two communities.

OPERATIONS OFFICER. U.S. Army, Germany (1999-00). Served as second-in-command of a 312-person company providing repair and maintenance support to communications sites throughout the country.
- Maintained 100% accountability of a $4 million inventory.
- Received valuable management experience during absences of the general manager.
- Kept the maintenance backlog to well below required performance goals.

HUMAN RESOURCES CONSULTANT. U.S. Army, Fort Jackson, SC (1996-99). Kept a personnel recruiting chief executive up-to-date on matters related to personnel recruiting and retention while providing sound advice regarding the recommended solutions for labor relations issues and human resources problems.
- Authored strategic action plans which identified the need for human resources in specialized areas.
- Earned a reputation as a dynamic and persuasive public speaker while handling a busy schedule of public speaking engagements.
- Was a member of a committee that produced personnel recruiting videotapes which were used as "models" by other organizations.

GENERAL MANAGER. U.S. Army, Italy (1995-96). Planned short-term and long-range activities for communications support of criminal investigation personnel in the Europe area.
- Handled a wide range of management objectives including conducting technical inspections and overseeing support from acquisition, through the installation stage, and on to maintenance and operation.
- Coordinated arrangements to obtain a new type of radio with the data encryption functions to ensure security for classified transmissions.

DEPARTMENT MANAGER/CHIEF INSTRUCTOR. U.S. Army, Fort Bragg, NC (1994-95). Supervised 14 instructors and conducted training courses at a major training center.
- Contributed to the success of the program by implementing cross training for instructors and developing a concise reference guide.

Other experience:
First-line Supervisor: Learned to be an effective leader as the supervisor of 44 technicians maintaining communications-electronics equipment, U.S. Army, Fort Bragg, NC.
Division Manager: Earned promotion on the basis of outstanding performance after only six months in the management training program of the retail giant Belk, Richmond, VA.
- Was handpicked over other senior managers to direct the operation of four departments in a new mall location.

CLEARANCE	Entrusted with a **Top Secret** security clearance with Special Background Investigation/Sensitive Compartmented Information.
EDUCATION	**B.A., Speech/Drama**, University of South Carolina, Columbia, SC, 1993.
TRAINING	In addition to the one-year Training With Industry Program in cooperation with GE, excelled in extensive management and technical training.
PERSONAL	Was honored with several medals of commendation and for "meritorious service." Earned the National Defense Service Medal for contributions in support of the War on Terror.

TWO-PAGE RESUME

DARRYL JENSEN

1110½ Hay Street, Fayetteville, NC 28305 • preppub@aol.com •
(910) 483-6611

OBJECTIVE

To offer my expertise in the specialized areas of environmental remediation/environmental management compliance to an organization that can use my organizational, communication, and leadership skills refined in critical and highly visible roles as a U.S. Army officer.

ENVIRONMENTAL LOGISTICS MANAGER & EMERGENCY RESPONSE TEAM MANAGER

EXPERIENCE

ENVIRONMENTAL LOGISTICS MANAGER and **EMERGENCY RESPONSE TEAM MANAGER.** U.S. Army, Fort Stewart, GA (2005-present). For a 145-person company, supervised the acquisition of equipment and services for six environmental remediation projects with a combined budget exceeding $2.5 million; on a rotating basis, directed emergency response teams responding to on-post chemical accidents or incidents.
- Prepared statements of work and contracted for the renovation and upgrade of seven facilities valued at $179,500.
- Procured $750,000 worth of goods and services during a six-month period while managing supplies, chemical equipment, and a motor pool valued in excess of $20 million.

GENERAL MANAGER. U.S. Army, Fort Stewart, GA (2003-05). Selected because of exceptional performance, managed 22 specialists responsible for responding to worldwide emergencies during chemical accidents/incidents; conducted environmental remediation on formerly used defense (FUD) sites and was subcontractor for $750,000 of FUD reclamations.
- Was cited for my expertise in supervising 14 separate teams which escorted toxic chemical agents to installations and laboratories throughout the United States.

CHEMICAL OPERATIONS MANAGER. Germany (2002-03). As advisor to the commander regarding nuclear, biological, and chemical (NBC) defense matters, assisted in planning and supervising the removal of nuclear weapons back to the U.S. for a 380-person company.
- In preparation for the removal operation, played a key role in planning a highly successful nuclear accident response exercise, which was recognized as "best in the brigade."

OPERATIONS MANAGER and **COMPANY COMMANDER.** Italy (2000-02). Handpicked to oversee the removal of American chemical weapons stores from Italy, managed the storage, maintenance, security, and accountability of the American chemical weapons in Europe; directed operations at two storage sites with 477 employees.
- Once the weapons were removed, was handpicked to dismantle the 159-person ordnance company; completed the reduction of an overstrength and overequipped organization with more than $400 million in assets ahead of schedule with no losses.

CHEMICAL OPERATIONS MANAGER. U.S. Army, Fort Bragg, NC (1999). Prepared contingency plans for a 2,300-person organization as the NBC subject matter expert and advisor.

- Directed maintenance, logistical, and administrative support activities while managing a major project which transferred personnel and assets to Germany for training.

MAINTENANCE AND TRAINING MANAGER. U.S. Army, Fort Benning, GA (1998). Fine-tuned my organizational and combat leadership skills handling multiple responsibilities as supervisor of 30 persons in both mechanized smoke and decontamination platoons; maintained and accounted for $6 million worth of tactical vehicles and equipment.

INTELLIGENCE MANAGER. U.S. Army, Fort Benning, GA (1997-98). Cited for superb performance as the advisor on intelligence matters, ensured security for classified documents and communications equipment and oversaw training for nuclear weapons security procedures.

CHEMICAL OPERATIONS OFFICER. U.S. Army, Fort Benning, GA (1996-97). In addition to helping run the organization's training programs, acted as the advisor on NBC defense activities.

- **Highlights of prior experience:** Managed a National Guard combat engineer organization with 30 employees and directed maintenance on more than $4 million worth of assets.

EDUCATION & TRAINING

M.S., Systems Management, Columbus State University, Columbus, GA, 1998.
B.S., Chemical Engineering, University of Nebraska, Omaha, NE, 1995.
Was a distinguished/honor graduate while attending more than one year of advanced training on hazardous material management, chemical safety, GA and NC state regulations, staff management, hazardous material packaging and handling, and logistics and procurement.

CERTIFICATION & AREAS OF SPECIAL INTEREST

Occupational Safety and Health Administration (OSHA) certification in hazardous waste materials handling/emergency response and hazardous waste operations supervision.
Have a general understanding of computer diagnostics and repair with hands-on experience.
Am familiar with commercial computer software packages including:
    Word   Excel   PowerPoint   Access   InDesign

PERSONAL

Have a Top Secret security clearance with BI. Am familiar with Department of Defense (DOD) procedures for contracts up to $3 million. Am willing to relocate.

Date

Exact Name of Person
Title or Position
Name of Company
Address
City, State, Zip

Dear Exact Name of Person: (or Dear Sir or Madam if answering a blind ad.)

I would appreciate an opportunity to talk with you soon about how I could contribute to your organization through my exceptionally strong problem-solving skills as well as my specialized experience in controlling transportation activities.

As you will see from my resume, I have been targeted for rapid future promotion as a military officer and was recently selected to attend a prestigious six-month course in advanced logistics and transportation concepts.

In a prior job as a Transportation Officer in Europe, I coordinated transportation needs for all military personnel sent to the middle east while evaluating 55 civilian employees implementing military contracts valued at up to $250,000. I have received extensive training related to Department of Defense contracting procedures and have gained an "insider's" view of how government contracting is supposed to work and how contracts are awarded. While in that job I oversaw transportation services for personnel in 20 separate organizations and was praised for expertly managing a complex transportation program. On my own initiative, I developed and implemented methods of improving numerous existing areas including air and ground transportation services, airfield operations, property shipping/accountability, and vehicle maintenance.

In a previous job I managed a truck company with 45 drivers and oversaw maintenance of a multimillion-dollar fleet of tractors and trailers. During the War on Terror, I managed a land transportation fleet consisting of more than 1,200 line-haul, cargo, and heavy equipment transporter trucks. I have also managed personnel administration sections supporting transportation organizations.

You would find me in person to be a congenial professional who is known for my attention to detail and for my resourcefulness in finding solutions to stubborn problems. I will provide outstanding personal and professional references upon request.

I hope you will welcome my call soon when I try to arrange a brief meeting at your convenience to discuss your needs and how I might serve them. Thank you in advance for your time.

Sincerely yours,

Mark Jones

Alternate last paragraph:
I hope you will call or write soon to suggest a time convenient for us to meet and discuss your current and future needs and how I might serve them. Thank you in advance for your time.

MARK JONES

1110½ Hay Street, Fayetteville, NC 28305 • preppub@aol.com • (910) 483-6611

OBJECTIVE To benefit an organization that can use a skilled planner, coordinator, and manager who offers extensive knowledge related to the transportation industry along with "hands-on" experience in controlling logistics, physical assets, human resources, and projects.

EXPERIENCE **EXECUTIVE LOGISTICS PROGRAM STUDENT.** U.S. Army, Fort Knox, KY (2005-present). By my selection as a captain to attend this six-month course designed to prepare logistics officers for senior-level line management and staff responsibilities, am being groomed for rapid promotion as an officer.

ASSISTANT MANAGER, MOVEMENT CONTROL CENTER. U.S. Army, Fort Myers, VA (2004). At the fast-paced Movement Control Center, developed and managed plans for transporting people and assets worldwide.
* Became skilled as a Dispatch Operations Chief, Movement Planner, and Shipping Consultant. Developed a traffic circulation plan for movement of cargo in a major project.

TRANSPORTATION OFFICER. U.S. Army, Europe (2003-04). At an air base in Europe, coordinated transportation needs for all U.S. military forces sent to the middle east while also serving as a Contracting Officer Representative evaluating 55 civilian employees implementing military transportation service contracts valued at up to $250,000.
* Oversaw transportation services provided to personnel in 20 separate organizations.
* Was recommended for rapid promotion and praised in writing for "expert management of a complex transportation program and expert management of hundreds of logistical and training support missions in the middle east."
* On my own initiative, significantly improved air and ground transportation services, airfield operations, property shipping/accountability, and vehicle maintenance activities.
* Organized a daily shuttle service to the Iraqi capital for commercial air travel customers and established a same-day airline ticketing service.
* Earned respect for my outstanding writing skills: developed and distributed consumer information explaining transportation services and wrote articles for the base newspaper.

PERSONNEL/ADMINISTRATIVE MANAGER. U.S. Army, Fort Lewis, WA (2002-03). Supervised seven personnel while managing personnel and administrative management programs for a transportation center supporting the needs of numerous organizations.

TRANSPORTATION OFFICER. U.S. Army, Afghanistan (2001-02). In preparation for and during the War on Terror, planned and managed the surface transportation of supplies and personnel to, from, and in a harsh desert environment.
* Managed a land transportation fleet consisting of more than 1,200 line-haul, cargo, and heavy equipment transporter trucks. Played a key role in planning and managing the movement of 110,000 personnel and 30,000 vehicles to Afghanistan in 23 days.

GENERAL MANAGER. U.S. Army, Fort Lewis, WA (2000-01). In charge of a truck company with 45 truck drivers, oversaw maintenance of 19 tractors and 38 trailers valued at more than $1.5 million for an organization which provided line-haul and local transportation.

EDUCATION **B.S. in Business Administration**, University of West Florida, Pensacola, FL, 1999.

PERSONAL Offer an extraordinary ability to pinpoint and anticipate problems before they happen. Am known for strict attention to detail. Subscribe to high standards of loyalty and honesty.

Date

Exact Name of Person
Title or Position
Name of Company
Address
City, State, Zip

FREIGHT PROCESSING SPECIALIST

Dear Exact Name of Person: (or Dear Sir or Madam if answering a blind ad.)

I would appreciate an opportunity to talk with you soon about how I could contribute to your organization through my background in the logistics field as well as through my skills and knowledge related to all phases of shipping/receiving, customer service, warehouse operations, and supply management gained while serving in the U.S. Army.

As you will see from my enclosed resume, I excelled as a Traffic Management Coordinator at Fort Stewart, GA, from 2002 until 2006. At the Central Receiving Point for this installation, which is one of the nation's largest military bases worldwide, I accepted and processed millions of dollars worth of supplies, equipment, and vehicles which were then distributed to customer units throughout the installation. Among my accomplishments in this position were providing supervision and guidance for up to ten people, training as many as 30 people in logistics policies and procedures, and applying computer skills while processing support documentation for multimillion-dollar inventories.

During this period of time at Fort Stewart, I was selected to receive special training in hazardous materials handling, storage, and transportation and then earned certification as a trainer in this specialized area. I earned my second Army Achievement Medal for my professionalism and dedication after earning my first Achievement Medal in Germany for contributions which included processing more than 10,000 pieces of freight during a large-scale joint services exercise.

If you can use an experienced logistics supervisor and manager who offers a reputation as an articulate and enthusiastic professional who can be counted on to find a way to achieve results and exceed goals, I hope you will contact me to suggest a time when we might meet to discuss your needs. I can assure you in advance that I could rapidly become an asset to your organization.

Sincerely,

Byron Coonse

BYRON COONSE

1110½ Hay Street, Fayetteville, NC 28305 • preppub@aol.com • (910) 483-6611

OBJECTIVE

To contribute through the application of my knowledge and experience in logistics, shipping and receiving, and customer service for the benefit of an organization that can use an enthusiastic, articulate, and results-oriented young professional.

EDUCATION & TRAINING

Completed one semester of course work at Savannah State University, Savannah, GA. Excelled in U.S. Army-sponsored training including a logistical operations/traffic management coordination course and hazardous materials/federal hazardous communications training as well as attending an Environmental Awareness Course at Savannah Community College.

SPECIAL SKILLS

Computers: Windows XP, MS Word, Excel, and proprietary systems specific to the logistics industry at K-Mart and the U.S. Army
Material-handling equipment: from forklifts ranging in capacity from 2,000 to 15,000 lbs. used to load and unload aircraft, trains, and trucks; pallet jacks; conveyer belts
Other: computer database entry using bar code scanners, readers, and printers; ensuring compliance with government laws and regulations including OSHA and HAZMAT

EXPERIENCE

FREIGHT PROCESSING SPECIALIST. K-Mart Distribution Center, Savannah, GA (2006-present). Ensure the timely and correct processing of freight being delivered by trucks to a regional distribution center.

- Am increasing my knowledge of the freight processing policies and procedures unique to this major retailer. Have been called on to train other personnel based on my demonstrated knowledge and skills gained in the U.S Army.

Gained a strong experience base in logistics while serving in the U.S. Army:
TRAFFIC MANAGEMENT COORDINATOR. Fort Stewart, GA (2002-06). Handled multiple duties while building a reputation as a reliable young professional who was always available to help train and guide other personnel in their responsibilities and duties during the processing of personnel and freight shipments.

- Gained experience in working with large amounts of materials, to include hazardous materials, at the Central Receiving Point at one of the nation's largest military bases worldwide.
- Supervised as many as ten people to include evaluating their job performance, preparing written monthly counseling statements, and developing plans for improving the performance of anyone not working up to expectations. Became skilled in establishing leadership while supervising personnel who were often older and more experienced.
- Trained approximately 30 people in logistics policies and procedures as well as in their individual responsibilities and duties.
- Accepted and processed millions of dollars worth of supplies, equipment, and vehicles which were then distributed to customer units throughout the installation.
- Received training in the storage, handling, and transportation of hazardous materials.

SHIPPING AND HANDLING SPECIALIST. Germany (2001-02). Became recognized as a thoroughly reliable and knowledgeable young professional while learning shipping and handling procedures, material handling equipment uses, and computer applications unique to the logistics industry in my first military assignment.

- Was awarded my first Army Achievement Medal for accomplishments which included processing more than 10,000 pieces of freight during a large-scale joint training exercise.

PERSONAL

Am known for my exceptional organizational and planning skills. Available for relocation.

Date

Exact Name of Person
Title or Position
Company Name
Address
City, State, Zip

Dear Exact Name of Person: (or Dear Sir or Madam if answering a blind ad.)

With the enclosed resume, I would like to formally begin the process of applying for positions with your organization.

As you will see from my resume, I have recently retired from the U.S. Army after 20 years of service. With most of my experience in supply and logistics, I received numerous medals and awards for distinguished service and in recognition of my professionalism and accomplishments. I was awarded the prestigious Meritorious Service Medal for my career achievements after earlier receiving four U.S. Army Commendation Medals, four Achievement Medals, six Good Conduct Medals, the National Defense Service Medal, and two Humanitarian Service Medals.

Since 2006 I have worked as an Independent Contractor handling a wide variety of carpentry, general, home repair, and remodeling services for area realty companies. I am skilled in such tasks as building and repairing decks and flooring systems, building and installing cabinetry, and painting home interiors and exteriors. I also do plumbing, minor electrical work and wiring, and install air conditioning and heating systems.

I offer skills in the operation of heavy equipment to include D-5 Caterpillar and Case 420 bulldozers, trucks up to five-ton size, up to 10,000-lb. forklifts, and boom cranes up to 15,000-lb. size. With military training and certification in equipment and vehicle operations, I also am certified in hazardous cargo handling procedures.

Entrusted with a Secret security clearance, I have built a reputation for personal integrity and high standards and have worked and lived overseas.

If you can use a mature professional with my diverse skills in heavy equipment operations, construction and carpentry, and logistics/supply management, I hope you will call or write soon to suggest a time when we might meet to discuss your needs and goals and how my background might serve your organization. I can provide outstanding references at the appropriate time.

Sincerely,

Anthony Brackett

Alternate last paragraph:
I hope you will welcome my call soon to arrange a brief meeting at your convenience to discuss your current and future needs and how I might serve them. I can provide outstanding references at the appropriate time.

ANTHONY BRACKETT

1110½ Hay Street, Fayetteville, NC 28305   •   preppub@aol.com   •   (910) 483-6611

OBJECTIVE	To contribute through my versatile skills in heavy equipment operation and carpentry as well as through extensive experience in logistics and supply operations management.
EDUCATION & TRAINING	Completed college course work in General Studies and Military Science. Received extensive training in supply operations, motor transportation, leadership, and employee supervision as well as in hazardous material handling.

SPECIAL SKILLS

Am skilled in the operation of heavy equipment including the following:

D-5 Caterpillar and Case 420 bulldozers	up to five-ton trucks
up to 10,000-lb. forklifts	up to 15,000-lb. boom cranes

EXPERIENCE

INDEPENDENT CONTRACTOR. Hopkinsville, KY (2006-present). Provide a wide variety of general carpentry, home repair, and remodeling services for area realty companies.

- Apply carpentry skills while building and repairing decks and flooring systems as well as building and installing cabinetry.
- Complete work which includes interior and exterior painting, assembling storage buildings, installing roof truss systems, and repairing holes in sheet rock and plaster.
- Handle plumbing to include replacing toilets and sinks in addition to minor electrical work and wiring as well as installing heating and air conditioning including vent systems.
- Operate bulldozers and heavy equipment in additional to all standard tools and equipment used in carpentry, electrical, plumbing, and general repair work.

Earned U.S. Army Commendation and Achievement Medals for expertise in the supply and logistics field as well as for my leadership and managerial skills:
SUPPLY OPERATIONS SUPERVISOR. Fort Campbell, KY (2001-06). Controlled a $5.5 million inventory while supervising three specialists and providing a 122-person airborne engineering company with support for its short-notice worldwide missions.

- Recognized as the organization's subject matter expert on supply issues, was cited on several occasions as having "the best" supply operation within the parent organization.
- Evaluated as "expertly" maintaining records for more than 2,300 property book items, became the first supply manager in the parent organization to complete full automation of supply records on the ULLS (Unit Level Logistics System).

SUPPLY OPERATIONS SUPERVISOR. Fort Riley, KS (1998-01). Managed a $9.5 million inventory of equipment and property for a military police company including providing security and accountability for the weapons utilized by the unit.

- Widely recognized for "unsurpassed knowledge" of supply operations, received commendable ratings in physical security inspections and achieved 100% accountability.
- Emphasized safety in the workplace and was cited for my skill in teaching and training personnel in job skills and computer applications.

SUPPLY MANAGER. Italy (1995-98). Directed supply support activities for a heavy maintenance company with four geographically dispersed divisions. Coordinated the movement of more than $30 million worth of equipment in support of various operations.

Highlights of earlier experience: Advanced to increasing responsibility for multimillion-dollar inventories with U.S. Army training, field artillery, and signal communications units.

PERSONAL

Offer extensive overseas experience gained while serving in Italy, Germany, and Korea.

Date

Exact Name of Person
Title or Position
Name of Company
Address (number and street)
Address (city, state, and zip)

**INDUSTRIAL SUPPLY
MANAGER**

Dear Exact Name of Person: (or Sir or Madam if answering a blind ad.)

With the enclosed resume, I would like to express my interest in exploring employment opportunities with your organization.

As you will see from my resume, I offer extensive expertise related to purchasing and procurement, including military contracting. For nearly 20 years, I have excelled as Territory Manager and Purchasing Agent with a major company that sells industrial equipment to the military, civilian contractors, and retail customers. In addition to providing outstanding service and support to 150 customers, I also act as a consultant as I provide safety guidance on a variety of equipment and tools. I have completed numerous OSHA safety seminars and have earned multiple safety certifications, including hazardous materials certifications. I am highly respected for my safety knowledge, and superintendents utilizing equipment in the field routinely call me when they have an emergency or an emerging problem they need help with.

As a Purchasing Agent purchasing thousands of dollars in tools and equipment weekly, I am skilled in utilizing technical manuals, catalogs, and the Internet in order to obtain hard-to-find parts. In addition to my duties related to customer service and industrial sales, I am responsible for purchasing and controlling the multimillion-dollar inventory of my employer. I was named Top Salesman out of six professionals for 10 out of my 16 years of service with the company.

With an outstanding personal and professional reputation, I can provide excellent references at the appropriate time. I am known for my ability to establish effective relationships, solve tough problems, and produce satisfied customers.

If you can use my extensive background in procurement and purchasing as well as my in-depth technical knowledge of industrial products and equipment, I hope you will contact me to suggest a time when we might talk in person. Thank you in advance for your time.

Sincerely,

Benjamin Warren

BENJAMIN WARREN

1110½ Hay Street, Fayetteville, NC 28305 • preppub@aol.com • (910) 483-6611

OBJECTIVE

To benefit an organization that can use a versatile professional with experience in industrial sales, industrial safety, and procurement, including military contracting, along with the ability to establish effective relationships, solve problems, and produce satisfied customers.

TRAINING

One year of coursework in Business Administration, Columbia Technical Community College. Graduated from Glendale High School, Glendale, AZ.

OSHA training: Completed numerous safety seminars including OHSA training related to plant/construction, hazardous materials, and equipment safety.

Safety certifications: Earned certifications related to scaffolding safety, body harness safety, drain cleaning equipment safety, powder actuated anchors tools safety, and fire extinguisher safety. Received Firestop safety rating.

Hazardous materials certifications: After training, received certifications related to Husquarna gas equipment, Poulan gas equipment, and Redmax gas equipment. Completed training and certifications related to operating Lenox band saw blades, and Diamond core bits, blades, machinery, and rigs.

EXPERIENCE

TERRITORY MANAGER & PURCHASING AGENT. Kriner Supply Co., Inc., Columbia, SC (1989-present). Provide outstanding service and support to 150 customers who purchase or rent tools, equipment, and construction products in multiple product lines.

- **Research and analysis:** Am skilled in utilizing technical manuals, catalogs, and the Internet in order to locate hard-to-obtain parts and tools for customers.
- **Purchasing agent responsibilities:** Am responsible for purchasing and controlling the multimillion-dollar inventory of this major industrial supplier. Secure quotations based on customer specifications. Obtain materials from suppliers at lowest price consistent with quality, reliability, and urgency considerations. Track procured items to ensure timely delivery.
- **Customer service and accounts receivable management:** On a weekly or monthly basis, provide customer service to electrical contractors, mechanical contractors, drywall contractors, acoustical ceiling contractors, steel erectors, concrete and masonry contractors, water and waste water treatment specialists, highway and bridge contractors, general contractors, facilities and plant management personnel, and specialty contractors. Monitor aging accounts receivable and coordinate with customers to obtain timely payment.
- **Military contracting:** Represent product line on military bases throughout NC, SC, and GA to customer organizations that include Special Operations and Delta Force. Am respected for my in-depth product knowledge and frequently provide consulting on OSHA matters. Knowledgeable of military, corporate, and municipal contracting process.
- **Honors:** Named Top Salesman out of six professionals for 10 out of 16 years.

ASSISTANT MANAGER. Columbia Gym and Living Well Fitness Center, Columbia, SC (1987-89). Designed and implemented fitness activities while managing the sale of memberships and store products. Led aerobics classes to groups of up to 15 people. Taught individuals of all skill levels including disabled and physically handicapped children. For Living Well Fitness Center, traveled throughout NC and SC to open new fitness facilities and design training programs.

PERSONAL

Outstanding references on request. Known for my strong personal initiative and integrity. Outstanding computer skills including expertise with Word, Excel, and PowerPoint.

Exact Name of Person
Title or Position
Name of Company
Address (number and street)
Address (city, state, and zip)

Dear Exact Name of Person: (or Sir or Madam if answering a blind ad.)

**INTERNATIONAL
LOGISTICS MANAGER**

    With the enclosed resume, I would like to express my interest in exploring employment opportunities with your organization. While serving my country in the U.S. Army, I have risen to the rank of Major while earning respect as an astute strategic planner, international diplomat, logistician, and manager.

Education in international relations and business management

    In spite of numerous deployments as a military officer, I have earned a Master's degree in International Relations as well as a B.S. degree in Business Management. I have also excelled in numerous graduate-level programs sponsored by the U.S. Army which expanded my international knowledge of Asia, Africa, Europe, Latin America, and the Middle East.

Experience as an international diplomat

    In my current position in Germany, I am the acknowledged expert on Civil Affairs in the European theater, and I have excelled as the single U.S. planner on a combined German-U.S. staff. Through my leadership, we modernized an outdated Civil Affairs structure as we developed the first Civil-Military operations framework for complex humanitarian emergencies. In my previous job as a Civil Affairs Officer, I managed a $13 million budget as I also served as Deputy Executive Officer of an organization with 3,981 employees. Evaluated as a "gifted, visionary leader," I personally developed a new concept which was implemented Armywide.

Extensive management and supervisory experience

    I have also excelled in challenging line management positions in high-tempo environments. As a Company Commander, I served as the "chief executive officer" of the largest maintenance and maintenance supply company in the Pacific. In that capacity, I supervised 230 soldiers while managing a budget of $1.6 million. In a prior assignment as a Maintenance Officer and Logistics Planner, I performed multifunctional logistics planning for units throughout the world and earned respect for my ability to quickly analyze a problem and determine the best solution.

    With a Top Secret/SCI security clearance, I can provide outstanding references at the appropriate time. Although I have been recommended for promotion to Lieutenant Colonel and was strongly encouraged to remain in military service, I have decided to leave the Army and enter the civilian work force. I hope you will contact me to suggest a time when we might meet to discuss your needs and goals.

Sincerely,

James Ray Jarvis

JAMES RAY JARVIS

1110½ Hay Street, Fayetteville, NC 28305   •   preppub@aol.com   •   (910) 483-6611

OBJECTIVE

To contribute to an organization that can use an outstanding strategic thinker and problem solver whose leadership ability has been refined through experience as a military officer involved in logistics management, interagency coordination, and team building.

CLEARANCE

Current Top Secret/SCI (TS/SCI), granted in 2002; valid until 2007.

EDUCATION

Master of Science in International Relations (M.S.), Webster University, Ft. Benning campus, GA, 2000. Excelled academically with a 3.2 GPA.
Bachelor of Science in Business Management (B.S.), University of Georgia, Columbus campus, GA, 1990.

EXPERIENCE

Excelled in a track record of achievement while advancing to Major, U.S. Army:
PLANS OFFICER. Germany (2005-present). As the acknowledged expert on Civil Affairs in the European theater, have excelled as the single U.S. planner on a combined German-U.S. staff. Utilized my organizational skills to implement high-level conferences on Civil Affairs, and was instrumental in restructuring an outdated Civil Affairs structure and transforming it from a weak into a strong area. Improved alliance relationships.
* Developed the first Civil-Military operations framework for complex humanitarian emergencies. The concept was presented to the Joint Chiefs of Staff and implemented.

SUPPORT OPERATIONS MANAGER & CIVIL AFFAIRS OFFICER. The Presidio, CA (2002-04). Served as Deputy Executive Officer of an organization with 3,981 employees in three infantry battalions, three other battalions, and six companies. Planned and coordinated civil-military activities in complex environments. Managed a $13 million budget.
* Was evaluated in writing as a "gifted, visionary leader."

GENERAL MANAGER ("COMPANY COMMANDER"). Ft. Huachuca, AZ (1997-98). Was the "chief executive officer" of the largest maintenance and maintenance supply company in the Pacific Command. Supervised 230 soldiers providing maintenance for automotive, communications and electronics, artillery, small arms, engineer, missiles, air conditioning, service and recovery, and Class IX parts for units in the Pacific. Managed a budget of $1.6 million. Provided oversight for multimillion-dollar assets that included 110 prime movers, 20 power generators, 25 trailers, and five crew-served weapons.
* Was commended in writing for reducing a maintenance backlog from 400 to 250 jobs in three months despite severe personnel shortages. Led my company to outstanding results in maintenance, transportation, dining, postal, finance, and police activities.

MAINTENANCE OFFICER & LOGISTICS PLANNER. Ft. Huachuca, AZ (1995-97). Served as a Liaison Officer among organizations in the Pacific. Identified maintenance and repair parts needs for multiple units, and performed multifunctional logistics planning.
* Was praised for demonstrating the ability to quickly analyze a problem and determine the best solution. Was described as "a world class team player and logistician."

Highlights of other U.S. Army experience: OPERATIONS SUPPORT OFFICER. Supervised one officer and 10 enlisted soldiers while overseeing intelligence gathering, communications, schools management, truck operations, logistics support, and other areas.

PERSONAL

Highly intuitive problem solver with a commitment to safety and quality assurance. Recipient of more than 23 medals, badges, and other honors for exemplary performance.

Date

Exact Name of Person
Title or Position
Name of Company
Address
City, State, Zip

LOGISTICAL OFFICER   Dear Exact Name of Person: (or Dear Sir or Madam if answering a blind ad.)

With the enclosed resume, I would like to make you aware of my interest in exploring employment opportunities with your organization.

As you will see from my resume, I have earned a reputation as one of the military's most astute logisticians and managers while serving my country in both the U.S. Army and the U.S. Army National Guard. My background also includes service as a Master State Trooper in the State of Iowa.

In my current position as a Logistical Officer with the Army Logistics Division, I am in charge of planning and organizing logistics needs for National Guard troops being sent to Afghanistan and Iraq for peacekeeping missions. I am proud that I have gained a reputation within the Army as someone who "trains the trainers," and it was my honor to plan and host a top-level conference in Washington, D.C., in 2006 which trained logisticians and operators who are in charge of logistics for the Army and National Guard. While in my current position, I was recognized for providing critical logistical support for the United States. Formal performance reports have praised my "total understanding of multi-function logistics" as well as my "outstanding planning and problem-solving skills."

Although much of my experience has involved training and preparing for the relocation of military professionals assigned to Europe, I have also excelled in line management positions. In one position in Iraq, I was called up from the National Guard to a nine-month active-duty assignment during which I managed 15 people. In a line management position with the National Guard as a Company Commander, I managed 75 people. Through my logistical background, I have developed a strong belief in the value of training, and I transformed that organization into a highly efficient unit with highly motivated and well-trained employees.

Although I am highly regarded in my current position and have been recommended for promotion to Lieutenant Colonel, I have decided to explore employment opportunities outside the military community. I can provide outstanding references at the appropriate time, and I would enjoy an opportunity to discuss your needs for a logistics expert with exceptional problem-solving ability.

Yours sincerely,

Alan Joseph

ALAN JOSEPH

1110½ Hay Street, Fayetteville, NC 28305   •   preppub@aol.com   •   (910) 483-6611

OBJECTIVE

To contribute to an organization that can use a knowledgeable professional who offers an extensive background related to logistics management and operations management along with strong communication, management, and organizational skills.

CLEARANCE

Current Secret clearance; previously was cleared to the Top Secret level.

COMPUTERS

Experienced with numerous software programs including Excel, PowerPoint, and Word; have completed training on various automated systems used in the logistics field.

Am qualified on the following Army logistics software programs which enable me to cross-level, source, coordinate, and integrate equipment for active duty and reserve forces:

- Logistics Integrated Data Base (LIDB)
- Deployment Asset Visibility System (DAVS)
- Automated Battlebook System (ABS 2000-2)

PUBLICATIONS

Have authored numerous Memoranda of Agreement and have contributed to the creation of annexes to Special Operations Procedures (SOPs) related to the logistical aspects of mobilization. Am highly skilled in research and analysis using AREM and LOGSA.

EXPERIENCE

Have served my country for seven years on active duty (current rank Major) and for 13 years in the U.S. Army Reserves (current rank Major) in the following track record of accomplishment:

LOGISTICAL OFFICER. U.S. Army, Army Logistics Division, Fort Drum, NY (2005-present). Was handpicked for this job which involves planning and organizing logistics for National Guard soldiers being sent to locations such as Afghanistan and Iraq for peacekeeping missions as well as locations in the U.S. for homeland defense activities. Have received the prestigious Meritorious Service Medal recognizing distinguished accomplishments.

- Continuously anticipate training needs and assure that soldiers are well trained for their missions. Have gained an outstanding reputation as a leading logistical thinker and planner within the Army, and am entrusted with the honor of training and advising other top logistics military leaders.

PRIMARY LOGISTICS PLANS OFFICER. U.S. Army, Fort Drum, NY (2003-04). As the leading logistical planner for the 10th Mountain Division, developed logistical sourcing strategies for critical worldwide activities.

- Planned and managed government contracting services and logistics activities related to two projects involving 7,800 military employees and an $8 million budget.

QUALITY CONTROL INSPECTOR. U.S. Army National Guard, Des Moines, IA (2002-03). Traveled to 20 organizations throughout IA in order to verify and inspect organizational efficiency and provide management consulting where problems existed.

GENERAL MANAGER. U.S. Army, Iraq (2000-01). Was called up from the National Guard to this nine-month active duty position in Iraq. As a Captain in charge of a 15-person organization, provided logistical expertise and leadership in combat.

EDUCATION

Pursuing MBA degree via online courses, Touro University, 2002-present.
Received a **BA degree in Law and Justice**, Drake University, Des Moines, IA, 1987.

PERSONAL

I believe my strong communication and problem-solving skills have been the key to my success as a top-level planner and leader. Exceptionally strong references on request.

Date

Exact Name of Person
Title or Position
Name of Company
Address
City, State, Zip

**LOGISTICAL
OPERATIONS
COORDINATOR**

Dear Exact Name of Person: (or Dear Sir or Madam if answering a blind ad.)

I would appreciate an opportunity to talk with you soon about how I could benefit your organization as a Warehouse Manager or Warehouse Supervisor by applying my outstanding motivational, supervisory, and managerial abilities.

While serving as a U.S. Army officer, I have had the opportunity to directly supervise as many as 140 employees in a variety of settings. I have been in charge of activities ranging from weapons systems maintenance to logistics operations.

As you will see from my resume, my most recent position involves contributing my expertise to a team of logistics specialists engaged in large-scale contingency planning. I was chosen for this role on the basis of my performance as Director of Logistics Support.

Throughout my career I have been consistently described as a "pace setter" who can be counted on to set high personal performance standards and guide employees to achieve their own high goals. I feel that my ability to respond to rapidly changing circumstances calmly and with control is one of my greatest strengths.

I hope you will call or write me soon to suggest a time convenient for us to meet and discuss your current and future needs and how I might serve them. Thank you in advance for your time.

Sincerely yours,

Dillon Kramer

Alternate last paragraph:
I hope you will welcome my call soon to arrange a brief meeting at your convenience to discuss your current and future needs and how I might serve them. Thank you in advance for your time.

DILLON KRAMER

1110½ Hay Street, Fayetteville, NC 28305　•　preppub@aol.com　•　(910) 483-6611

OBJECTIVE

To contribute to an organization that can benefit from my managerial skills as well as my specific knowledge and experience in the areas of budget and finance, logistics, production, and inventory control gained in a distinguished career as a junior military officer.

EDUCATION & TRAINING

M.S.A., General Administration, Central Texas College; to be awarded December 2006.
B.S., Industrial Technology, Elmhurst College, Elmhurst, IL, 1996.
* Was honored as the Distinguished Military Graduate.

EXPERIENCE

LOGISTICAL OPERATIONS COORDINATOR. U.S. Army, Fort Bragg, NC (2005-present). Was selected to join a team of specialists involved in developing complete logistical support plans to be used in combat as well as for peacetime projects when requested.

DIRECTOR OF LOGISTICS SUPPORT. U.S. Army, Fort Benning, GA (2002-04). During a period of rapid change due to functional reorganization, developed budget forecasting/planning improvements while coordinating activities in support of 320 people training more than 5,000 students a year in 18 advanced special operations programs.
* Controlled a $2 million annual operating budget including two- and six-year planning.
* Coordinated and oversaw construction of $15 million worth of new construction.
* Earned praise for developing comprehensive and workable two-year forecasts and six- and ten-year plans for improved budgeting processes.
* Excelled in passing my expertise to employees and updated the logistics section of corporate standard operating procedures which "clearly surpassed other contributions."

GENERAL MANAGER. U.S. Army, Germany (2001-02). Described as an "exceptional manager and natural leader," guided 140 employees and controlled more than $3 million worth of assets while overseeing training and performance of employees in the largest and most complex support unit in Italy.
* Handled the details of logistical support for other companies, ranging from mail service for 21 units to weapons storage space for seven and housing for five of the units.
* Implemented successful training programs which surpassed government requirements.
* Led employees to a 100% pass rate in physical fitness/weapons qualification testing.

Gained experience in both "staff" and "line" positions, U.S. Army, Fort Knox, KY:
SUPPLY MANAGER. (1999-00). Advanced rapidly from "second-in-command" to take charge of a $2,900,000 budget and provide advice to a chief executive on fiscal, property management, and logistics matters for a 552-person organization.
* Handpicked to manage an "overwhelming" project coordinating the shipment of personnel and equipment to Germany for a training mission, completed the project "flawlessly."
* Transformed a series of detailed plans which were in "complete disarray" and within two weeks received a commendable rating in an important inspection.

OPERATIONS MANAGER. (1998-99). Oversaw the operation and maintenance of 14 high-tech weapons systems worth in excess of $5 million as the "second-in-command."
* Displayed technical knowledge which resulted in a 94% operational readiness rates.

FIRST-LINE SUPERVISOR. (1997-98). Trained and supervised 22 employees operating and maintaining six weapons systems valued in excess of $13 million.

PERSONAL

Have a reputation for integrity and moral courage. Perform well under pressure and in stressful situations. Offer superior analytical and decision-making skills.

Date

Exact Name of Person
Exact Title
Exact Name of Company
Address
City, State, Zip

Dear Exact Name of Person (or Dear Sir or Madam if answering a blind ad):

With the enclosed resume, I would like to make you aware of my interest in exploring employment opportunities with your organization. As you will see from my enclosed resume, I have served my country with distinction as a military officer since graduating with a B.S. in Business Administration and Economics.

Extensive logistics management skills

Promoted rapidly to the rank of Captain, I was handpicked for jobs normally held by someone of more senior rank, and I proved my ability to manage multiple complex projects simultaneously. After completing a one-year graduate-level program called the Army Logistics Management College, I was specially selected for an important logistics planning/management job. I currently develop and implement plans to support logistical operations in 25 countries including Iraq, Afghanistan, Horn of Africa, and the entire Eastern Asia area. Logistical plans that I develop support the needs of **250,000** people and, on a daily basis, I prepare and deliver PowerPoint briefings on logistical matters for VIPs such the Secretary of Defense, U.S. Senators, presidents, ambassadors, and military executives. In my prior position, I utilized my training in transportation operations, HazMat procedures, and military contracting in order to improve organizational effectiveness, reduce costs, and boost morale.

Knowledge of logistics, transportation, and hazardous materials

In previous work as a Senior Logistics Officer, I planned and coordinated logistics support for thousands of military professionals involved in activities in Nepal, Sri Lanka, Cambodia, and other places in the Pacific. Trained in HazMat, I have certified HazMat materials transported internationally by air, sea, and land. As a military officer, I have become known for integrity and reliability, and I have been entrusted with extensive purchasing authority as well as responsibility for the use of government credit cards. I have been entrusted with one of our country's highest security clearances—Top Secret.

Although I have excelled as a military officer, I have decided to explore opportunities in the civilian world where I will be able to use my vast experience in logistics and transportation management as well as my B.S. in Business Administration and Economics. I can provide outstanding references at the appropriate time, and I would enjoy an opportunity to meet with you in person to discuss your current or future needs.

Yours sincerely,

Asacia Winkle

ASACIA WINKLE

1110½ Hay Street, Fayetteville, NC 28305   •   preppub@aol.com   •   (910) 483-6611

OBJECTIVE

I want to contribute to an organization that can use a highly motivated young professional who offers a proven ability to handle multiple simultaneous priorities while organizing and motivating others to work together to accomplish ambitious goals.

EDUCATION

B.S. degree in Business Administration and Economics, Winfield College, Winfield, NC, 1998; was on scholarship for two years.
Completed Combined Logistics Captain's Career Course (known as the Army Logistics Management College), Ft. Lee, VA, 2003-04. This is a one-year graduate-level program.
Completed Transportation Officer Course and HazMat School. Certified HazMat materials for numerous international projects.

EXPERIENCE

Have served my country with distinction as a military officer:
LOGISTICS CHIEF. U.S. Army, Kuwait (2005-present). Develop plans to support combat and logistical operations in 25 countries including Iraq, Afghanistan, Horn of Africa, and the entire Eastern Asia area. Travel frequently throughout those countries in order to analyze, plan, and develop recommendations for operations plans supporting 250,000 people.

- Create daily oral presentations utilizing 10-20 PowerPoint slides which I use to provide logistical updates and transportation status. Delivered briefings to U.S. VIPs such as the Secretary of Defense, U.S. Senators and Congressmen, and military executives. Also briefed foreign dignitaries, presidents, ambassadors, and senior military leaders.
- Continuously perform cost-benefit analyses and compare vendor prices and capabilities in order to maximize the efficiency of taxpayer dollars.
- Develop transportation plans utilizing air, ground, and sea while utilizing my logistics expertise. Apply my knowledge of distribution procedures, inventory management and asset management, contracting procedures, and logistics network designs.

TRANSPORTATION OPERATIONS MANAGER. U.S. Army, Ft. Hood, TX (2001-2004). As a Lieutenant in a Captain's job, managed 10 people including administrative specialists, supply operations personnel, and others involved in overseeing a fleet of light to medium industrial vehicles associated with a 150-person Psychological Operations organization which supports Special Operations. Was evaluated as "an officer with unlimited potential."

- **Budgeting and cost control:** Controlled a $220,000 budget along with other budgets which ranged up to $600,000; using Excel and PowerPoint, developed a budget tracking system which tracked "to the penny" every dollar spent. Resourcefully utilized military IMPAC credit cards. Briefed senior officers on spending patterns and budget projections.
- **Project management:** Accounted for property valued at more than $1 million. Coordinated the turn-in and resourceful reutilization of excess property, which saved thousands of dollars. Installed a computer local area network (LAN) in only two weeks.
- **Logistics management:** Planned and organized logistics for thousands of people during major training projects in Nepal, Sri Lanka, Cambodia, Thailand, Korea, and other places in the Pacific.

GENERAL MANAGER ("Platoon Leader"). U.S. Army, Ft. Bragg, NC (1999-01). Excelled as a Platoon Leader in two separate assignments; in one assignment, managed 23 people while overseeing a fleet of air defense vehicles, Stinger missiles, and other equipment valued at $4.5 million.

PERSONAL

Outstanding references. Enjoy working as part of a team dedicated to quality results.

Date

Exact Name of Person
Title or Position
Name of Company
Address (number and street)
Address (city, state, and zip)

LOGISTICS
MANAGEMENT
OFFICER

Dear Exact Name of Person: (or Sir or Madam if answering a blind ad.)

With the enclosed resume, I would like to express my interest in exploring employment opportunities with your organization. I am single (no dependents) and could relocate worldwide to suit your needs.

As you will see from my resume, I proudly served my country as an officer after graduating from New York Military Academy and then from Hofstra University on an ROTC scholarship. As a military officer for four years, I was promoted on the "fast track" to Captain and excelled in every assignment.

Most recently as a Logistics Management Officer, I managed a $3 million budget and applied my knowledge of the government contracting process as I managed property for five companies, including three newly activated National Guard units. On my own initiative, I saved the government $300,000 through aggressively and resourcefully pursuing rebates while filling all shortages and even purchasing new items not on the property books—all within budget. Trained and certified as a Billing Officer, I supervise government credit card holders.

In a previous position as a Service Operations Manager and Supply Manager, I directed a 15-person team providing logistical support in the combat environment of Iraq. While managing a $20 million warehouse and a fleet of 30 wheeled vehicles and trailers, I established "from scratch" contracts for food, fuel, trash removal, and other services and supplies. As I maintained flawless inventory control and perfect cash management, I refined my skills in international diplomacy in the process of negotiating sensitive, essential items with multinationals. During a previous assignment in Iraq, I was specially selected to manage a 64-person platoon during a three-month deployment throughout Saudi Arabia and Iraq. In that assignment, I directed the establishment of a fuel system supply point providing 20,000 gallons of fuel daily and a water purification point that delivered 1,000 gallons of water per day. In my first job in the U.S. Army, I excelled as a Logistics Officer in Korea and was commended for "flawless planning and execution of logistical and transportation support."

If you can use a capable young individual who possesses genuine enthusiasm for the challenges associated with logistics, contracting, purchasing, and supply management, I hope you will contact me to suggest a time when we might discuss your needs. Thank you in advance for your time.

Sincerely,

Gloria Nijawhan

GLORIA NIJAWHAN

1110½ Hay Street, Fayetteville, NC 28305 • preppub@aol.com • (910) 483-6611

OBJECTIVE

To benefit an organization that can use an astute young professional who offers extensive experience in managing contracting and acquisitions in international environments while utilizing my ability to establish effective working relationships and achieve difficult goals.

EDUCATION

Graduated with **B.A. in Sociology,** minor in Biology, Hofstra University, Long Island, NY, 2001. Completed two years of college at Norwich University, NY, 1996-98. Financed education with ROTC scholarship.

Graduated from high school at New York Military Academy, Cornwall-Hudson, NY, 1996.

EXPERIENCE

Although I have excelled in the U.S. Army and was promoted on a "fast track" to Captain, I am resigning my commission as a military officer (and I will not be a member of the Reserve forces):

July 2004-2006: **LOGISTICS MANAGEMENT OFFICER (S-4).** U.S. Army, Ft. Hood, TX. As a Captain, supervised two mid-managers, one clerk, and one maintenance technician while managing property for five different companies, including three recently activated National Guard units, with 680 employees.

- **Contracting and Budgeting:** Managed a $3 million budget. Applied my knowledge of the government contracting process as well as my negotiating skills while directing the procurement of parts and equipment. Filled all shortages and even purchased new items not on the property books—all within budget. On my own initiative, saved the government $300,000 through aggressively pursuing rebates.

June 2003-June 2004: **SERVICE OPERATIONS MANAGER & SUPPLY MANAGER.** U.S. Army, Iraq. As a Lieutenant, directed a 15-person team providing logistical support in support of Operation Iraqi Freedom while managing a $20 million warehouse and a company maintenance program. Managed a fleet of 30 wheeled vehicles.

- In support of the War on Terror, deployed to Iraq, where I established an aerial operating base for 3,000 military professionals. Set up "from scratch" contracts for food, fuel, trash removal, and other services and supplies. Worked with companies in other countries to procure items including candy. Organized the delivery of fuel and ammunition deliveries throughout Iraq. Operated a warehouse that provided supplies from lumber, to oil and lubricants, to office supplies.
- In Iraq, maintained perfect inventory control and flawless cash management while expending large amounts of cash in the purchasing process.

Nov 2002-June 2003: **GENERAL MANAGER.** Ft. Hood, TX, and Iraq. Was specially selected to manage a platoon supporting the Joint Special Operations Forces which deployed for three months to Baghdad International Airport. Established a fuel system supply point and a water purification point while accounting for $1 million in property; provided over 20,000 gallons of fuel and 1,000 gallons of water per day throughout three airfields.

Nov 2001-Nov 2002: **LOGISTICS OFFICER.** Korea. Managed 50 employees including 39 Korean nationals while serving as a Lieutenant in a position normally filled by a Captain. Was commended for "flawless planning and execution of logistical and transportation support."

PERSONAL

Fluent in Spanish—speaking, writing, and reading. Outstanding references on request. Known for my strong personal initiative and integrity. Held Secret security clearance. Outstanding computer skills including expertise with Word, Excel, and PowerPoint.

Date

Exact Name of Person
Title or Position
Name of Company
Address
City, State, Zip

Dear Exact Name of Person: (or Dear Sir or Madam if answering a blind ad.)

    With the enclosed resume, I would like to make you aware of my experience in all aspects of supply, logistics, and warehouse management including my ability to account for all types of materials in large quantities as well as my strong computer skills and budgetary knowledge.

    As you will see from my resume, I offer knowledge of numerous software programs which include the Microsoft XP as well as programs for inventory control and supply management. In my current job as Logistics Management Supervisor in charge of two employees, I have become recognized as the "internal expert" on all logistics matters within my organization while flawlessly accounting for property valued at more than $35 million and managing a budget of more than $100,000. On my own initiative, I have provided the leadership required to establish new automated systems which have boosted productivity and efficiency. I have also served as Instructor for the Unit Level Logistics System S4 (ULLS-S4). I have earned a reputation as a skilled problem solver.

    While gaining expertise in logistics and supply management, I have been selected for difficult assignments which required an astute problem solver and strategic thinker who could accurately forecast future needs. I have established highly effective logistics systems in field and headquarters environments, and I once supervised the closure of a military installation and the geographical relocation of the unit with no loss of accountability.

    In my previous position, I worked in human resources administration and managed five employees while supervising a Customer Service Desk. I offer excellent communication and negotiating skills.

    If you can use a highly motivated self-starter known for unlimited personal initiative, I hope you will contact me to suggest a time when we might meet to discuss your needs. I can assure you in advance that I could rapidly become an asset to your organization.

Sincerely,

Cornelius Whitaker

CORNELIUS WHITAKER

1110½ Hay Street, Fayetteville, NC 28305 • preppub@aol.com • (910) 483-6611

OBJECTIVE

To offer my experience related to all aspects of supply, logistics, and warehouse management as well as my strong computer skills and budgetary knowledge.

EDUCATION & TRAINING

Have completed 52 hours of general studies, Central Texas College, Killeen, TX.
Studied Principles of Banking/Teller Training, Baylor University, Waco, TX.
Excelled in extensive military-sponsored training which included the following courses:

Standard Property Book Systems Redesign
Unit Level Logistics Systems (ULLS-S4) Instructor
Defense Reutilization and Marketing
Personnel Records

Defense Property Disposal
Research and Development
Equipment Records and Parts
German

EXPERIENCE

Am advancing in leadership roles while building a reputation for my knowledge of logistics management, personnel supervision, and warehouse operations, U.S. Army:
LOGISTICS MANAGEMENT SPECIALIST. Fort Hood, TX (2005-present). Have handled multiple areas of responsibility in similar consecutive assignments which have included maintaining accountability for property valued in excess of $35 million; am recognized as a subject matter expert in the field of logistics.

- Advanced to supervise two people.
- Maintain records and parts inventories for more than 200 items of equipment.
- Was a key player in the establishment of new automated systems which are a vital factor in units receiving "commendable" ratings in inspections.
- Control a $100,000 annual unit budget.
- Was cited for my proficiency in maintaining the property books for two separate units.
- Displayed communication skills and technical knowledge which led to my selection as an instructor for the Army's new Unit Level Logistics System S4 (ULLS-S4); was chosen from among a group of 15 well-qualified professionals and trained more than 80 people including specialists, supervisors, and managers.
- Supervised a military installation closing project and physical relocation of all organizational assets with no losses of equipment or funds. Oversaw the design and renovation of new facilities with little assistance and within severe time constraints.

PERSONNEL RECORDS TEAM SUPERVISOR and **CUSTOMER SERVICE SUPERVISOR.** Germany (1998-05). Selected to supervise a customer service desk in a Personnel Services Company, directed the workflow of five subordinates in an out-processing section which serviced more than 100 people each week.

- Maintained personnel records for in excess of 800 people.
- Supervised personnel with varied skills and duties including mail clerks, computer operators, and customer service specialists. Trained subordinates.
- Applied my German language skills while working, living, and traveling extensively in Germany. Was awarded five Army Achievement Medals for my positive impact on productivity and efficiency.

COMPUTERS

Am adept at diagnosing, identifying, and correcting malfunctions to ULLS-S4 systems as well as in loading program software and solving operator and system problems.
Programs and software: Microsoft Word, Excel, PowerPoint, Form Flow, ULLS (S4 and Ground), and Standard Property Book Systems-Redesign.

PERSONAL

Am known for my ability to react quickly and make sound decisions under pressure. Offer expert skills in varying areas including purchasing, budgeting, forecasting, and contracting.

Date

Exact Name of Person
Title or Position
Name of Company
Address
City, State, Zip

LOGISTICS MANAGER   Dear Exact Name of Person: (or Dear Sir or Madam if answering a blind ad.)

I would appreciate an opportunity to talk with you soon about how I could benefit your organization through my outstanding communication, problem-solving, and decision-making skills, as well as my management ability refined as a junior military officer.

As a Captain in the U.S. Army, I have gained extensive experience in managing personnel, assets, logistics, and transportation activities. Known for my keen analytical skills, I currently analyze trends, determine needs, and solve potential problems while managing transportation activities for 1,600 people. An excellent planner and organizer who works well under pressure, I have developed plans for the emergency transport of people and assets.

With a reputation as a dynamic leader and persuasive coach, I once coached a team to its first-ever first place finish in a technical competition. While acquiring on-the-job experience with several popular computer software packages, I have earned awards for my skill in cutting costs and increasing efficiency.

You would find me to be a "born motivator" who is capable of providing the guidance and enthusiasm needed to bring your ideals "to life."

I hope you will welcome my call soon to arrange a brief meeting at your convenience to discuss your current and future needs and how I might serve them. Thank you in advance for your time.

Sincerely yours,

Melanie Moses

Alternate last paragraph:
I hope you will call or write me soon to suggest a time convenient for us to meet and discuss your current and future needs and how I might serve them. Thank you in advance for your time.

MELANIE MOSES

1110½ Hay Street, Fayetteville, NC 28305 • preppub@aol.com • (910) 483-6611

OBJECTIVE
To contribute to an organization that can use a dedicated professional who offers outstanding communication skills, as well as problem-solving, decision-making, and management abilities refined as a military officer.

EXPERIENCE
LOGISTICS MANAGER. U.S. Army, Fort Richardson, AK (2005-present). Manage a team controlling diversified transportation assets for 1,600 people involved in worldwide training projects.
- Became known as an exceptional decision maker while analyzing trends, determining priorities, and resolving potential problems.

TRANSPORTATION MANAGER. U.S. Army, Fort Richardson, AK (2004-05). Coordinated the highway/railway transport of thousands of personnel while developing strategic plans for the emergency transportation of people and assets.
- Played a key role in the implementation of an advanced cargo air transport planning system.
- Designed detailed analytical studies of international transport operations.

TRAINING/ADMINISTRATIVE DIRECTOR. U.S. Army, Fort Bragg, NC (2003). Established an "orientation" program for new personnel while overseeing training, supply, and housing activities for an organization of 300 people; excelled in assuming the role of "chief executive officer."
- Expertly counseled employees on personal and professional matters.

EXECUTIVE AIDE/OPERATIONS MANAGER. U.S. Army, Fort Bragg, NC (2002-03). As the "second in command" of this 400-person central headquarters operation, oversaw a five-person administrative services office. Was credited with "revitalizing" a troubled in-house publication system previously known for mismanagement and low productivity.
- Designed a standardized training program for administrative personnel.

LOGISTICS CHIEF. U.S. Army, Fort Bragg, NC (2001-02). Trained, motivated, and managed 39 people involved in receiving, sorting, and distributing tons of cargo daily; oversaw the operation and maintenance of $1.6 million in heavy equipment.
- During an international training project in Honduras, monitored the loading of two commercial vessels transporting Army assets.

OPERATIONS MANAGER. U.S. Army, Germany (1999-00). Earned a respected medal while overseeing a 79-person vehicle maintenance/driver testing operation with 267 vehicles worth over $1.8 million.
- Dramatically cut costs by almost eliminating unnecessary trips.
- Reduced the number of vehicles needing repairs to below 7%.

EDUCATION & TRAINING
B.A. in Sociology, Boston University, Boston, MA, 1999.
- Was selected for the National Dean's List and chosen as a member of the Beta Chi Honor Society.
- Because of my leadership skills, was granted a three-year ROTC scholarship.
Excelled in Army training for professional managers related to personnel and assets management, transportation systems, logistics, and maintenance.

PERSONAL
Hold Top Secret security clearance with SBI. Am a "born motivator.

Date

Exact Name of Person
Title or Position
Name of Company
Address
City, State, Zip

LOGISTICS MANAGER   Dear Exact Name of Person: (or Dear Sir or Madam if answering a blind ad.)

Can you use a "hard charger" who offers a background of exceptional performance and a reputation as a superior manager of human, fiscal, and physical resources during a distinguished career as a military officer?

Throughout my career in the U.S. Army I was repeatedly singled out to take over substandard operations, find solutions to problems, and implement changes which established successful "turnarounds" to above-standard performance.

As you will see from my resume, I have managed multimillion-dollar projects and have been heavily involved in budgeting for numerous organizations. In one earlier job I managed the logistical support for the Multinational Forces and Observers in the middle east, a 3,000-person community with members from 11 nations. I supervised 350 people in a location described as "the end of the supply trail."

I feel that my experience and education related to accounting and auditing combine with my personal qualities as an energetic and resourceful professional to make me a person who can add to an organization's "bottom line."

I hope you will welcome my call soon to arrange a brief meeting at your convenience to discuss your current and future needs and how I might serve them. Thank you in advance for your time.

Sincerely yours,

Matt Fisher

Alternate last paragraph:
I hope you will call or write soon to suggest a time convenient for us to meet and discuss your current and future needs and how I might serve them. Thank you in advance for your time.

MATT FISHER

1110½ Hay Street, Fayetteville, NC 28305   •   preppub@aol.com   •   (910) 483-6611

OBJECTIVE

To apply managerial as well as accounting and auditing abilities to an organization that can use a mature professional who has excelled as a military officer.

EXPERIENCE

LOGISTICS MANAGER. U.S. Army, Rolla Army Depot, Rolla, MO (2002-06). Earned praise for my "initiative and enthusiasm" displayed in coordinating with several major military commands and private industry while developing, analyzing, implementing, and documenting the Integrated Logistic Support (ILS) Programs for 25 new weapons systems.
- Managed a $40 million project processing specialized equipment for worldwide delivery.
- Established an automated database which resulted in improved project tracking.
- Earned official praise for my "capacity to quickly grasp and translate complex concepts."
- Assumed another specialist's workload and managed several additional projects.
- Was cited for serving "often and flawlessly" in acting upper-level management roles.

Advanced in this "track record," U.S. Army, Fort Ord, CA:
MANAGER OF LOGISTICAL SUPPORT. (2001-02). Provided supply, maintenance, budget, and support services for 600 people in 10 units at two locations 350 miles apart.
- Controlled a $2.5 million annual operating budget from the development stage.
- Developed the standard operating procedures for property accountability and supply.
- Was officially described by one senior executive as "the best I have seen in my 23 years."

GENERAL MANAGER. (2000-01). Recognized for my ability to manage multiple tasks, was selected ahead of my peers to manage a newly formed unit and described as "tremendous" in producing thoroughly trained employees despite the harsh arctic environment.
- Administered assets worth $2 million while providing day-to-day and training support.
- Turned around a chaotic and disorganized supply operation within four months.

MEDICAL SUPPLY MANAGER and **SECURITY AND COMMUNICATIONS SUPPORT MANAGER.** (1999). Was handpicked for successive positions as the interim manager for two separate dysfunctional operations and quickly revitalized both companies.
- Brought medical supply customer satisfaction to an all-time high, led employees to exceed performance testing standards, and produced a rare 100% rate on vehicle readiness.
- Directed planning, security, and communications for thousands of people.

WHOLESALE SUPPLY MANAGER. (1998-99). Cited for my "exceptional ability to anticipate problems and develop practical solutions," maintained ordering and status monitoring on repair parts and special tools during modernization of the Army's vehicle fleets. Created a workable plan for using outdated vehicles after reissuing 900 new ones.

LOGISTICAL SUPPORT OFFICER. U.S. Army, Korea (1997). Managed more than $15 million in equipment and supplies in support of the 11-nation, 3,000-member multinational forces; supervised 350 employees.
- Gained experience in "juggling" multiple tasks in a complex international operation.
- Created a detailed audit trail, the first in the organization's history.

EDUCATION & TRAINING

B.A., Business Administration, Bemidji State University, MN, 1996; graduated **cum laude**. Excelled in more than 1,800 hours of supply and management executive training courses.

PERSONAL

Was awarded numerous medals for "meritorious service." Have been consistently described as one who "sets the standards" and for performing "head and shoulders above his peers."

Date

Exact Name of Person
Title or Position
Name of Company
Address
City, State, Zip

LOGISTICS MANAGER Dear Exact Name of Person: (or Dear Sir or Madam if answering a blind ad.)

I would appreciate an opportunity to talk with you soon about how I could contribute to your organization through my management and marketing experience as well as my technical expertise related to telecommunications, communications-electronics, and automated data processing.

Telecommunications and communications-electronics expertise

As you will see from my resume, I have excelled as a military officer in top-level jobs which involved planning and implementing communications services including telecommunications, centralized computer operations, radio communications, and procedures for implementing emergency security plans. In my most recent job, I used my resourceful problem-solving style to reduce the organization's long-distance telephone costs by 30%, and I used my technical know-how to install a new device that tracked unauthorized calls. In a previous job I planned, engineered, and installed command and control communications for the Special Operations Forces. I am skilled in using several popular software programs including Microsoft Word, Excel; and Adobe InDesign.

Finance and logistics knowledge

In one job I managed a logistical operation cited as "the best" among 25 similar logistics activities. While planning and controlling a budget of $1 million, I organized and coordinated the turn-in and receipt of new equipment worth $210 million.

Management skills

With a reputation as a powerful motivator who believes in "leadership by example," I have also excelled as a "company commander" responsible for managing 163 people in a company with over $28 million in equipment. I led that company to be named "the best" out of six companies in the parent organization because of my success in transforming inefficient administrative, supply, maintenance, and training programs into top-notch service operations.

I hope you will call or write me soon to suggest a time convenient for us to meet and discuss your current and future needs and how I might serve them. Thank you in advance for your time.

Sincerely yours,

Albert Knutson

ALBERT KNUTSON

1110½ Hay Street, Fayetteville, NC 28305 • preppub@aol.com • (910) 483-6611

OBJECTIVE

To benefit an organization that can use a professional with expert experience in telecommunications, communications-electronics, automated data processing, and logistics.

SUMMARY

Over ten years of increasing management responsibility in all facets of engineering, installing, operating, maintaining, and merging a wide array of communication and information systems.

EXPERIENCE

LOGISTICS MANAGER. U.S. Army, Fort Leonard Wood, MO (2005-present). Supervised supply management for a 2,500-person organization including force modernization integration and movements; planned and coordinated the fielding of Tactical Quiet Generators (TQG).

TELECOMMUNICATIONS OFFICER. U.S. Army, Germany (2004). Planned and implemented communications support for a division headquarters organization; trained 1,000 personnel on Mobile Subscriber Equipment (MSE); planned and coordinated the movement to a new location of the entire headquarters along with its 3,000 telephones and computer systems. Reduced long distance telephone costs 30% by installing a new device that tracked unauthorized calls.

SYSTEM INTEGRATION OFFICER. U.S. Army, Fort Bragg, NC (2003). Developed operational procedures used to implement emergency contingency plans in this top-level strategic planning and consulting position; acted as a consultant to numerous subordinate organizations in developing support concepts and procedures related to emergency response.
• Planned and coordinated the training of the Texas National Guard.

GENERAL MANAGER. U.S. Army, Fort Bragg, NC (2000-02). Was "Company Commander" of a 163-person company with over $28 million in equipment. Led the company to be named "the best" out of six companies because of my success in transforming mediocre maintenance, supply, administrative, and training programs into top-notch service operations.
• Received a prestigious medal for my extraordinary leadership and management.

LOGISTICS OFFICER. U.S. Army, Fort Bragg, NC (1998-00). Managed a logistical operation that was cited as "the best" among 25 similar logistics activities; planned and coordinated the turn-in and receipt of new equipment worth $210 million while acting as the "right arm" and trusted advisor to a top military executive.
• Planned and administered a budget of $1 million. Received "commendable" rating in assets movement, property accountability, and budgeting.

COMMUNICATIONS-ELECTRONICS OFFICER. U.S. Army, Germany (1997-98). Established the first-ever communications system from a command post to Navy ships while planning, engineering, installing, and maintaining command and control communications for all U.S. Special Operations Forces (S.O.F.).

COMMUNICATIONS-ELECTRONICS OFFICER. U.S. Army, Fort Knox, KY (1994-97). Developed a communications vehicle that combined three communications vans in one vehicle while planning, engineering, and installing command and control communications support for an infantry brigade.

EDUCATION

Earned a **Bachelor of Science (B.S.) degree in Business Administration and Marketing**, University of Southern Maine, Gorham, ME, 1993.

Date

Exact Name of Person
Title or Position
Name of Company
Address (number and street)
Address (city, state, and zip)

**LOGISTICS
MANAGER**

Dear Exact Name of Person: (or Sir or Madam if answering a blind ad.)

With the enclosed resume, I would like to express my interest in exploring employment opportunities with your organization.

Expertise in logistics management, contracting, and operations

While serving my country in the U.S. Army as a military officer, I have demonstrated my resourcefulness, analytical skills, and problem-solving ability in complex logistics roles. Early in my career, I developed and maintained support for projects in Saudi Arabia, Kuwait, and Haiti. Later as a Logistics Management Officer, I worked as a top-level consultant to eight major headquarters in Louisiana, Arkansas, and Kuwait while providing logistics expertise to more than 200 separate organizations. During the War on Terror, I have been tapped to assume major responsibilities for moving human resources and multimillion-dollar assets. In my current position as International Operations Chief in Kuwait, I plan and manage vital support operations in the "gateway to Iraq." U.S. and Coalition soldiers involved in Operation Iraqi Freedom arrive at this base in Arifjan with their equipment prior to entering Iraq and, after their combat tours, they spend time here as they prepare to return home with their equipment. I function as more or less of a "city manager" as I oversee the provision of vital services and supplies required by these transient human resources.

Personnel management skills and general management experience

During my military service, I have also excelled in demanding line management positions. On two different occasions, I served as a Company Commander. In one job as a Company Commander overseeing 780 employees and controlling $87 million in property, I was evaluated in writing as "a caring commander" and recognized for my leadership in improving employee morale.

Extensive software knowledge

Proficient with a variety of software programs including Word, Excel, Access, and PowerPoint, I am experienced in using numerous automated programs used to control supplies at the wholesale and retail level. Entrusted with a Top Secret (TS/SI) security clearance, I frequently work with specialized intelligence software.

If you can use a visionary logistics executive who possesses genuine enthusiasm for the challenges associated with logistics, contracting, purchasing, and supply management, I hope you will contact me to suggest a time when we might discuss your needs.

Sincerely,

Juan Camaro

JUAN CAMERO

1110½ Hay Street, Fayetteville, NC 28305 • preppub@aol.com • (910) 483-6611

OBJECTIVE

To benefit an organization that can use a professional who offers extensive experience in managing contracting, acquisitions, and logistics in international environments while establishing effective relationships, solving tough problems, and achieving ambitious goals.

EDUCATION

Masters in Logistics Management, Florida Inst. of Technology, Melbourne, FL, 1995.
Bachelor of Science, Business Administration, Mississippi College, Clinton, MS, 1986.

EXPERIENCE

INTERNATIONAL OPERATIONS CHIEF. U.S. Army, Arifjan, Kuwait (2004-present). At the base in Kuwait which is the "gateway to Iraq" for U.S. and Coalition soldiers involved in Operation Iraqi Freedom, manage support operations for soldiers preparing to enter Iraq and exiting Iraq. Prior to entering Iraq, soldiers live and train in Kuwait for up to one month while awaiting the arrival of vehicles and equipment. After combat tours are finished, soldiers live in Kuwait for a period of time as equipment and vehicles are loaded onto ships while they await air transportation that will take them home. I am excelling in a job equivalent to "City Manager."

- **Contracting and budgeting**: Manage a $30 million budget that supports soldiers in transition. Contract for $31 million in support which includes 500 vehicles, 250 buses, and 1200 cell phones. Coordinate housing and food service for a constantly changing population ranging from 50,000 to 100,000, and have deployed/redeployed more than 500,000 service members for combat operations. Identified the need and procured funding for additional contracted items valued at $5 million.

SUPPORT OPERATIONS MANAGER. U.S. Army, New Orleans, LA (2002-03). Was handpicked for this position because of my reputation as a superior logistician. Described as "aggressive, articulate, and intelligent," assumed responsibility for the planning involved in deploying 10,000 soldiers to Iraq and establishing a Logistical Support Area (LSA) to provide essential supplies and services for Army, Air Force, Marine, and Coalition forces.

STAFF OPERATIONS OFFICER. U.S. Army, Ft. Hood, TX (2001-02). For an organization with 27,000 soldiers, was in charge of planning two major training projects. On my own initiative, made contributions that improved organizational effectiveness and efficiency.

LOGISTICS MANAGEMENT OFFICER. U.S. Army, New Orleans, LA (1999-01). Acted as a top-level logistics consultant to eight major headquarters in Louisiana, Arkansas, and Kuwait while guiding more than 200 separate organizations. Advised units on all kinds of logistics issues while serving as the technical expert on the Standard Army Retail Supply System (SARSS) and other programs. Was evaluated in writing as "a superstar among outstanding performers; easily rates in the top 1% of all majors."

GENERAL MANAGER ("COMPANY COMMANDER"). U.S. Army, Ft. McPherson, GA (1997-98). Excelled in a job equivalent to "Chief Executive Officer" (CEO) of a company with 780 employees, a fleet of 217 prime movers and vehicles, and $87 million in property.

LOGISTICS OPERATIONS OFFICER. U.S. Army, Headquarters FORSCOM, Ft. McPherson, GA (1996-97). Developed and maintained support for projects in Saudi Arabia and Kuwait, and coordinated the contract for logistics support for operations in Haiti.

PERSONAL

Outstanding references on request. Known for my strong personal initiative and integrity. Received numerous medals including the Bronze Star.

Date

Exact Name of Person
Exact Title
Exact Name of Company
Address
City, State, Zip

Dear Exact Name of Person (or Dear Sir or Madam if answering a blind ad):

With the enclosed resume, I would like to make you aware of my interest in exploring employment opportunities with your organization and introduce you to my talents and skills.

With a Top Secret/SCI security clearance (valid until 2010), I rose to the highest enlisted rank—Command Sergeant Major—while serving my country in the U.S. Army. I began my military service as a Psychological Operations Specialist and excelled in a field which refined my analytical, problem-solving, and writing skills. Because of my outstanding communication skills, I was handpicked for a key training role as a Drill Sergeant, and I was named "Drill Sergeant of the Year" for the Ft. Huachuca military installation. In subsequent supervisory positions, I supervised employees, managed multimillion-dollar assets, developed professional development programs, and was promoted ahead of my peers based on leadership ability and resource management skills.

Within the famed Special Forces, I was handpicked for senior positions as a trainer and writer. At the John F. Kennedy Special Warfare Center & School (USAJFKSWCS), I served as the "subject matter expert" for the psychological operations field. In one position, I directed administration and training of 400 entry-level trainees and 600 officers trained annually in psychological operations and civil affairs.

In my final position in the military, I served as the senior "middle manager" in an airborne psychological operations battalion. I was praised for creating conditions which allowed the organization to win two major awards for supply excellence and maintenance excellence while aggressively developing training programs that enhanced employee skills. I have earned widespread respect for my ability to inspire and motivate others, and I have led our organization to achieve outstanding employee morale, with the result that our organization was ranked highest in employee retention.

If you can use a proven leader with unquestioned integrity along with an ability to manage change, lead people, and build coalitions, I hope you will contact me to suggest a time when we might discuss your needs.

Yours sincerely,

Caesar Rodriguez

CAESAR RODRIGUEZ

1110½ Hay Street, Fayetteville, NC 28305 • preppub@aol.com • (910) 483-6611

OBJECTIVE   To benefit an organization that can use an experienced leader and problem solver with an ability to manage complex investigative programs while demonstrating my ability to manage change, lead people, and build coalitions while expressing ideas in a convincing fashion.

EXPERIENCE   **Promoted to the highest enlisted rank—Command Sergeant Major—while serving my country in the U.S. Army in the following "track record" of advancement:**
COMMAND SERGEANT MAJOR. Ft. Benning, GA, and Iraq (2001-06). As the senior enlisted professional in an airborne psychological operations battalion, provided guidance to top-level military officers while overseeing activities of 120 employees. Created conditions which allowed the organization to win two major awards for supply excellence and maintenance excellence while aggressively developing training programs that enhanced employee skills.

COMMAND SERGEANT MAJOR. Ft. Benning, GA (2000-01). Handpicked to serve as the senior enlisted professional for the Army's only airborne psychological operations battalion serving organizations operating worldwide. Trained employees for 37 different exercises, and was commended for my emphasis on "junior leader training."

GENERAL MANAGER. Ft. Benning, GA (1999). For a company that conducted seven programs of instruction within the Special Forces, directed administration and training of 400 entry-level trainees and 600 officers annually who received training in psychological operations and civil affairs. Oversaw 13 mid-managers.

GENERAL MANAGER. Ft. Bragg, NC (1998-99). Handpicked to serve as a senior manager of the Army's only Civil Affairs and Psychological Operations Advanced Individual Training company. Administered training requirements for 1,500 students annually while supervising 25 supervisors. Praised for "improving unit performance and soldiers' abilities." Received a Meritorious Service Medal for "initiative, resourcefulness, and untiring efforts."

GENERAL MANAGER. Ft. Bragg, NC (1995-98). As the senior personnel manager of a psychological operations company with 57 employees and $2.6 million in property, developed an outstanding professional development program and was commended for my "excellent approach to training" as well as my "superb leadership and resource management abilities."

TRAINING COORDINATOR. Ft. Bragg, NC (1995). In this critical position in the Design and Development Branch at the Warfare Training Group, provided oversight for programs of instruction taught in 22 courses graduating 4,000 students annually. Commended for "innovative ideas and common sense" in rewriting and updating the operating procedures for course administration and programs of instruction.

EDUCATION   Completed 68 college credit hours towards a Computer Science degree, Wake Technical Institute, Raleigh, NC.
Graduated from executive leadership development programs including the U.S. Army Sergeants Major Academy, 2000. Graduated from the U.S. Special Operations Forces Pre-Command Course, 2000. Graduated from the First Sergeant Course, 1997.
Completed training programs including the U.S. Air Force Cargo Preparation Course, Airlift Load Planners Course, and the Air Movement Operations HAZMAT Course.

PERSONAL   Received numerous medals, certificates, and ribbons for exemplary performance.

Date

Exact Name of Person
Title or Position
Name of Company
Address
City, State, Zip

LOGISTICS MANAGER and ADVISOR

Dear Exact Name of Person: (or Dear Sir or Madam if answering a blind ad.)

I would appreciate an opportunity to talk with you soon about how I could contribute to your organization through my proven expertise in logistics, my skill as a trainer, and my general management experience.

While proudly serving my country as a junior military officer in the U.S. Army, I have earned a reputation for my analytical abilities and technical knowledge of logistics. I have been placed in jobs normally reserved for more experienced and higher ranking officers and have excelled in these positions through my talents, motivational skills, and drive for perfection.

I have managed NATO supply facilities controlling $125 million-dollar inventories, been recognized as the "subject matter expert" on logistics for a military community, and directed activities of as many as 32 employees in a headquarters operation.

I am certain that the combination of my specialized experience in logistics management, education, and general background as a hard worker who can handle pressure and deadlines, would make me a valuable asset to your organization.

I hope you will welcome my call soon to arrange a brief meeting at your convenience to discuss your current and future needs and how I might serve them. Thank you in advance for your time.

Sincerely yours,

Jeffrey Smith

JEFFREY SMITH

1110½ Hay Street, Fayetteville, NC 28305   •   preppub@aol.com   •   (910) 483-6611

OBJECTIVE To offer my experience to an organization that can use my analytical, technical, and leadership abilities along with management skills refined as a junior military officer.

EXPERIENCE **LOGISTICS MANAGER** and **ADVISOR.** U.S. Army, Italy (2005-present). Serve as the "subject matter expert" on logistics requirements for supplying ammunition to a 4,500-person military community.
- Inspected supply operations and verified their compliance with safety guidelines.
- Initiated revisions to training and inspection programs.
- Directed logistics support during major training projects: projected use, arranged for storage facilities, and provided transportation.

MATERIEL MANAGEMENT OPERATIONS MANAGER. U.S. Army, Italy (2005). Handpicked for this position normally held by a more experienced manager, supervised 25 people in five separate departments providing logistics support for 4,500 people.
- Excelled in a position usually reserved for a more experienced, higher ranking manager. Earned praise for my innovations in streamlining operations to provide outstanding customer service.

STORAGE FACILITY SUPPLY MANAGER. U.S. Army, Italy (2004). Controlled $125 million worth of ammunition and explosives while prioritizing storage, packaging, and maintenance requirements and managing 20 people at two separate storage sites.
- Guided the operation to one of only three "no-deficiency" ratings awarded by the Department of Defense to European explosives storage facilities.
- Reduced prior "negative management trend indicators" from 20% to under 1%.

SUPERVISORY LOGISTICS MANAGER. U.S. Army, Germany (2003-04). Supervised a 24-person team which maintained, inspected, calibrated, and assembled nuclear weapons systems in support of NATO. Ensured the security of ammunition support for seven scattered companies. Contributed to improvements in technical logistics operations by developing standard operating procedures and an inspection program.

FIRST-LINE SUPERVISOR. U.S. Army, Germany (2002-03). Managed 32 supply, training, and communications specialists in a headquarters administrative department responsible for the security and storage of Top Secret and communication security (COMSEC) materials.
- Received "outstanding" ratings in a major security inspection after only a short time as the security manager. Trained employees who received the highest individual scores in the unit's history during an inspection of emergency actions procedures.

EDUCATION & TRAINING **B.A., Political Science**, University of North Carolina at Chapel Hill, NC, 2001.
Excelled in more than six months of specialized training in supply and logistics management, microcomputers, and hazardous materials handling.

HONORS 2006—received the Army Commendation Medal for "exceptional performance."
2004—selected as the "Company Grade Officer of the Year" in very tough competition among the Germany community.
2003—honored as "Outstanding Young Man of America" for professional accomplishments, leadership, and community service.

PERSONAL Possess a Top Secret security clearance with BI. Certified as a Hazardous Cargo Handler.

Date

Exact Name of Person
Title or Position
Name of Company
Address
City, State, Zip

LOGISTICS OPERATIONS DIRECTOR

Dear Exact Name of Person: (or Dear Sir or Madam if answering a blind ad.)

I would appreciate an opportunity to talk with you soon about how I could apply my managerial experience and knowledge of maintenance, production, logistics, and distribution activities for the benefit of your organization.

I am known as a professional who can be counted on to direct operations which are respected for efficiency and profitability. As a military officer I earned promotion to ever-increasing management levels while advancing in a "track record" of accomplishments.

Throughout my career, every company or department I have managed has succeeded in reducing work backlogs, earned consistently "commendable" ratings in major inspections, and enjoyed being known for achieving higher-than-average operational readiness rates.

I offer a reputation as a high-energy individual with the drive to accomplish any job I take on. Easily adaptable to rapidly changing priorities, I handle pressure and stress effectively. I feel that my greatest accomplishments are still ahead of me and that I have many valuable skills and personal qualities to contribute.

I hope you will welcome my call soon to arrange a brief meeting at your convenience to discuss your current and future needs and how I might serve them. Thank you in advance for your time.

Sincerely yours,

Paul Wright

Alternate last paragraph:
I hope you will call or write soon to suggest a time convenient for us to meet and discuss your current and future needs and how I might serve them. Thank you in advance for your time.

PAUL WRIGHT

1110½ Hay Street, Fayetteville, NC 28305   •   preppub@aol.com   •   (910) 483-6611

OBJECTIVE

To contribute my managerial experience and special knowledge of logistics, maintenance, and production operations to an organization that can use a professional who has excelled as a military officer known for outstanding skills in maximizing productivity and profitability.

EDUCATION & TRAINING

Completed 18 graduate-level credits (800 hours) in Logistics Management, the U.S. Army Logistics Management College, May 2006.

B.S., Biology, Princeton University, Princeton, NJ, 1995.

EXPERIENCE

Rose to increasing managerial levels in this "track record," U.S. Army, Germany:
LOGISTICS OPERATIONS DIRECTOR. (2004-present). Earned consistently "commendable" ratings in annual inspections of my programs while controlling a $2.5 million budget which provided subcontractors, management, and customers with logistics support.
- Applied my skills and technical knowledge to plan and develop programs after analyzing contractual commitments, customer specifications, and design changes.
- Saved the government approximately $104,000 annually by applying stringent cost effectiveness standards in contract management.

MAINTENANCE COMPANY GENERAL MANAGER. (2002-04). Directed operations in a 270-person company with a reputation for outstanding performance and quality.
- Controlled a $4.5 million operating budget and a $20 million equipment inventory.
- Analyzed budget requests and made determinations on the most cost-effective and productive use of funds. Received "commendable" ratings three consecutive years in Army-wide inspections of supply and maintenance operations.
- Outperformed four "sister" companies and held the record for the most "commendable" ratings as well as being the three-time winner of an "excellence in supply" award.

MATERIEL MANAGER. (2000-01). Supervised a 20-person work force involved in maintenance, repair, quality control, and parts requisitioning for a multimillion-dollar fleet.
- Reduced the number of vehicles sidelined for more than 30 days from 60 to 24 in an organization where the acceptable standard was 30 "deadlined" vehicles.
- Held the operational readiness rate at approximately 8% above standards.
- Controlled the support for 1,500 wheeled vehicles, 50 heavy construction vehicles, and 300 power generation and radio/special electronics items.

MAINTENANCE MANAGER. (1999-00). Streamlined procedures for reporting maintenance and repair parts supply activities to higher management levels while ensuring quality control and high levels of productivity in an intermediate-level facility.
- Reduced production backlogs and overtime by developing and writing improved standard operating procedures (SOPs).

DIRECT SUPPORT MAINTENANCE MANAGER. (1998-99). Received numerous "commendable" ratings for my leadership of a 100-person company which provided maintenance, repair, and quality control for a fleet of 1,000 wheeled vehicles, 200 power generators, and radio/special electronics devices; controlled a $750,000 operating budget.
- Directed a project to field new equipment and increased operational readiness rates to 5% above standards.

PERSONAL

Hold lifetime membership in the Society of Logistic Engineers. Am very adaptable and handle pressure and challenges effectively. Offer strong problem-solving skills.

Date

Exact Name of Person
Title or Position
Name of Company
Address (number and street)
Address (city, state, and zip)

Dear Exact Name of Person: (or Sir or Madam if answering a blind ad.)

I would appreciate an opportunity to talk with you soon about how I could contribute to your organization through my expertise in supply and logistics management as well as my diversified experience in areas ranging from sales and marketing, to personnel counseling and training.

As you will see from my resume, in my most recent position with a civilian contractor, I worked as a Logistics & Operations Officer in Taji, Iraq. In that high-threat environment, I played a key role in establishing "from scratch" a training facility on a 50-acre site, and I managed logistical activities which supported the training of 600 Iraqi Security Officers who are now providing security for Iraqi oil assets and electrical power facilities. In part because of my logistical leadership, the training camp became an "operational model," and it has been chosen as the site where the Iraqi National Guard will be trained. While supervising 35 Iraqi nationals, I managed a budget of $500,000 as I coordinated contracts and worked with vendors in the process of ordering items ranging from bulldozers to uniforms. I also conducted inspections, operated automated systems, and was involved in security management.

In previous experience with the U.S. Marine Corps, I excelled in positions as a Logistics Chief, Combat Cargo Chief, and Transportation Specialist. I prepared load plans and monitored the loading of supplies, cargo, equipment, and personnel aboard aircraft, ship, and rail, and I was evaluated in writing as "a superb organizer and administrator." I provided safety training for combat cargo personnel, and I once instituted a hazardous waste handling and disposal program. In my position as a Combat Cargo Chief supervising 25 people, I was credited with saving over $250,000 through my outstanding knowledge of the supply, logistics, and materiel management systems.

In spite of frequent travel and deployments, I earned A.A. and B.A. degrees while fulfilling the obligations of a demanding military career. I am highly computer proficient.

If you are searching for a hard-working leader, I am an enthusiastic self-starter with an eye for detail and a proven ability to maximize available resources in order to get the job done. I hope you will welcome my call soon to arrange a brief meeting to discuss your current and future needs and how I might serve them. Thank you in advance for your time.

Sincerely,

Dominique Racas

DOMINIQUE RACAS

1110½ Hay Street, Fayetteville, NC 28305   •   preppub@aol.com   •   (910) 483-6611

OBJECTIVE

To contribute to an organization that can use a skilled logistics professional who offers experience in acquisitions and contracting, transportation and traffic management, as well as hazardous materials handling, personnel training, and automated systems operations.

EDUCATION

Earning **Master and Bachelor in Logistics Management,** Columbus University online, Picayune, MS; completing degree online—degree anticipated 2006. Previously completed 45 credit hours at the master's degree level.

Earned **B.A.B.S. in Behavioral Science,** National University, San Diego, CA, 1993.

Completed **A.A. in Liberal Arts,** Chicago Citywide College, Chicago, IL, 1987.

EXPERIENCE

LOGISTICS & OPERATIONS DIRECTOR. Bluewater Services, Inc., Taji, Iraq (2004-06). In a formal performance evaluation when this contract ended, was commended for "exceptional work as a Logistics Officer." In a hazardous combat environment, trained and directed 35 Iraqi nationals performing logistical activities related to the training of Iraqi Security Officers for the Iraqi Oil Ministry and Ministry of Electricity. In part because of my logistical leadership, this camp in Taji became the model for three additional training camps which have been established. Because of its success as an "operational model," the 50-acre camp in Taji has been selected to train the Iraqi National Guard.

- **Budget management and reporting:** Formulated and managed a budget of $500,000 used to order items ranging from bulldozers to uniforms. Reviewed expenses with the facility manager, and prepared forecasts for future needs. Prepared daily, weekly, and monthly reports containing analysis and recommendations.
- **Training operations:** After playing a key role in setting up the first training camp in Taji for Iraqi Security Officers, participated in training 600 Iraqi Security Officers who are now involved in protecting Iraq's oil assets and electrical power facilities.
- **Acquisitions and contract management:** Managed contracting activities and worked with international vendors including Halliburton and Iraqi companies.
- **Inspections and warehousing:** Inspected maintenance progress and verified maintenance compliance; planned maintenance schedules. Audited inventory and ensured prudent reordering. Ensured proper warehousing of materials.
- **Automated systems:** Operated electronic monitoring and communication equipment. Utilized the Internet and other sources in locating needed items.
- **Security management:** Coordinated with the Security Team Leader on security.

While serving in the U.S. Marine Corps, received numerous awards for my accomplishments and professional knowledge:
LOGISTICS CHIEF. San Diego, CA, and Quantico, VA (1991-2004). Became recognized as a knowledgeable and dedicated professional while planning, conducting, and supervising traffic management activities related to the loading, transportation, and delivery of personnel, supplies, and equipment. Earned outstanding performance evaluations. Played an important role in my unit's recognition with a Meritorious Unit Ribbon for support of worldwide activities.

TRANSPORTATION AND LOGISTICS SUPPORT SPECIALIST. Camp Lejeune, NC (1982-90). Contributed to the smooth operation of support activities during which personnel, equipment, and supplies were loaded, transported, and unloaded in order to meet the requirements of training exercises and real-world missions.

PERSONAL

Working knowledge of Arabic. Am very adaptable. Excel in motivating others to build their skills and strengths. Can provide outstanding references at the appropriate time.

Exact Name of Person
Title or Position
Name of Company
Address (number and street)
Address (city, state, and zip)

**LOGISTICS
OPERATIONS
MANAGER**

Dear Exact Name of Person: (or Sir or Madam if answering a blind ad.)

   With the enclosed resume, I would like to express my interest in exploring employment opportunities with your organization. As you will see from my resume, I proudly served my country while excelling in the logistics field.

   Most recently as a Logistical Operations Manager, I managed a $1.3 million budget and applied my knowledge of the government contracting process as I coordinated 17 civilian contractors and supervised 15 people. On my own initiative, I increased logistical productivity 25% through reorganizing and streamlining procedures while directing logistical support in countries including Iraq and Afghanistan.

   In my previous position as a Supply Manager, I managed a facility with 1,500 line items of repair parts valued at more than $20 million. I developed a HAZMAT certification training program recognized as outstanding and was described in a formal performance evaluation as "an unparalleled property manager." On my own initiative, I saved money by identifying 300 items no longer needed and turning in $2 million in excess equipment.

   In prior positions in the supply and logistics field, I managed multimillion-dollar assets while providing logistics support for sensitive missions worldwide. I also managed government credit card programs, trained employees to utilize Access database programs and other software used for logistics management, and provided leadership in automating manual accounting systems. I am accustomed to managing multimillion-dollar inventories without a single loss while monitoring the transportation of equipment and supplies worldwide under short notice.

   Proficient in computer operations, I am skilled at utilizing Word, PowerPoint, Excel, and databases used for inventory control. I hold a Top Secret (TS/SCI) security clearance.

   If you can use a capable individual who possesses genuine enthusiasm for the challenges associated with logistics, contracting, purchasing, and supply management, I hope you will contact me to suggest a time when we might discuss your needs. I can provide outstanding personal and professional references. Thank you in advance for your time.

                                        Sincerely,

                                        Wilson Yarborough

WILSON YARBOROUGH

1110½ Hay Street, Fayetteville, NC 28305 • preppub@aol.com • (910) 483-6611

OBJECTIVE

I want to contribute to an organization that can use an experienced professional who offers outstanding skills related to logistics management, supply and inventory control.

EDUCATION

Completing **B.S. degree in Business Administration,** Campbell University, Buies Creek, NC; earned 125 college credit hours; am four courses short of graduation with 3.6 GPA.

EXPERIENCE

Have excelled in the following track record of promotion, U.S. Army:
LOGISTICAL OPERATIONS MANAGER. Ft. Huachuca, AZ (2002-present). Managed a budget of $1.3 million annually and supervised 15 people while hiring, training, and coordinating 17 civilian contractors as well as cross training 10 associates in logistical functions. Managed logistical support for the Army's highest priority combat unit.
- **Overseas logistics:** Managed logistics in countries including Iraq and Afghanistan. Provided logistical support for 120 employees and maintained accountability of $10 million in assets. Directed the movement of 200 tons of equipment with total success. Served as Hazardous Material Certifier.
- **Efficiency management:** Increased logistical productivity 25% through reorganizing and streamlining procedures.

SUPPLY MANAGER. U.S. Army, Ft. Huachuca, AZ (2000-02). Managed a weapons maintenance facility with 1,500 line items of repair parts valued at more than $20 million. Managed a $750,000 facility budget. Trained and supervised a highly proficient 8-person staff dedicated to the highest levels of customer service despite the challenges of fielding multiple new systems. Developed a HAZMAT certification training program recognized as "outstanding." Described as "an unparalleled property manager," was praised for the ability to analyze and solve complex problems.
- **Customer service:** Provided outstanding service to 900 customers.
- **Personal initiative:** On my own initiative, saved money by identifying 300 items no longer needed and turned in excess equipment valued at $2 million. Produced a 10% savings by establishing new vendor contracts that increased purchasing power.
- **Safety management:** Emphasized safety with the result that there was no accidents.

SUPPLY MANAGER. Washington, DC (1998-00). Managed $24 million in assets while providing logistical support for sensitive missions in Bosnia. In an additional duty, took charge of logistics during the 12-week Unit Assessment and Selection Course.
- **Equipment fielding and evaluation:** Led the organization in fielding a new weapon system. Promoted stringent supply discipline; turned in $1.4 million in excess equipment.
- **Database management:** Mastered utilization of the ULLS S-4 and Access database which led to highly proficient property management.
- **Strategic planning and multiple task management:** Coordinated hand receipts for 25 separate missions in 12 countries.

Highlights of other U.S. Army experience:
SUPPLY MANAGER. Was the internal expert on supply matters for an African-oriented organization. Controlled more than $30 million in property.
LOGISTICS MANAGER. Served as Property Book Officer for the Special Operations Task Force in support of the United Nations mission in Haiti, and worked with U.N. logistical personnel in developing resupply operations for land, sea, and air.

PERSONAL

Outstanding references on request. Known for my strong personal initiative and integrity.

Date

Exact Name of Person
Title or Position
Name of Company
Address
City, State, Zip

LOGISTICS OPERATIONS SUPERVISOR

Dear Exact Name of Person: (or Dear Sir or Madam if answering a blind ad.)

With the enclosed resume, I would like to make you aware of my background as an articulate, experienced manager with exceptional planning and organizational skills who offers a track record of excellence in operations management and supervision, training, and staff development in logistics and supply environments.

As you will see from my resume, I am currently excelling in the U.S. Army where I have earned respect for my ability to maximize human, material, and fiscal resources while developing expertise in the logistics field. Among my greatest strengths are transforming poorly functioning operations into models of efficiency as well as motivating others to exceed expected standards. I am a strong believer in "leadership by example."

In my present job as a Logistics Operations Supervisor, I manage a property book account of over $42 million and have been credited with "turning around" a troubled operation. This communications organization, which had been suffering extensive losses, has now been recognized with the coveted and prestigious Supply Excellence Award given by the U.S. Army Chief of Staff.

As a recipient of numerous honors including two Commendation Medals and six Achievement Medals, I have been cited for my personal accomplishments and professionalism as well as for contributions to unit success in numerous functional areas. In addition to success in a military career, my time management and organizational skills have allowed me to succeed as an honors student at Hopkinsville Community College where I am maintaining a 3.6 GPA and have been named to the National Dean's List. I will receive my B.S. degree in Psychology in December 2006.

If you can use a skilled supervisor and trainer with excellent computer and office operations skills as well as extensive logistics experience, I hope you will welcome my call soon when I try to arrange a brief meeting to discuss your goals and how my background might serve your needs. I can provide outstanding references at the appropriate time.

Sincerely,

Paige Taylor

Alternate last paragraph:
I hope you will write or call me soon to suggest a time when we might meet to discuss your needs and goals and how my background might serve them. I can provide outstanding references at the appropriate time.

PAIGE TAYLOR

1110½ Hay Street, Fayetteville, NC 28305   •   preppub@aol.com   •   (910) 483-6611

OBJECTIVE
To benefit an organization that can use an experienced manager who offers exceptional planning and organizational skills as well as the proven ability to train productive and efficient teams and revitalize operations performing below accepted standards.

EDUCATION & TRAINING
B.S. in Psychology, Hopkinsville Community College, NC; to be awarded December 2006. Named to the **National Dean's List**, maintaining a **3.6 GPA** while excelling in a demanding military career simultaneously with my college attendance.
A.A., Logistics, Yankee University, Fort Drum, NY, 2001.
Completed nearly a year of additional college-level course work related to the Management of Defense Acquisition Contracts.

SPECIAL SKILLS
Computers: possess skills with Microsoft Word, Excel, PowerPoint, and Access as well as Logistics Intelligence Files (LIF), Delrina Forms Flow, Standard Property Book System Redesign (SPBS-R), and the DCAS budget system.

EXPERIENCE
Am building a reputation as a knowledgeable logistics professional, U.S. Army:
LOGISTICS OPERATIONS SUPERVISOR. Fort Campbell, KY (2003-present). Trained and now supervise nine personnel while managing property valued at $42 million.
- Took over a troubled operation, reorganizing the property accounting system of an organization that had been suffering extensive losses of equipment; received the Army Chief of Staff's prestigious Supply Excellence Award for the changes our office initiated.
- Located sources for needed equipment, saving more than $500,000 in the process.
- Identified excess equipment and developed methods for eliminating it from the total inventory; supervised the transfer and turn-in of more than $3.5 million worth of excess.
- Maintain both automated and manual records of all supply transactions and have become extremely familiar with the Modern Army Record Keeping System (MARKS).
- Established internal evaluation standards; inspect subordinate supply operations.
- Singled out as supervisor/approving authority for five government credit card holders, oversee a $385,000 annual budget used to obtain supplies, equipment, and services.
- Apply tact and an impartial manner as an Equal Opportunity advisor.
- Established an Automated Unit Equipment Listing (AUEL) for a 400-person organization so that all equipment can be quickly moved by air, sea, land, or ground transportation.

ASSISTANT LOGISTICS SUPERVISOR. Fort Bragg, NC, and Iraq (2001-03). Selected for a special assignment, spent six months overseeing preparations for what was evaluated as a well-planned and carried out transfer of a 700-person unit and all equipment from North Carolina to Iraq both by sea and air.
- After arriving in Iraq, assisted five managers while holding sole responsibility for maintaining equipment shortage listings and requisitioning.
- Maintained property book records on $282 million worth of inventory which included 24 helicopters valued at $10 million each.

SUPPLY SUPERVISOR. Fort Drum, NY (1996-01). Controlled more than $13 million worth of equipment for a financial support services organization.
- Requisitioned, purchased, issued, and received equipment and supplies.

PERSONAL
Received numerous honors including two U.S. Army Commendation and six Achievement Medals as well as NCO of the Quarter. Offer experience in bookkeeping, filing, and typing.

Date

Exact Name of Person
Title or Position
Name of Company
Address
City, State, Zip

LOGISTICS PLANNING MANAGER

Dear Exact Name of Person: (or Dear Sir or Madam if answering a blind ad.)

I would appreciate an opportunity to talk with you soon about how I could contribute to your organization through my expertise in managing human and material resources for maximum productivity and effectiveness.

While advancing as a military officer, I have built a reputation as a talented and assertive leader with exceptional decision-making and problem-solving skills in demanding management roles. In my present job at one of the nation's military base, I direct the activities of a logistics center which provides the post with equipment and supplies in support of worldwide no-notice missions.

In earlier managerial positions I excelled in activities such as the development of operational guidelines, creation of improvements to operational procedures, and in guiding my personnel to set new standards for their performance levels and accomplishments.

I am confident that I offer a natural leadership style which has been refined in the competitive and demanding military environment. I am bright, articulate, and highly motivated and I will succeed in anything I attempt while applying my positive attitude, talent for building cohesive well-trained teams, and ability to coordinate complex activities.

I hope you will call or write me soon to suggest a time convenient for us to meet and discuss your current and future needs and how I might serve them. Thank you in advance for your time.

Sincerely,

Michael Hancock

Alternate last paragraph:
I hope you will welcome my call soon to arrange a brief meeting to discuss your current and future needs and how I might serve them. Thank you in advance for your time.

MICHAEL HANCOCK

1110½ Hay Street, Fayetteville, NC 28305 • preppub@aol.com • (910) 483-6611

OBJECTIVE   To offer my supervisory and managerial skills as well as my inventory management expertise and motivational abilities skills to an organization in need of a mature professional.

EXPERIENCE   *Earned advancement to the rank of captain in a competitive environment which is undergoing rapid change and downsizing, U.S. Army:*
LOGISTICS PLANNING MANAGER. Fort Campbell, KY (2005-present). Develop supply plans and procedures for an organization with four major divisions affiliated with both direct and general support centers while providing the 101st Airborne Division with the equipment and supplies needed for any situation which arises worldwide.
- Developed and maintained open lines of communication with customer units so that their requirements could be filled on time and accurately.
- Assisted in the development and publication of a functional handbook providing guidance for material management personnel preparing for overseas assignments.
- Was cited as the key figure in the development of control center and service/support center operating procedures which increased readiness rates an impressive 80%!

STUDENT—LOGISTICS MANAGEMENT SCHOOL. Fort Leonard Wood, MO (2004).

CHIEF OF THE MATERIAL MANAGEMENT CENTER. Fort Jackson, SC (2003-04). Exceeded standards for maintenance operations while managing an 87,000-square-foot warehouse with 2,300 authorized lines of supplies valued in excess of $11 million.
- Supported six separate organizations of approximately 1,000 employees each while managing all aspects of requisitioning, excess supplies, and stockage levels.
- Managed an office which provided computer hardware service and repair, software support, and software training as well as testing and evaluating new ADP equipment.
- Provided 31 supported units with new computer systems within only three days.

MAINTENANCE MANAGER. Fort Jackson, SC (2002-03). Cited for my ability to quickly grasp and apply complex concepts, managed one of the military's largest direct support maintenance organizations with 200 employees and which accepted more than $14 million in requisitions annually.
- Directed the performance of five maintenance support teams, four maintenance shops, and a large inventory of equipment available for parts.
- Maintained operational readiness rates above 90% during a month-long training exercise and was awarded an achievement medal for my outstanding performance.
- Was cited for my dynamic and enthusiastic leadership style which impacted favorably on the success of two large-scale sessions at a national training center.

FIRST-LINE SUPERVISOR. Fort Jackson, SC (2000-02). Supervised and trained 15 people who operated and maintained four state-of-the-art battle tanks valued in excess of $4 million.
- Led my personnel to recognition as the best of 47 similar sized units at a national training center training and evaluation session.

EDUCATION   **B.S., Education**, University of Utah, Salt Lake City, UT, 1999.
A.A., Education with a concentration in Biology, Kemper Military School and College, Booneville, MO, 1997.

PERSONAL   Offer a reputation as an articulate, enthusiastic, and energetic leader.

Date

Exact Name of Person
Title or Position
Name of Company
Address
City, State, Zip

Dear Exact Name of Person: (or Dear Sir or Madam if answering a blind ad.)

With the enclosed resume, I would like to make you aware of my interest in exploring employment opportunities with your organization as a logistician. As you will see from my resume, I have served my country with distinction in the U.S. Army and have been promoted to Major. Although I have been strongly encouraged to remain in military service and have been recommended for promotion to Lieutenant Colonel, I have decided to resign my commission as an officer and seek employment in the private sector.

I was handpicked for my current position as a senior logistics professional, and I am in charge of distributing all wheeled tactical vehicles within the Army National Guard in 50 states and four U.S. territories. While managing a $120 million inventory of wheeled tactical vehicles, I also develop and implement training plans for fielding $25 million in modernized vehicles and implementing those assets into existing inventory. I manage a $20 million budget for five vehicle repair and restoration facilities located throughout the United States. I work closely with officials all over the U.S. and I am respected for my knowledge of the U.S. Government Defense Budgeting and Execution Process.

In my previous position, I was the "resident expert" on logistics matters for National Guard and Reserve units and provided support to training conducted over a seven-state area. I supervised 23 military employees and five Department of the Army professionals while managing an inventory of 750 major end items along with an operating budget of $374,000. I was also in charge of a $14 million construction project, from the design through the final stages. Formal performance evaluations described me as "thorough and aggressive in a business requiring great judgment and initiative."

In a previous position I was in the role of an Inspector and Quality Assurance Chief as I provided expert logistical advice to 274 Army Reserve and National Guard units. Early in my military career, I was chosen as company commander of a maintenance organization, and I managed 213 American employees and ten Bosnian soldiers who assured the timely provision of repair parts, data processing services, and communication and electronic maintenance support to organizations throughout Bosnia.

If you think you could benefit from my vast logistics knowledge and my extensive training background, I hope you will contact me soon to suggest a time when we might discuss your needs. I hold a Top Secret clearance and can provide outstanding references.

Yours sincerely,

Christopher Foster

CHRISTOPHER FOSTER

1110½ Hay Street, Fayetteville, NC 28305   •   preppub@aol.com   •   (910) 483-6611

OBJECTIVE
To contribute to an organization that can use a skilled logistics professional who offers extensive expertise in training and supervising personnel, utilizing automated systems for maximum efficiency, as well as planning new programs to improve customer satisfaction.

EDUCATION
Master of Arts in History, University of Tennessee, Chattanooga, TN, 2005.
Bachelor of Arts in History, Norwich University, Northfield, VT, 1986.

CLEARANCE
Top Secret SBI secret clearance

EXPERIENCE
Excelled in a track record of promotion to Major, U.S. Army; have been recommended for promotion to Lieutenant Colonel and strongly encouraged to remain in military service, but I have decided to pursue opportunities in the private sector:
LOGISTICS STAFF OFFICER. Army National Guard, Waterbury, CT (2005-present). Because of my logistics knowledge, was handpicked for this position in charge of distributing all wheeled tactical vehicles within the Army National Guard in 50 states and U.S. territories.
- Manage a $120 million inventory of wheeled tactical vehicles while also developing and implementing training plans for fielding $25 million in modernized vehicles and implementing those assets into existing inventory.

LOGISTICS OFFICER. Chattanooga, TN (2002-04). Was the "resident expert" on logistics matters for National Guard and Reserve units, and provided support to training conducted over a seven-state area.
- Supervised 23 military employees and five Department of the Army professionals while managing an inventory of 750 major end items along with an operating budget of $374,000. Was in charge of a $14 million construction project; monitored the design, advertisement, and awarding of the project.

EXECUTIVE OFFICER & LOGISTICS OFFICER. Spokane, WA (2000-02). Managed 21 employees providing supply and maintenance services along with mobilization and administrative support for Army Reserve and National Guard organizations in Washington, Oregon, and Idaho. Coordinated with the Federal Emergency Management Agency in my role as manager of a Mobilization and Support Team.

INSPECTOR & QUALITY ASSURANCE CHIEF. Spokane, WA (1999-00). Provided expert logistical advice to 274 Army Reserve and National Guard units in Washington and Idaho; managed six senior military managers and one civilian manager.
- Provided timely guidance and assistance to a military police organization during their processing in preparation for deployment to Kuwait. Took charge of an inefficient property book operation and transformed it into a model of efficiency.

LOGISTICS OFFICER. Military Intelligence Brigade, Bosnia (1998-99). In Bosnia, provided logistical support for 1,600 personnel stationed in 20 locations throughout the country. Managed complex logistics systems providing supply, maintenance, transportation, services, engineer, and procurement support. Supervised a fleet of 120 commercial vehicles.

LOGISTICS SUPPORT OFFICER. Boise, ID (1997-98). In this top-level role in charge of providing training support, conducted training for 244 officers and senior enlisted managers.

PERSONAL
Proven ability for visionary, future-oriented thoughts and actions. Excellent references.

Date

Exact Name of Person
Title or Position
Name of Company
Address (number and street)
Address (city, state, and zip)

Dear Exact Name of Person: (or Sir or Madam if answering a blind ad.)

   With the enclosed resume, I would like to express my interest in exploring employment opportunities with your organization.

Expertise in maintenance management and logistics management

   While serving my country in the U.S. Army, I have demonstrated my resourcefulness, analytical skills, and problem-solving ability in complex maintenance management roles. In one position with NATO in Greece, I excelled as a Fleet Operations Manager and Quality Assurance Inspector. While overseeing a $2.1 million fleet of commercial vehicles—including busses and sedans—used to transport NATO officials and VIPs, I single-handedly created and implemented the first-ever maintenance program for the Joint Command SouthCent (JCSC). In a subsequent position as a Fleet Operations Supervisor and Hazardous Materials Manager, I supervised 16 mechanics and three automated logistics specialists while directing maintenance performed on a fleet of 170 vehicles and 15 generators.

Extensive safety and hazardous materials knowledge

   Throughout my military career, I was commended for my exceptional emphasis on safety in the workplace. In every job I have held, I improved the safety knowledge of employees as well as their technical maintenance know-how, and I consistently managed fast-paced operations that had no workplace accidents or incidents. While in Panama, I was specially selected as Maintenance Inspector for the U.S. Army South Command Inspection Program and, in that capacity, I inspected 15 different operations and developed the Inspector General Checklist for Preventive Maintenance and Services. My extensive technical training included numerous safety programs as well as the Hazardous Materials and Hazardous Waste Handlers Course.

Excellent supervisory skills and management ability

   In numerous assignments, I demonstrated my ability to "start up" maintenance operations "from scratch" and to transform underperforming operations. In one assignment in Panama overseeing vehicle maintenance operations at the U.S. Army Jungle Operations Training Center, I was recognized as the critical factor in bringing a struggling transportation operation back to its feet.

   If you can use a strong leader with outstanding problem-solving and troubleshooting skills, I hope you will contact me to suggest a time when we might discuss your needs. I can provide outstanding references at the appropriate time.

                                            Sincerely,

                                            Kevin Doyle

KEVIN DOYLE

1110½ Hay Street, Fayetteville, NC 28305   •   preppub@aol.com   •   (910) 483-6611

OBJECTIVE I want to contribute to an organization that can use an experienced problem solver and supervisor with extensive experience in maintenance management along with a background related to the handling, transportation, and storage of hazardous materials.

EXPERIENCE **Proudly served my country for 24 years as a member of the U.S. Army:**
MAINTENANCE & CONTRACTS MANAGER. Iraq (2003-06). Supervised up to 25 individuals performing maintenance and correcting malfunctions on 32 power generator sets and a fleet of 256 tactical wheeled vehicles while controlling tool boxes and equipment.
- Deployed to Iraq and led numerous patrols which confiscated weapons and captured insurgents. Trained soldiers in mounted patrol operations.

FLEET OPERATIONS SUPERVISOR & HAZARDOUS MATERIALS MANAGER. Ft. Benning, GA (2001-2003). Supervised 16 mechanics and three automated logistics specialists while performing as the "in-house expert" on automotive maintenance and administrative operations. Directed maintenance performed on a fleet of 170 vehicles and 15 generators as well as howitzer weapons systems. Took over a maintenance facility with numerous deficiencies, and developed a maintenance training program that became the standard.
- Developed and taught the organization's Operator and Supervisor Maintenance Training Program, with the result that the readiness rate improved by 3%. Saved hundreds of wasted labor hours through new procedures which I developed.

QUALITY ASSURANCE INSPECTOR & FLEET OPERATIONS MANAGER. Greece (2000-01). At the U.S. Army NATO, trained and managed 10 people while providing maintenance management guidance on a fleet of commercial vehicles including busses and sedans valued at $2.1 million that transported NATO officials and VIPs. Conducted thorough technical inspections of equipment to determine serviceability.
- Single-handedly created and implemented the first-ever maintenance program for the Joint Command SouthCent (JCSC). Maintained 100% readiness for the NATO fleet.

SHOP FOREMAN & MAINTENANCE SUPERVISOR. Ft. Bragg, NC (1998-00). Trained and managed 15 employees performing maintenance on wheeled, ground support, and special purpose equipment while conducting repairs and troubleshooting major assemblies, systems, and subsystems. Accounted for $1.5 million in equipment while ensuring the operational readiness of 130 vehicles, 25 generators, and 18 howitzers.

SENIOR MECHANIC & MAINTENANCE INSPECTOR. Ft. Bragg, NC and Panama (1993-1997). Trained and supervised 16 maintenance personnel performing scheduled and unscheduled maintenance on 211 pieces of equipment ranging from 1¼ ton to 5-ton trucks and tractors, HMMWVs, and trailers of all sizes. Trained 158 personnel on boat operations.

EDUCATION Completed 100 hours of college credits from the University of Minnesota.
U.S. Army training included Special Forces Assessment and Selection Course, Wheel Vehicle Mechanic Course, Environmental Awareness, Prescribed Load List (PLL) Course, Airborne and Air Assault Schools, Hazardous Materials and Hazardous Waste Handlers Course, Unit Level Logistics System Course (ULLS), Motor Sergeant Orientation Course, Safety Officers/ NCOs Course, Army Maintenance Management (TAMM) Course, and other courses.

PERSONAL Received numerous medals, certificates, and ribbons for exemplary performance. Outstanding references available on request. Tireless hard worker known for initiative.

Date

Exact Name of Person
Title or Position
Name of Company
Address
City, State, Zip

Dear Exact Name of Person: (or Dear Sir or Madam if answering a blind ad.)

I would appreciate an opportunity to talk with you soon about how I could contribute to your organization through my extensive knowledge of the medical/health services field, my research and development experience, as well as my technical expertise related to biology, electronics, and computer applications.

With prior experience as a military officer, I have had my hands in R&D all my life, beginning with a job testing aircraft engine modifications for a civilian company, to jobs as an officer working with the 150-person Aeromedical Center performing developmental and operational testing of flight systems, flight crew equipment, and human factors.

In other jobs as a military officer I combined my management skills with my creativity and research know-how to develop new programs and establish new systems. In one job as a company commander, I managed operations of a medical clinic and, in that capacity, developed a new program to provide free medical treatment to German nationals and to a local orphanage.

Most recently while completing my second bachelor's degree, I have been involved in medical research projects using animal models and I have become skilled at numerous tests and procedures used to further medical knowledge.

You will see from my resume that I offer extensive knowledge related to software used for data management, statistical analysis, graphics, and word processing. I have creatively applied my software knowledge on numerous occasions to reduce operating costs and increase the efficiency of operating systems.

I hope you will write or call me soon to suggest a time when we might meet to discuss your needs and goals and how I might contribute to them. I can provide outstanding personal and professional references.

Sincerely yours,

Phillip Jimmie

Alternate last paragraph:
I hope you will call or write me soon to suggest a time convenient for us to meet and discuss your current and future needs and how I might best serve them. Thank you in advance for your time.

PHILLIP JIMMIE

1110½ Hay Street, Fayetteville, NC 28305 • preppub@aol.com • (910) 483-6611

OBJECTIVE

To benefit an organization that can use a versatile professional who has excelled as a research and development specialist, project manager, pilot, and military officer with technical expertise in aviation, electronics, and computer applications.

EDUCATION

Bachelor of Science, Biology, University of Maryland, to be awarded 2006.
Bachelor of Science, Aeronautical Sciences, University of Maryland, 1997.

EXPERIENCE

MAINTENANCE & LOGISTICS OPERATIONS MANAGER. U.S. Army, Germany (2005-present). As "second-in-command" of a 390-person organization, directed aircraft and vehicle maintenance, dining facilities for 500 people, logistical support, and budgeting.

- Reorganized aircraft parts ordering and stocking procedures for an 18% fiscal year budget reduction and developed the $4,385,000 2006 budget.
- Established an automated system for property accounting and increased vehicle and aircraft availability rates to 90% from 70% through a functional reorganization.

GENERAL MANAGER. U.S. Army, Germany (2003-04). Excelled in developing innovative programs and was promoted to Maintenance/Logistics/Operations Manager on the basis of my leadership and management skills while directing a 235-person attack helicopter headquarters company. Implemented two successful training programs: reduced ground vehicle accidents 77% through driver safety training and increased the pilot availability rate to a **perfect 100%**.

Excelled in research and development, U.S. Army, Fort Eustis, VA:
DIRECTOR OF INSTRUMENTATION DEVELOPMENT. (2002-03). Supervised 46 people involved in the design and installation of aircraft instrumentation data collection devices. Reduced overhead costs 12% through changes in operational procedures.

CHIEF OF UTILITY AND CARGO AIRCRAFT DEVELOPMENT. (2000-02). Performed developmental and operational testing on all types of aircraft and flight systems and was able to conduct customer testing approximately 15% below the $12.5 million budget.

- Performed Aircraft Survivability Equipment (ASE) as well as Reliability, Availability, Maintainability (RAM) testing.

TEST PROJECT OFFICER. (1999-00). Led a team of 12 specialists in the test procedures for aircraft, aircraft systems, and air crew equipment while designing major projects including the Army's aircraft survivability vest and "next-generation" voice-activated avionics.

- Applied my analytical and written communication talents preparing test design plans, test methodology, detailed test plans, and test reports.

FIRST-LINE SUPERVISOR. U.S. Army, Germany (1998-99). Managed supply, maintenance, and performance of 32 employees with nine AH-1 aircraft.

- Introduced changes which resulted in a 23% increase in aircraft availability by reorganizing the parts department and also by automating maintenance record keeping.

AIRCRAFT DESIGNER AND BUILDER. Experimental Aircraft Association, AL (1991-97). Designed/built/flew 14 types of aircraft; tested engine modifications.

PERSONAL

Troubleshoot/repair to the component level computer systems, electromechanical devices, avionics, airframes/power plants, and analog/digital circuitry. Secret security clearance.

Date

Exact Name of Person
Title or Position
Name of Company
Address
City, State, Zip

Dear Exact Name of Person: (or Dear Sir or Madam if answering a blind ad.)

I would appreciate an opportunity to talk with you soon about how I could contribute to your organization through my strong background related to purchasing, supply, and contracting operations as well as through my energy, optimism, and enthusiasm.

During my years of service in the U.S. Air Force, I advanced to increasing levels of responsibility while becoming known for my creativity and innovative ideas. Always focused on the bottom line, I continually found ways to reduce costs, increase the life of assets, and improve productivity levels and morale.

Throughout my career, I have been singled out for numerous awards including twice being named a "Professional Performer," an honor given to only a select few during major Inspector General visits. On numerous other occasions, I have been selected by my peers as one of the very best logistics professionals in every community where I have worked.

Having lived and worked in diverse areas, I possess the experience and diplomatic abilities to represent the U.S. in positions anywhere in the world. I offer a strong working knowledge of Italian and German.

My background as a purchasing agent has given me experience in writing telecommunications contracts, maintenance contracts, and purchase agreements. Known as a team player with well-developed leadership skills, I can handle stress and deadlines while keeping a keen eye on the details in order to ensure that projects are completed on time.

I hope you will call or write me soon to suggest a time convenient for us to meet and discuss your current and future needs and how I might serve them. Thank you in advance for your time.

Sincerely yours,

Roger Owens

ROGER OWENS

1110½ Hay Street, Fayetteville, NC 28305 • preppub@aol.com • (910) 483-6611

OBJECTIVE

To offer an organization my broad base of knowledge and experience in supply operations and material control along with my diplomatic skills, enthusiastic personality, and strong customer service orientation.

EXPERIENCE

MATERIAL CONTROL CHIEF. U.S. Air Force, Ramstein AB, Germany (2001-present). Developed numerous time- and money-saving ideas while coordinating supply actions and material requisitions between a civil engineering office and the community supply center.

- Initiated a program in which 75% of all assets in a $1.6 million furniture account were replaced after completing a 100% inventory of all furniture and appliances on the air station and getting all applicable records organized and updated.
- Saved more than $100,000 in Air Force funds by processing the turn in of more than $350,000 worth of worn-out property.
- Supervised two specialists while controlling the furniture and appliance inventory for military family housing, off-base contracted housing, and barracks for single personnel.
- Managed other supply and equipment inventories including tools, bench stock, equipment, and special accounts for space warning mission equipment and utility systems.
- Was personally credited with improving the level of team work, morale, and customer satisfaction while reducing paperwork backlogs and requisition processing time.
- Evaluated as a "super budget defender," was cited for keeping tight controls on spending and wisely prioritizing requirements.
- Was one of a select few to earn the distinction of "Professional Performer" during a major inspection, April 2005; had also earned this honor in 2003.

SUPERVISOR, LOGISTIC SUPPORT OPERATIONS. U.S. Air Force, Cannon AFB, NM (1996-01). Provided an Air Force recruiting headquarters with management support in areas ranging from control of a 75-vehicle fleet, to local purchase requests, to General Services Administration (GSA) supplies, to telecommunications, to meal/lodging/carrier tickets.

- Provided technical guidance and training for 50 recruiting offices and a headquarters while performing staff assistance visits and processing supply and equipment requests for 312 geographically scattered offices. Processed payments and reports on monthly vehicle costs and ensured telephone, vehicle, and medical bills were paid on time.
- Became known for my outstanding time management skills and ability to prioritize actions in order to accomplish diverse objectives. Installed a telephone system and prepared requests for telephone installation and removals as well as accounting for use of each phone.
- Wrote telecommunications contracts and coordinated with various telephone companies.

Highlights of previous experience: Gained a reputation as a thoroughly knowledgeable professional in positions in the fields of supply and inventory control, locations in the U.S. Asia, and Europe.

EDUCATION & TRAINING

B.A., Geography, University of Wyoming, Laramie, WY, 1993.
A.A., Liberal Arts, University of Wisconsin, Green Bay, WI, 1990.
Completed more than 600 hours of advanced training programs emphasizing managerial, supervisory, and leadership techniques as well as resource management and procurement.

PERSONAL

Have a working knowledge of Italian. Received four Air Force Commendation Medals for professionalism, initiative, and leadership. Operate office equipment including computers.

Date

Exact Name of Person
Title or Position
Name of Company
Address
City, State, Zip

Dear Exact Name of Person: (or Dear Sir or Madam if answering a blind ad.)

With the enclosed resume, I would like to express my interest in exploring employment opportunities with your organization.

As you will see from my resume, I offer a strong background in logistical support and inventory control management gained while serving in the Department of Defense. During my military career, I have been singled out for my sound judgment, ability to gain the cooperation and best efforts of others, and talent for guiding and motivating personnel to excel.

In my final assignment before retirement from the DoD, I continue to build on my reputation for honesty, personal integrity, and mental toughness. As the supervisor of a 14-person department, I am known for my ability to apply analytical skills and technical knowledge while developing workable methods for tracking and reconciling supply discrepancies. Significant accomplishments have been (1) a 75% reduction in the level of repairable parts as well as (2) the aggressive implementation of procedures used to track millions of dollars in discrepancies.

I achieved similar results in earlier assignments while controlling multimillion-dollar inventories of all classes of supplies in locations throughout the world. In recognition of my technical and managerial skills and knowledge, I was awarded numerous medals including a Joint Service Achievement Medal. I have also been recognized for my ability to maximize scarce resources and operate within tight time constraints while achieving excellent results in all measurable areas of performance.

If you can use a logistics and supply professional who is highly self-motivated and thrives on pressure and deadlines, I hope you will contact me soon to suggest a time we might meet to discuss my qualifications for this position. I can provide excellent professional and personal references at the appropriate time. Thank you for your time and consideration.

Sincerely,

Jerry Godwin

JERRY GODWIN

1110½ Hay Street, Fayetteville, NC 28305   •   preppub@aol.com   •   (910) 483-6611

OBJECTIVE   To contribute through a strong background in logistical support and inventory control management to an organization that can use an experienced professional with excellent motivational, planning, instructing, and supervisory skills.

EDUCATION   Pursuing an Associate of Arts (A.A.) degree, Central Michigan University.

EXPERIENCE   *Advanced to management positions in the Department of Defense while building a reputation as a dedicated and knowledgeable professional in the logistics field:*
MATERIAL MANAGEMENT SECTION SUPERVISOR. Fort Meade, MD (2005-present). Am credited with improving daily operations, morale, and cohesiveness as supervisor of a supply Class IX section of 14 people in a Supply Discrepancy and Overage Repairable Item management section.
- Provide technical guidance to six supply support activities with a total of 6,218 lines worth $42 million. Reduced the level of overage repairable items 75% while researching more than $25 million worth of items.
- Cited for my ability to identify, analyze, and solve problems, implemented procedures which tracked more than 750 discrepancy reports valued in excess of $2.3 million.

MATERIAL MANAGEMENT OPERATIONS SUPERVISOR. Fort Bragg, NC (2004-05). Cited for my willingness to share my knowledge with others and inspire them to set and achieve high performance standards, reviewed approximately $24 million worth of requisitions, each valued at over $5,000, every month; supervised six people.
- Tracked approximately 2,450 referrals a month to ensure timely issue and receipt of repair parts between units while providing technical guidance to six subordinate units.
- Applied "exceptionally efficient managerial skills" to save $12 million in repair parts.

SUPERVISOR OF STORAGE, REPAIRABLE EXCHANGE, PACKING, AND CRATING SECTIONS. Germany (2003-04). Respected for my knowledge of supply procedures "from unit to wholesale level," managed storage and issuing of 2,350 lines valued in excess of $18 million.
- Trained and supervised 22 people including German civilian and American military personnel while supporting 83 customer units and two Forward Support Battalions.
- Was credited with several important achievements which included completing a wall-to-wall inventory in under five days, maintaining a denial rate under 1% for Material Release Orders, and processing 60,000 MROs within two days of their receipt.

PERISHABLE GOODS SECTION SUPERVISOR. Fort Carson, CO (2003). Planned activities and trained personnel in a department which received, stored, distributed, and issued perishable food items while overseeing maintenance of $4 million worth of equipment.

WAREHOUSE MANAGER. Fort Carson, CO (2002). Described as a professional who resolved problems before they could escalate while mentoring well-trained teams, controlled the receipt, storage, issue, and distribution of more than $20 million worth of weapons and night vision devices. Supervised 11 people while controlling 4,900 sensitive items.

SUPERVISOR, MATERIAL HANDLING EQUIPMENT OPERATIONS. Fort Carson, CO (2001-02). Singled out for my ability to maximize scarce resources and use a positive and fair approach to solving problems, supervised 15 people.

PERSONAL   Highly motivated individual with outstanding character. Secret security clearance.

Date

Exact Name of Person
Title or Position
Name of Company
Address (number and street)
Address (city, state, and zip)

**MEDICAL SUPPLY AND
LOGISTICS MANAGER**

Dear Exact Name of Person: (or Sir or Madam if answering a blind ad.)

With the enclosed resume, I would like to express my interest in exploring employment opportunities with your organization. As you will see from my resume, I have proudly served my country in the Department of Defense while acquiring expertise related to supply and logistics, including medical supply and logistics.

During the past three years, I rose to senior management positions. In my most recent position as Medical Emergency Operation Center Manager, I controlled sensitive equipment valued at $5 million. In a previous position, I managed supply and logistics for a 296-bed deployable medical systems combat support hospital. I routinely managed multimillion-dollar inventories while controlling the purchasing and distribution of medical supplies.

Once I was selected for a job as Medical Supply Sergeant over 20 other qualified managers; in that position, I managed the purchase and distribution of medical supplies while training customers on medical supply procedures. In a prior position as a Financial Analyst and Stock Control Manager, I handled the financial management of a 630-line stock record account. In a previous job as an Office Manager, I was praised for superior administrative skills as I ordered $5 million in supplies for 157 customers.

Throughout my career, I have been praised for resourcefulness and initiative. As a Medical Supply Manager and Logistics Manager in Georgia, I saved more than $400,000 through attention to detail and skillful financial analysis. In another job as a Medical Logistics Manager, I oversaw the Class VIII Quality Assurance Program and was instrumental in implementing the Guaranteed Returns Program for the Division Medical Supply Office.

Although I greatly enjoyed the challenge of serving in the Department of Defense, I decided to leave the government and establish my career in the civilian world. I can provide outstanding references at the appropriate time. I hope you will contact me to suggest a time when we might meet to discuss your needs and goals.

Sincerely,

Jennifer Macias

JENNIFER MACIAS

1110½ Hay Street, Fayetteville, NC 28305 • preppub@aol.com • (910) 483-6611

OBJECTIVE   To offer extensive logistical skills to an organization that can use a professional with specialized experience in medical supply and logistics along with knowledge of inventory control, purchasing, hazardous materials management, and logistical planning.

EDUCATION   Completed 68 hours of Criminal Justice coursework, Cameron University, Lawton, OK, and 62 hours of coursework in Logistics Management, Troy State University, Columbus, GA.

EXPERIENCE   **Excelled in a track record of promotion in the Department of Defense:**
MEDICAL EMERGENCY OPERATION CENTER MANAGER. Ft. Benning, GA (2004-2005). Controlled sensitive equipment valued at $5 million while acting as liaison between the Army Medical Center and Ft. Benning. Trained personnel on computer systems and was described in writing as "a results-oriented problem solver who always found innovative ways to accomplish the mission."

MEDICAL SUPPLY MANAGER & LOGISTICS MANAGER. Ft. Benning, GA (2002-2003). Served as the assistant to the logistics manager of a 296-bed deployable medical systems combat support hospital. Controlled the logistical integration of supply, transportation, medical logistics and supply, acquisition, laundry and bath for the hospital and all affiliated organizations. Managed one mid-manager and two junior employees.

SENIOR MEDICAL SUPPLY MANAGER. Ft. Benning, GA (2002-2003). Was specially selected for this position because of my broad knowledge of military and unit supply. Trained and managed four employees while overseeing the requisition, issue, disposition, and accountability of unit property valued at $13 million. Managed a 900-line-item inventory of medical supplies and equipment.

MEDICAL LOGISTICS MANAGER. Atlanta, GA (2001-2002). For an organization with 10,000 employees, was responsible for processing Class VIII requisitions for 32 customers while assisting in managing the annual budget. Directed maintenance of tactical vehicles and equipment valued at $2,500,000. Oversaw the Class VIII Quality Assurance Program, and managed a Guaranteed Returns Program for expired items that resulted in credits of over $80,000 to the Division Class VIII account. Coordinated the redistribution of thousands of dollars of excess medical materiel among units.
- **Program management:** Was commended as being "instrumental in the implementation of the Guaranteed Returns Program for the Division Medical Supply Office." Developed a simple customer handout and coordinated turn-ins between customers and the program manager.
- **Outstanding evaluations:** Was cited for "superb managerial skills" that contributed to the first-ever integration of a U.S. Army Medical Activity and a Division Medical Supply Office. Developed internal and external supply procedures between the customer and medical organizations.

MEDICAL SUPPLY SERGEANT. Ft. Drum, NY (2000-01). Was selected for this position over 20 other capable NCOs. Inventoried and maintained 13 hand receipts valued at $1.2 million. Was commended for a "firm yet approachable leadership style" and was chosen by the Commander as Equal Opportunity Representative in a 10,000-employee organization.

PERSONAL   Outstanding references on request. Known for my strong personal initiative and integrity.

Date

Exact Name of Person
Title or Position
Name of Company
Address
City, State, Zip

OPERATIONS MANAGER   Dear Exact Name of Person: (or Dear Sir or Madam if answering a blind ad.)

Can you use a versatile and adaptable professional who offers strong hands-on managerial abilities, a keen intellect, and a strong background in research, technical writing, and public speaking?

While serving my country in the U.S. Army, I consistently excelled in demanding roles which varied from managing multimillion-dollar maintenance and logistics support operations, to instructing and counseling students at the U.S. Military Academy, to conducting studies and planning real-world activities for Special Operations Forces.

Throughout my career I have been handpicked for advanced training and educational opportunities as well as sensitive and critical jobs which required highly developed problem-solving, decision-making, and analytical skills.

I feel that I am a very versatile individual who has demonstrated the ability to think on my feet and adapt to change and pressure. Through my experience, excellent communication skills, and motivational abilities I could prove to be a valuable addition to an organization such as yours.

I hope you will welcome my call soon to arrange a brief meeting at your convenience to discuss your current and future needs and how I might serve them. Thank you in advance for your time.

Sincerely yours,

Theodore Woodburn

Alternate last paragraph:
I hope you will call or write me soon to suggest a time convenient for us to meet and discuss your current and future needs and how I might serve them. Thank you in advance for your time.

THEODORE WOODBURN

1110½ Hay Street, Fayetteville, NC 28305   •   preppub@aol.com   •   (910) 483-6611

OBJECTIVE   To offer my reputation as an extremely adaptable, articulate, and innovative individual to an organization that can use a mature professional who has consistently excelled as a military officer through applying superior planning, communication, and leadership abilities.

EXPERIENCE   *Advanced in the U.S. Army in managerial roles at Fort Shafter, HI:*
OPERATIONS MANAGER. (2005-present). As second-in-command of a 700-person organization, act as the chief executive's right arm while overseeing the daily administrative, logistical, and budget support activities.
- Supervised a 15-person administrative staff and five mid-level managers. Led the organization to receive its highest-ever scores in a maintenance inspection.

DIRECTOR OF LOGISTICS AND MAINTENANCE SUPPORT ACTIVITIES. (2004-05). Handled the intricate details of providing a 2,300-person organization with logistics and maintenance support while overseeing three dining halls, a $1.35 million annual budget, material reporting, and maintenance for 250 vehicles.
- Coordinated transport of 170 fully loaded vehicles to Honolulu, HI, and on to Australia.

OPERATIONS MANAGER. (2003-04). Conducted research, prepared reports, and presented briefings to a senior official while making decisions on when, where, and how to send Special Operations Forces personnel to real-world trouble spots.
- Communicated regularly with United Nations representatives and non-government organizations while arranging to send and bring back personnel from overseas activities.

ASSISTANT PROFESSOR. U.S. Army, The United States Military Academy at West Point, NY (2000-03). Handpicked from a pool of 200 highly qualified executives for one of only 20 instructor positions, was recognized with the Department of History's 2002 "Excellence in Teaching Award" for my effectiveness as a classroom instructor and mentor.
- Singled out as a course director, directed 19 instructors who dealt daily with 935 cadets during the 2001 fall semester.

GRADUATE STUDENT. U.S. Army, University of Florida, Gainesville, FL (1998-00). Refined in-depth research and investigative skills while serving as an advisor for students in the university's ROTC program; earned a master's degree in my spare time.

Excelled in highly visible and critical roles with the U.S. Army in Italy:
GENERAL MANAGER. (1997-98). Provided outstanding leadership and guidance for 155 personnel working in a highly stressful environment, which called for constant alertness.
- Applied my communication skills while dealing regularly with Italian and British allies.

OPERATIONS MANAGER. (1995-97). Was handpicked for the General Manager's position on the basis of outstanding human and material resource management skills demonstrated while planning and scheduling training for a 750-person organization.
- Controlled the organization's $2.5 million annual ammunition budget.

EDUCATION   **M.A., History**, University of Florida, Gainesville, GA, 2000.
&   **B.S., Social Sciences**, University of Kentucky, Lexington, KY, 1995.
TRAINING   - Maintained a 3.74 GPA and completed two years of courses in only ten months.

PERSONAL   Known for my loyalty and honesty, was entrusted with a Top Secret security clearance.

Date

Exact Name of Person
Title or Position
Name of Company
Address
City, State, Zip

Dear Exact Name of Person: (or Dear Sir or Madam if answering a blind ad.)

With the enclosed resume, I would like to express my interest in exploring employment opportunities within your organization and introduce you to my reputation as a results-oriented professional with proven management and motivational skills.

As you will see from my resume, I was one of the youngest-ever individuals to advance to the rank of sergeant major in the U. S. Army. I have been praised for my strong verbal and written communication skills, and I have been consistently evaluated as a bright and articulate professional with a talent for getting the most out of people by setting high standards and leading the way to achieving them.

With a Bachelor of Business Administration degree (concentration in Logistics Management) earned while excelling in demanding logistics and personnel administration and management jobs, I was singled out as Honor Graduate in several advanced training programs emphasizing instructional techniques, employee supervision, and logistics management. The recipient of numerous medals and honors, which included being named "Soldier of the Year" twice, I am especially proud of the medals I received from Indiana Governor Adam Finkle for my community service as a coach and mentor for young people. As a senior advisor on personnel and supply issues since 2005, I have produced exceptional bottom-line results which included bringing personnel retention rates from 78% up to an average of 116%, and leading the organization to pass rigorous operational inspections with high scores. I have earned respect for my accomplishments in providing sound management oversight and for building cohesive teams of personnel who are committed to excellence. My computer skills are top-notch, and I am proficient with Word, Access, Excel, PowerPoint, and numerous other programs. I am also a Total Quality Management (TQM) Facilitator.

If you can use a proven leader and self starter with the ability to produce outstanding results for your organization, I hope you will welcome my call soon when I try to arrange a brief meeting to discuss your goals and how my background might serve your needs. I can provide outstanding references at the appropriate time.

Sincerely,

Aaron Anderson

Alternate last paragraph:
If you can use a proven leader and self-starter with the ability to produce outstanding results, I hope you will write or call me soon to suggest a time when we might meet to discuss your needs and how my background might serve them. I can provide outstanding references at the appropriate time.

AARON ANDERSON

1110½ Hay Street, Fayetteville, NC 28305 • preppub@aol.com • (910) 483-6611

OBJECTIVE

To contribute my exceptional skills in motivating, instructing, and guiding others to excel as well as through my strong base of experience in logistics management to an organization that can use an energetic, enthusiastic, and articulate professional.

EDUCATION & TRAINING

Bachelor of Business Administration with a concentration in **Logistics Management**, Butler University, Indianapolis, IN, 2003.
Was an **Honor Graduate** of several courses while completing advanced training in personnel management and employee supervision, logistics management, and instructional techniques. Completed additional course work in Total Quality Management (am a **TQM Facilitator**), computer applications and automated systems operations, and maintenance management.

EXPERIENCE

Earned rapid advancement in logistics management roles while gaining recognition as a team builder, instructor, and mentor, U.S. Army; was one of the youngest people ever promoted to the rank of Sergeant Major and named "Soldier of the Year" twice: PERSONNEL ADMINISTRATION AND SUPPLY OPERATIONS MANAGER. Jefferson Proving Ground, IN (2005-present). In a dual leadership role with an aviation unit, assisted the senior executive in planning and coordination of company activities as Senior Advisor on personnel issues, training, and supply support.

- Earned recognition for my ability to analyze and see all sides of a question and then apply creativity while solving problems and setting priorities and goals. Developed and implemented an internal training program which resulted in exceptional ratings during several evaluations as well as a "Governor's Unit Citation."
- Provided leadership and focus which allowed the unit to pass every inspection and become recognized as **the highest quality maintenance program in the state.**
- Maintained personnel strength at 116% with exceptionally low personnel losses.
- Officially described as a **"dynamic, far-sighted role model,"** was rated as possessing a **"superb blend of hands-on and executive-level management abilities."**
- Brought annual test results of professional knowledge and skills to above 95%.
- Was credited with volunteering personal time to improve quality of life, training, and professional development of unit employees.

LOGISTICS OPERATIONS MANAGER. Jefferson Proving Ground, IN (2003-05). Cited for my sound judgment and ability to find ways to maximize resources, assisted in managing, supervising, and carrying out supply support operations for an aviation organization.

- Ensured headquarters and subordinate unit personnel were thoroughly trained in the Army Logistical System and its procedures and operation.
- Evaluated as a proactive manager who was always alert to new methods and ways to conserve resources, led the unit to extremely low equipment and personnel losses.

Highlights of earlier U.S. Army experience: In various locations throughout the world, advanced to senior managerial and supervisory roles in the logistics and supply field.

- Earned U.S. Army medals for my accomplishments including a Meritorious Service Medal, six Commendation Medals, five Achievement Medals as well as the **Indiana Meritorious Service Medal and Indiana Commendation Medal awarded by Indiana Governor Adam Finkle** for community service as a coach and mentor for young people.
- Was recognized as **"Soldier of the Year"** in two different divisions (1996 and 1993).

PERSONAL

Secret security clearance. Proficient with Word, Excel, Access, PowerPoint, other software.

Date

Exact Name of Person
Title of Person
Name of Company
Address
City, State, Zip

PLANS OFFICER   Dear Exact Name of Person: (or Dear Sir or Madam if answering a blind ad.)

I would appreciate an opportunity to talk with you soon about how I could contribute to your organization through my management experience and leadership ability.

As you will see from my resume, I have excelled in a "track record" of accomplishments while being promoted to the rank of Major in the U.S. Army. On numerous occasions I was selected for "hotseat" jobs that required an articulate communicator with outstanding strategic planning, problem solving, and motivational skills. In one job I developed the organization's first strategic plan forecasting personnel and equipment needs into the 21st century. In my current job as a Plans Officer I brief top-level government officials on plans for pooling the resources of Navy, Army, Air Force, and Marine Corps forces in special projects worldwide.

A physically fit and health-conscious person who enjoys body building in my spare time, I practice "leadership by example" in everything I do. In one job as an assistant professor at the Kansas State University, I became a popular instructor and leader whom the college cadets wanted to emulate. In another job as a "company commander," I set the example for other officers to follow through my resourceful problem-solving style and ability to find new ways to maximize scarce resources.

You would find me to be a loyal and selfless person who is accustomed to making personal sacrifices so that the organization's goals can be achieved. I am single and would relocate according to your needs. I can provide outstanding personal and professional references upon your request.

I hope you will welcome my call soon when I try to arrange a brief meeting with you at your convenience to discuss your needs and how I might serve them. Thank you in advance for your time.

Yours sincerely,

Clifford Mosely

Alternate last paragraph:
I hope you will write or call me soon to suggest a time when we might meet to discuss your needs and goals and how I might meet them. Thank you in advance for your time.

CLIFFORD MOSELY

1110½ Hay Street, Fayetteville, NC 28305　•　preppub@aol.com　•　(910) 483-6611

OBJECTIVE

To benefit an organization that can use a resourceful and adaptable professional consistently described in performance evaluations as an "action person who makes things happen."

EDUCATION & TRAINING

Earned **Bachelor of Science (B.S.) degree**, University of Georgia, Athens, GA, 1988.
- Was named **Distinguished Military Graduate**.

Completed extensive graduate-level training as a military officer related to operations management, financial administration, production control, and leadership.

EXPERIENCE

PLANS OFFICER. U.S. Army, Fort Riley, KS (2005-present). Continuously brief top-level officers on plans for projects that pool the resources of the Army, Navy, Air Force, and Marines.

DIRECTOR OF SUPPORT OPERATIONS. U.S. Army, Fort Riley, KS (2003-04). Managed a variety of service operations supporting the overall mission of an 800-person organization; organized and directed special projects which required relocating personnel and assets; planned and supervised training programs; managed the safe implementation of an 11,000-hour flying-hour program to include 1,000 accident-free flying hours flown in a 30-day period during the Hurricane Isabel Relief Effort.
- Was praised for thrifty management of human resources and multimillion-dollar assets which included 50 aircraft, 51 wheeled vehicles, and other air ground support equipment valued at over 90 million dollars.

RESOURCES MANAGER. U.S. Army, Fort Riley, KS (2003). Was evaluated in writing as a "multi-talented self starter and team player" because of the multiple contributions I made, on my own initiative, to the largest aviation brigade in the U.S. Army; developed a strategic plan forecasting the organization's needs for equipment and personnel into the 21st century.

AVIATION STAFF OFFICER. U.S. Army, Iraq (2002). During the War on Terror, played a key role in planning and orchestrating the air support which is credited with "winning the war" while coordinating aviation issues with French, British, and Royal Saudi land forces.

ASSISTANT PROFESSOR OF MILITARY SCIENCE. Kansas State University, Manhattan, KS (1999-02). Was responsible for the recruiting, administration, and training of 187 college cadets and was the primary instructor for freshmen and senior cadets; was described as "endowed with matchless leadership, managerial, and instructor abilities."

GENERAL MANAGER ("COMPANY COMMANDER"). U.S. Army, Fort Drum, NY (1998-99). Was the chief executive officer of an aviation organization with 23 officer pilots and 15 flight instructors; became respected for my pro-active approach to problem solving while identifying solutions for backlogs and finding ways to optimize the use of scarce resources.

Highlights of other experience: Gained expert knowledge related to aviation.
- **Research & Development**: Determined user-oriented priorities for helicopter research, development, and acquisition; managed engineering change proposals (ECPs) and product improvement proposals (PIPs).
- **Operations management**: Maintained over 135 sets of flight records.
- **Aircraft/crew management**: Managed operations for an attack helicopter organization.

PERSONAL

Am fully bilingual in Spanish and English. Can use Word and Adobe PageMaker. Am single and will travel/relocate to suit my employer's needs. Hold a private pilot's license.

Date

Exact Name of Person
Title or Position
Name of Company
Address
City, State, Zip

Dear Exact Name of Person: (or Dear Sir or Madam if answering a blind ad.)

With the enclosed resume, I would like to introduce you to my background in supply and logistics operations as well as to my personal reputation as an energetic and enthusiastic manager of fiscal and material resources.

As you will see from my resume, I am presently serving in the U.S. Army as a Supply Supervisor in Europe. Handpicked to serve on a task force assigned to Iraq in April 2006, I was described as a talented performer who "juggles many jobs to help (the) mission." Faced with numerous obstacles while trying to provide soldiers with housing, laundry, mail, and other support services, one of my proudest accomplishments was successfully developing a system for getting laundry done locally within 24 hours, thus eliminating the previous system, which took three days and involved shipping laundry to remote destinations within the middle east.

With a talent for quickly mastering computer applications, I have been singled out to oversee multimillion-dollar inventories of supplies, equipment, and ammunition valued in the millions of dollars for organizations with up to 4,800 employees. I offer excellent time management skills and the ability to find ways to improve productivity and build effective teams, as well as a keen eye for an organization's bottom line.

I hope you will welcome my call soon when I try to arrange a brief meeting to discuss your goals and how my background might serve your needs. I can provide outstanding references at the appropriate time.

Sincerely,

Luke Thornhill

Alternate Last Paragraph:
I hope you will write or call me soon to suggest a time when we might meet to discuss your needs and goals and how my background might serve them. I can provide outstanding references at the appropriate time.

LUKE THORNHILL

1110½ Hay Street, Fayetteville, NC 28305　　•　　preppub@aol.com　　•　　(910) 483-6611

OBJECTIVE

To offer expertise in logistical operations and the supply management field to an organization that can use an energetic and hard-charging professional with outstanding verbal and written communication skills and a keen eye for the bottom line.

EDUCATION & TRAINING

Studied Accounting at Fayetteville Technical Community College, Fayetteville, NC. Completed training in customer service, supply operations, and leadership development.

SPECIAL SKILLS

Functional areas of expertise: hand receipt maintenance; physical security for sensitive items; ordering, tracking, receiving, inspecting, transporting, and issuing equipment: planning and coordinating services; implementing SOPs; and file maintenance.
Computer operations: quickly master new computer programs and am familiar with MS PowerPoint, Word, Excel, and Exchange as well as numerous government programs – AMDF, ARMYLOG, FEDLOG, and ULLS S4.
Other: type 40 wpm and operate most standard office equipment; am licensed to operate vehicles up to 2-1/2 tons as well as standard military weapons.

EXPERIENCE

Am advancing through my inventory management know-how and ability to find ways to improve productivity while serving in the U.S. Army:
PROPERTY ACCOUNTABILITY SECTION SUPERVISOR. Italy and other worldwide locations (2004-present). Built a results-oriented team of six supply specialists while overseeing an inventory valued in excess of $50 million; was recognized for my strong problem-solving ability.
- Turned in $2 million worth of unserviceable items and eliminated 30 lines of excess.
- Reconfigured the largest U.S. Army weapons storage and issuing section in Europe and was credited with developing workable SOPs and meeting physical security standards.
- Managed a $20 million furniture account and another $2 million office equipment account which were the largest of their kind in Europe.

Special Project in 2005: **SUPPLY SUPERVISOR.** Iraq. Handpicked to oversee supply support for a special project, supervise one assistant while controlling more than $30 million worth of supplies, equipment, and ammunition for 4,800 task force members.
- Created and now oversee a program which provides local 24-hour laundry service in an area where the wait had been 72 hours and required flying laundry to and from remote destinations in the middle east.

Special Project in 2004: **SUPPLY SUPERVISOR.** Kuwait. Chosen to supervise one subordinate and control a $400,000 property inventory for a four-month project, worked with peers from the military services of other countries and learned new supply procedures.

SPECIAL INVENTORY CONTROLLER. Korea (2002). Received an Army Achievement Medal for my accomplishments in restructuring a 24-hour-a-day "arms room" for $700,000 worth of weapons and ammunition used by 400 members of a joint military operation.

SUPPLY MANAGER. Fort Bragg, NC (2000-02). Was awarded a prestigious U.S. Army Commendation Medal for maintaining reports-of-survey records for 4,000 employees.

SUPPLY CLERK. Germany (1999-00). Received my first U.S. Army Commendation Medal for my outstanding work ethic and tactful, professional manner.

PERSONAL

Secret security clearance. Excel in handling the details of organizing, planning, and carrying out projects which provide efficient customer service. Certified drug free.

Date

Exact Name of Person
Title or Position
Name of Company
Address
City, State, Zip

PROPERTY CHIEF   Dear Exact Name of Person: (or Dear Sir or Madam if answering a blind ad.)

I would appreciate an opportunity to talk with you soon about how I could contribute to your organization through my extensive background in supply administration, including financial management and computer operations.

As you will see from my resume, most recently I was handpicked to take over a troubled organization as its Property Chief. Although the organization was widely regarded as being "out of control" when I took it over, I retrained staff, installed new computer programs, and corrected numerous deficiencies so that we passed a recent rigorous inspection with "no faults" noted. In a previous job as Supply Chief, I managed the provision of inspection, training, and consulting services related to contracting, purchasing, warehousing, financial management, and all other areas of supply administration. In that job I also performed extensive public relations duties with activities and organizations.

You will also see from my resume that I have administered supply operations for nearly all kinds of items, from communications-electronics to clothing, as well as professional services. In one job as Operations Chief, I trained and supervised 29 people while managing purchasing and requisitioning related to a 150-page current accounts file containing 2500 pending requisitions.

Proficient with both Windows operating systems, I am experienced in using Word and Excel; and I am skilled in using spreadsheets and databases to maximize efficiency and solve problems. In addition to my extensive formal training in all aspects of supply, I have benefited from recent training in Total Quality Leadership (TQL).

I hope you will welcome my call soon to arrange a brief meeting at your convenience to discuss your current and future needs and how I might serve them. Thank you in advance for your time.

Sincerely yours,

Alice Jones

Alternate last paragraph:
I hope you will call or write me soon to suggest a time convenient for us to meet and discuss your current and future needs and how I might serve them. Thank you in advance for your time.

ALICE JONES

1110½ Hay Street, Fayetteville, NC 28305 • preppub@aol.com • (910) 483-6611

OBJECTIVE

To contribute to an organization that can use a versatile supply administrator with excellent financial and accounting knowledge, extensive computer expertise, and in-depth operations management experience.

COMPUTERS

Proficient with Word, Excel, and PowerPoint, and skilled in working in Windows.

EXPERIENCE

Rose to top positions in the supply career field while serving my country in the U.S. Marine Corps in the following positions:

PROPERTY CHIEF. Electronics School, Jacksonville, NC (2005-present). Was specially recruited for this position which involved turning around a disorganized operation riddled with accountability, human resources, and other problems; received an Achievement Medal for my exceptional management results.
- Supervise the transfer of records from Access to ATLASS System.
- Implement the transfer of more than $3 million in computer assets to customer accounts.
- Was commended for my skill in reorganizing internal operations, streamlining procedures, and installing new computer programs; led my team to excel in a major rigorous inspection in which "no faults" were observed.

SUPPLY CHIEF/CONSULTANT. Instruction and Inspection Staff, Oceanside, CA (2001-04). Managed a $60,000 supply budget while supporting the training for a 185-person organization; provided inspection, instruction, and consulting services.

RETAIL STORE MANAGER. Defense Support Stock Control, Thailand (2000-01). Received a respected Certificate of Recognition for my outstanding bottom-line results in managing all aspects of a clothing sales store which retailed up to $3,000 in uniforms monthly.
- Supervised two clerks while overseeing inventory control, merchandising, and sales.

SUPPLY COORDINATOR. Recruiting Station, Richmond, VA (1995-00). Supported the recruiting efforts of 65 recruiters located at ten recruiting sites throughout Virginia while managing the payment and accountability of $125,000 in telephone bills, $65,000 in recruiter travel claims, and other budget items valued at more than $100,000. Earned a medal for my extraordinary efforts related to purchasing, contracting, and financial management.

OPERATIONS CHIEF. Material Issue Point, Camp Lejeune, NC (1993-95). Trained, motivated, and supervised 29 people while overseeing a 150-page current accounts file which contained more than 2500 pending requisitions. Became skilled in purchasing management.

SUPPLY COORDINATOR. Management Unit, Camp Lejeune, NC (1992-93). Received unusually rapid promotion to corporal and then to sergeant while working for the Officer in Charge; utilized computers to prepare correspondence for executive signature.

EDUCATION

Excelled in more than two years of college-level courses in supply administration, financial management, and human resources sponsored by the U.S. Marine Corps; courses included:
- Total Quality Leadership (TQL), 2005
- Human Resources and Operations Management, NCO Leadership Academy, 2004
- Supply Service and Support Schools, 1990-05

PERSONAL

Am a highly motivated self starter who can provide excellent personal and professional references. Offer the ability to solve difficult problems through applying my analytical skills.

Date

Exact Name of Person
Title or Position
Name of Company
Address
City, State, Zip

Dear Exact Name of Person: (or Dear Sir or Madam if answering a blind ad.)

With the enclosed resume, I would like to make you aware of my background in logistics and distribution operations with an emphasis on experience in purchasing.

As you will see from my resume, during my approximately seven years of military service I have become proficient in operating and training others in the operation of the Unit Level Logistics Supply System 4 (ULLSS-4) database. With experience in procuring supplies and equipment, supervising and mentoring employees, and presenting briefings which allow executives to gain information concerning supply activities, I have earned a reputation as a self-motivated professional who can be counted on to get the job done right the first time.

Familiar with the Department of Defense (DoD) contracting process, in several assignments I have been credited with saving government funds through my initiative and resourcefulness. I have been cited as the key force in developing sources for obtaining equipment and supplies from outside the standard military channels by using civilian sources for lower cost and reduced waiting times. Presently in control of purchasing for a 120-person organization, I purchase an average of $13 million in equipment quarterly while controlling a $10 million inventory of electronics and communication gear, food, furniture, and other classes of supplies.

The recipient of two U.S. Army Commendation Medals and two U.S. Army Achievement Medals in recognition of my professionalism and dedication, I also was awarded the Humanitarian Service Medal for my contributions during hurricane clean-up efforts.

If you can use a resourceful and creative professional who is known for sound judgment and for getting results, I hope you will welcome my call soon when I try to arrange a brief meeting to discuss your goals and how my background might serve your needs. I can provide outstanding references at the appropriate time.

Sincerely,

Fred Hall

Alternate last paragraph:
I hope you will write or call me soon to suggest a time when we might meet to discuss your needs and goals and how my background might serve them. I can provide outstanding references at the appropriate time.

FRED HALL

1110½ Hay Street, Fayetteville, NC 28305 • preppub@aol.com • (910) 483-6611

OBJECTIVE

To contribute a strong base of experience in logistics and distribution operations to an organization that can use a natural leader who offers superior communication and motivational abilities gained while excelling in inventory management activities.

EDUCATION & TRAINING

Completed U.S. Army-sponsored training with the ULLSS-4 (Unit Level Logistics Supply System 4) as well as courses in Microsoft Excel, Word, and PowerPoint.

EXPERIENCE

Am known for my persistence, ability to maximize resources, and dedication to ensuring the job is done by motivating others to excellent results, U.S. Army: **PURCHASING AGENT** and **SUPPLY SECTION SUPERVISOR.** Fort Benning, GA (2005-present). Display resourcefulness while purchasing and procuring supplies and equipment through negotiation with sources outside the normal military channels in order to provide a 120-person company with the best possible equipment within the shortest time frame.
- Purchase an average of $13 million worth of equipment each quarter.
- Apply planning and organizational skills arranging the details of ensuring adequate supplies and equipment in categories which include electronics and communication gear, food, furniture, and chemicals while accounting for $10 million worth of equipment.

SUPPLY OPERATIONS SUPERVISOR. Fort Benning, GA (2003-05). Cited for my willingness to share knowledge with others and dedication to doing whatever was needed to get the job done, oversaw a large-scale supply operation with $75 million worth of equipment.
- Supervised two people and was frequently sought out to counsel and advise others.
- Purchased $2 million worth of equipment and managed a $2 million annual budget.
- Developed more efficient methods for purchasing needed supplies and equipment from civilian markets with the result that the government achieved $50,000 in annual savings.
- Received "no discrepancies 100%" evaluations during three consecutive high-level inspections of the weapons and ammunition supply room as well as for the supply section during a maintenance assessment inspection.

ASSISTANT SUPERVISOR FOR SUPPLY ACTIVITIES. Fort Benning, GA (2003). Created improvements to the annual budget which resulted in saving the government $75,000 while accounting for more than $25 million worth of equipment.
- Became familiar with the most economical sources for purchasing materials from civilian sources and ordered all classes of supplies from both civilian and military sources.
- Supervised five people and maintained a $150,000 quarterly operations budget.

SUPERVISORY SUPPLY SPECIALIST. Germany (2001-02). Was cited as a force for positive change in American-German relations while supervising five people and controlling a $7 million property inventory and in excess of $20 million worth of equipment
- Implemented improvements to purchasing plans for a company which spent an average of $200,000 a quarter and earned 14 commendable ratings during a major inspection.

SUPPLY CLERK. Fort Jackson, SC (1999-01). Gained experience in time management and human relations while accounting for $10 million worth of property and ordering all classes of supplies; planned, designed, and implemented a two-year $160,000 budget.
- Filed reports, organized files, and investigated cases of loss, damage, or theft.

PERSONAL

Have earned two U.S. Army Commendation Medals, two Achievement Medals, and a Humanitarian Service Medal in recognition of accomplishments. Secret security clearance.

Date

Exact Name of Person
Title or Position
Name of Company
Address
City, State, Zip

Dear Exact Name of Person: (or Dear Sir or Madam if answering a blind ad.)

I would appreciate an opportunity to talk with you soon about how I could contribute to your organization as a Purchasing Agent through my experience in purchasing and inventory management gained in the U.S. Army. I am skilled in locating the sources which provide the most equipment for the best price, developing good working relations with vendors, and maintaining accountability for multimillion-dollar assets.

As you will see from my enclosed resume, I am a talented young professional with a reputation for always giving my best efforts and striving to excel in everything I attempt. In my present job as a Purchasing Agent and Unit Supply Specialist, I ensure that computer assets are distributed throughout a 1,000-person organization so that $10.5 million worth of equipment ends up with the people who most need it while controlling a $35 million budget.

In a previous assignment as a Material Control Accounting Specialist, I performed purchasing, accounting, and sales functions with direct responsibility for a supply materials account valued in excess of $1.5 million. In that position, I worked with major civilian contractors.

My technical knowledge covers the operation of PC hardware—hard drives, modems, rams, and floppy drives—and the use of software programs such as MS Office, Adobe PageMaker, and QuickBooks Pro.

I am an airborne-qualified young professional who enjoys contributing to the community by volunteering as a Boy Scout leader. I am certain that, through my creativity and knowledge, I have a great deal to offer to an organization that can use a detail-oriented and mature young professional.

I hope you will call or write me soon to suggest a time convenient for us to meet and discuss your current and future needs and how I might serve them. Thank you in advance for your time.

Sincerely,

Annette Morris

ANNETTE MORRIS

1110½ Hay Street, Fayetteville, NC 28305 • preppub@aol.com • (910) 483-6611

OBJECTIVE   To offer my experience in purchasing and inventory management to an organization that can use a knowledgeable professional known for excellent communication and motivational skills as well as the ability to develop and maintain effective customer relations.

EXPERIENCE   *Earned a reputation as a very energetic and enthusiastic professional who can be counted on to locate sources which result in the most effective use of funds and for accepting the responsibility for accounting for multimillion-dollar inventories, U.S. Army, Fort Knox, KY:*

PURCHASING AGENT & UNIT SUPPLY SPECIALIST. (2005-present). Provide an ordering and contracting officer with assistance during all phases of purchasing and contracting activities while ensuring the error-free maintenance and control of a $25 million dollar budget.

- Ensured that computer assets were distributed throughout a 1,000-person organization so that approximately $10.5 million worth of computer equipment requiring constant upgrading ended up with the end users who could get the most from it.
- Reduced contract supply costs 30% by researching suppliers and soliciting the best prices.
- Maintain records accounting for all equipment purchases.
- In November 2006, was appointed as the accounting manager in charge of accepting, accounting for, and distributing the equipment to the customers.

MATERIAL CONTROL ACCOUNTING SPECIALIST. (2002-04). Held direct accountability for a supply materials account valued in excess of $1.5 million while performing accounting, purchasing, and sales functions in support of the 25,000-customer 101st Airborne Division.

- Established accountability and maintained inventory control over sensitive commodities valued at more than $30 million.
- Transferred my knowledge while taking an organization with average ratings to one which was evaluated as "outstanding" after six months of hard work and dedication.
- Maintained regular communication with major civilian contractors.

ADMINISTRATIVE ASSISTANT. (2000-02). Became recognized for my ability to learn and apply computer skills while planning, organizing, and carrying out office support functions.

- Learned to provide budget analysis in a company which provided maintenance support for the 101st Airborne Division.
- Applied my technical knowledge while establishing databases and spreadsheets used in budget analysis activities.
- Gained a high level of familiarity with PC hardware and with software programs including MS Office, Adobe PageMaker and InDesign, Excel, Access, and QuickBooks Pro.
- Earned a one-year appointment as the marketing manager for the unit budget on the basis of my expertise and knowledge displayed while setting up and maintaining the budget process.

TRAINING   Completed a two-month advanced individual training program for supply specialists as well as additional programs emphasizing budgeting and finance.

TECHNICAL KNOWLEDGE
- Am experienced in using software programs including MS Office and Adobe PageMaker.
- Offer familiarity with the operation of PC hardware—hard drives, modems, and rams.

Date

Exact Name of Person
Title or Position
Name of Company
Address
City, State, Zip

**SALES REPRESENTATIVE,
WARRANTY MANAGER,
& SHIPPING MANAGER**

Dear Exact Name of Person: (or Dear Sir or Madam if answering a blind ad.)

I would appreciate an opportunity to talk with you soon about how I could contribute to your organization through my demonstrated track record of accomplishments in sales, customer service, and management.

As you will see from my enclosed resume, I offer a proven ability to rapidly become a valuable resource to my employer. I began with my current employer in 2003 as a supply/equipment delivery person and was quickly placed in charge of all the company's deliveries because of my ability to analyze routes and develop the most efficient plans for delivering products. I was then promoted to responsibilities in the area of sales and customer service, and my sales efforts have greatly boosted the company's overall annual sales. In inside sales, I have served customers over the counter and by telephone, and in outside sales, I have set up numerous new accounts while personally servicing the company's most valuable contracts.

Because of my public relations style and customer service skills, I am the person who troubleshoots the company's most difficult customer problems. In the last couple of years, I have added responsibilities in the management area. For example, I now manage the company's warranty program and am the internal expert on the warranty requirements of more than 900 vendors. I routinely handle numerous responsibilities in the area of purchasing, inventory control, and budgeting.

You would find me in person, I am sure, to be a good natured individual who relates well to people. Even in my spare time, I am considered a leader; for example, I was elected Baptist Man of the Year by my church. I can provide excellent personal and professional references.

I hope you will welcome my call soon to arrange a brief meeting at your convenience to discuss your current and future needs and how I might serve them. Thank you in advance for your time.

Sincerely yours,

Guy Nelson

Alternate last paragraph:
I hope you will call or write me soon to suggest a time convenient for us to meet and discuss your current and future needs and how I might serve them. Thank you in advance for your time.

GUY NELSON

1110½ Hay Street, Fayetteville, NC 28305 • preppub@aol.com • (910) 483-6611

OBJECTIVE   To contribute to an organization that can use a hard-working young professional who offers exceptionally strong sales and customer relations skills along with proven abilities related to managing operations, boosting profitability, controlling inventory, directing shipping and receiving, and solving a wide range of problems related to product quality and service.

EXPERIENCE   **SALES REPRESENTATIVE, WARRANTY MANAGER, & SHIPPING MANAGER.** Fitzgerald Supply, Inc., Killeen, TX (2003-present). Began with this company as a salesman and supply/equipment delivery person, and have become a respected part of the company's management team while advancing to handle a wide range of responsibilities.

- **On-time delivery:** As a Delivery Person, single-handedly performed work normally handled by two people, and became known for my strong time management skills.
- **Shipping and receiving:** As Shipping and Receiving Manager, prepared a daily Back Order Report and Order Hangout Report and checked those reports against current inventory; created invoices and then packaged merchandise for shipping by FedEx and other carriers; filled out bills of lading and palletized items.
- **Inside sales:** As a Counter Sales Representative, was in contact with dozens of customers daily face-to-face and by telephone; was respected by customers for my expert ability to match up parts from air conditioning, heating, and refrigeration units as well as major appliances and mechanical devices by utilizing my expert ability to use microfiche machines, technical data books, and knowledge gained from past experience.
- **Outside sales:** Have excelled as an Outside Sales Representative; on my own initiative, prospected for customers and set up 12-14 sales calls per day which tremendously increased company sales; have personally serviced the company's most valuable contracts at Fort Hood.
- **Bottom-line orientation:** Have become known as the company's most effective problem solver in difficult customer relations situations; have learned the art of satisfying the customer without compromising the company's bottom line; through my effective style of sales and customer service, have greatly increased overall company sales.
- **Vendor relations/warranty management:** In 2005, took over management of the company's complex warranty programs; now oversee warranties provided by more than 900 vendors and personally established the company's internal procedures for warranty management; am now considered an expert in obtaining credit for in-warranty merchandise and carefully monitor the warranty program to assure satisfaction.
- **Inventory control:** Continuously control inventory and oversee purchasing of stock; installed new inventory control procedures that minimized inventory investment costs.

SALESMAN. Texan Appliance Parts, Killeen, TX (2002-03). Learned the nuts and bolts of the appliance parts business while becoming an expert in using microfiche to cross reference parts to determine their potential for utilization in various products.

ASSISTANT MANAGER. Taco Bell, Killeen, TX (2002). Was groomed for management; excelled in dealing with the public and fellow employees while ordering inventory, overseeing maintenance and sanitation, and scheduling employees on all shifts.

TRAINING   Completed training related to motors and ventilation and HVAC controls; completed a course in public speaking and sales. Am a notary public.

PERSONAL   Was elected Baptist Man of the Year by my church in 2005. Was ordained as a Deacon in 2005. As a hobby, enjoy restoring used cars and making minor repairs on them.

Date

Exact Name of Person
Title or Position
Name of Company
Address
City, State, Zip

Dear Exact Name of Person: (or Dear Sir or Madam if answering a blind ad.)

With the enclosed resume, I would like to make you aware of my interest in offering my versatile background and track record of accomplishments to an organization that can use a dynamic, articulate, and results-oriented professional.

As you will see from my resume, I offer a strong work history in managing maintenance and supply operations as well as in planning and developing training, special projects, and all types of support for large-scale organizations working under tight time constraints. During a distinguished career culminating in promotion to one of the highest enlisted ranks, I have built a reputation for my sound judgment, ability to gain the cooperation and best efforts of others, and talent for guiding and motivating others to excel in every endeavor.

I offer a reputation for honesty, integrity, physical and mental toughness while producing excellent results. My ability to apply creativity and sound judgment to the decision-making and planning process is resulting in improvements to the quality of training as well as other operational areas.

Consistently described as an "invaluable" and "exceptional" manager, I have brought about improvements in areas which included quality-of-life issues as well as training, logistics and maintenance support, safety and quality control, and security support for the rapid response missions of the 10th Mountain Division and its parent organization. I have been honored with the Legion of Merit, two prestigious Meritorious Service Medals, five U.S. Army Commendation Medals, and five Army Achievement Medals in recognition of my accomplishments and dedication.

If you can use an articulate communicator with high levels of enthusiasm, energy, and drive, I hope you will contact me soon to suggest a time we might meet to discuss how I could contribute to your organization. I can provide excellent professional and personal references at the appropriate time. Thank you for your time and consideration.

Sincerely,

Gerald Campbell

Alternate last paragraph:
If you can use an articulate communicator with high levels of enthusiasm, energy, and drive, I hope you will welcome my call to suggest a time we might meet to discuss how I could contribute to your organization. I can provide excellent professional and personal references at the appropriate time. Thank you for your time and consideration.

GERALD CAMPBELL

1110½ Hay Street, Fayetteville, NC 28305   •   preppub@aol.com   •   (910) 483-6611

OBJECTIVE   To offer a distinguished track record of accomplishments built while managing maintenance and supply operations while also expertly supervising, counseling, and training personnel through innovative and dynamic leadership skills.

EDUCATION   Completed 73 semester hours toward a **B.S. in Management**, Mt. San Antonio College,
& TRAINING   Walnut, CA. Received intensive management training for senior military leaders including the Command Sergeants Major Course and an advanced program for maintenance managers.

EXPERIENCE   *Advanced to the rank of Command Sergeant Major, U.S. Army, Fort Drum, NY:*
SENIOR LOGISTICIAN and **CONSULTANT FOR TRAINING AND PERSONNEL SUPPORT.** (2005-present). Cited for my ability to take charge and produce results, serve as the senior enlisted advisor and training manager for more than 600 people.
- Provide expert leadership in a center which controls support ranging from food service, to maintenance, to security, to coordinating planning and use of resources; serve as the liaison for coordinating modernization issues and the fielding of new equipment.

SENIOR SUPPORT AND LOGISTICS MANAGER and **ADVISOR FOR PERSONNEL AND TRAINING SUPPORT.** (2003-05). Earned praise for results achieved in the management of the largest and most diverse unit in the parent organization which included more than 1,000 people in ten subordinate units.
- Ensured fast and reliable loading of supplies and equipment and high-quality logistical support which allowed the organization to respond worldwide within 18 hours of notice.
- Described as a "trusted and invaluable advisor," was cited as a key factor in the 100% success of numerous inspections, exercise, and missions.

SENIOR ADVISOR ON PERSONNEL ADMINISTRATION and **COUNSELOR.** (2002). Cited as the "driving force" in the unit's recognition for having the best training program in the region, acted as the senior advisor on personnel issues for 720 people.

SENIOR ADVISOR FOR LOGISTICS AND PERSONNEL ADMINISTRATION. (2000-02). Became the "resident expert" on planning and preparing for external evaluations, loading equipment and supplies, and field operations; played a major role in preparing for one of the military's largest-ever moves from a logistical standpoint as 8,500 paratroopers and 700 container deliveries were made in support of operations in Afghanistan.

SENIOR ADVISOR, PERSONNEL ADMINISTRATION. (1999-00). Received special praise for my ability to inspire cooperation and confidence in others even under the most adverse conditions while ensuring personnel matters such as housing, training, assignments, and promotions were carried out fairly.
- Managed successful special projects including a self-help construction project which saved more than $150,000 and a national training center cycle for which I set the example of physical and mental courage despite adverse weather conditions.

MAINTENANCE COMPANY PERSONNEL MANAGER. (1996-98). Directed support issues as the senior supervisor for training and professional development of 236 people.

PERSONAL   Secret security clearance. Honors include Legion of Merit, two Meritorious Service Medals, five Army Commendation Medals, and five Army Achievement Medals. Enjoy volunteering with Special Olympics and Cub Scouts as well as organizations assisting the elderly.

TWO-PAGE RESUME

DAVID McQUEEN

1110½ Hay Street, Fayetteville, NC 28305   •   preppub@aol.com   •
(910) 483-6611

SENIOR LOGISTICS ADVISOR

OBJECTIVE

To offer a broad base of expertise related to logistics operations, planning, and management to an organization in need of a mature leader who has excelled as a senior military officer through sound decision-making skills and an assertive, dynamic style.

EXPERIENCE

Advanced to the rank of Lieutenant Colonel while earning recognition as a subject matter expert in the international logistics community, U.S. Army locations worldwide:

SENIOR LOGISTICS ADVISOR. Iraq (2005-present). Singled out for this critical assignment based on my background as an expert in the field, am the principal advisor to the mission's senior executive on all matters pertaining to logistics plans, operations, and support for more than 6,000 members of a multinational force.

- Developed the initial logistics support and base camp construction plans which addressed the arrival of international personnel into the facility as well as all areas of transportation, medical care, food, lodging, and security.
- Created the long-range plans which detailed the breakdown and return of all assets to the country of ownership at the end of the mission.
- Provided oversight for various contractors involved in the project after developing the initial requirements for each area.
- Managed the daily operation of the material management, movements control, and logistics support centers which included 16 British heavy cargo trucks and two U.S. utility landing craft.
- Supervised a multinational staff of 55 people supporting the mission, international relief and monitoring organizations, and the Iraqi government.

HUMAN AND MATERIAL RESOURCES OPERATIONS ADVISOR. Fort Bragg, NC (2002-05). Advanced to positions of increasing responsibility as senior advisor to the chief executive of a 32,000-person organization with seven separate divisions and was selected to oversee activities in international locations such as Afghanistan and Iraq.

- Directed a staff of 13 managers and 51 employees involved in the planning and coordination of arrangements for relocating more than 32,000 people and all their equipment when their presence was required during rapid responses to international situations.
- Cited for my thorough grasp of all aspects of planning on such a large scale, initiated sound procedures for logistical operations which will be followed for many years.
- Earned praise for my ability to remain calm and in control under intense pressure.
- Created a fully mobile integrated logistical and tactical operations center.
- Selected as senior logistician in Bosnia, was in charge of every aspect of planning and providing support for five large

organizations of approximately 1,000 people each.

- Was evaluated as "the best logistician I have ever worked with" by several officials and was known for my honesty along with my sensitivity to employees and their concerns.
- Joined this organization as an advisor on plans, security, intelligence, and training and was quickly able to revitalize an 11-manager and 31-employee staff and make the most of short amounts of time available to improve training effectiveness appreciably.

ADMINISTRATIVE OPERATIONS MANAGER. Korea (2001-02). Initiated sweeping reforms in an administrative center where questions of protocol, administration, and official and social personal matters were of great concern in an environment where a senior official dealt routinely with his international counterparts and officials.

- Was cited as a clear thinker with a dynamic leadership style and the vision to see how change could be made which would streamline operations and reduce interruptions.

SENIOR LOGISTICS OPERATIONS ADVISOR. Italy (1999-01). Promoted on the basis of my performance in this position, provided logistics support on every aspect of sustainability, assessment, and reporting of the logistics capabilities of American forces.

- Handled arrangements for supplying personnel from throughout Europe in advance of and for the duration of the War on Terror and received praise for my performance in this critical position with little advance notice.
- Managed several projects and was described as consistently making valuable contributions during one project to assess the logistics portion of information system needs and requirements.
- Was often singled out for my professionalism and diplomacy to escort and brief VIPs.
- Reviewed, edited, and wrote sections of several Standard Operating Procedures (SOPs).

LOGISTICS MANAGER. Fort Drum, NY (1997-98). Provided expertise in logistics and resource management activities in a very fast-paced environment where the organization had to be available to relocate worldwide within 18 hours.

- Was officially described as creative, articulate, and dedicated with meticulous planning skills and superior attention to detail.

DIVISION PLANS AND OPERATIONS MANAGER. Fort Drum, NY (1995-97). Served as chief advisor on plans and operations as well as intelligence, security, force modernization, and training manager for a 2,000-person organization with a $7.5 million annual budget.

Highlights of earlier U.S. Army experience: Developed a reputation as a technically proficient professional in the logistics field and also expanded my general managerial skills in worldwide locations including Italy and Germany.

EDUCATION
&
EXECUTIVE
TRAINING

M.A., History, University of Indianapolis, Indianapolis, IN, 2002.
B.A., History, Madonna University, Livonia, MI, 1992.
Excelled in extensive graduate-level programs for military executives including the Army, Marine, and Air Force Command and General Staff Colleges along with the Supply Management Officers and Logistics Management Development Courses.

PROFESSIONAL
MEMBERSHIPS

Hold membership in the following professional organizations:
    The Association of the United States Army (AUSA)
    The Airborne Association

PERSONAL

Completed Ranger School, the military's "stress test" of physical and mental limits, as well as specialized training in the airborne, pathfinder, and jumpmaster schools. Speak Spanish.

Date

Exact Name of Person
Title or Position
Name of Company
Address
City, State, Zip

SENIOR SUPPLY OPERATIONS MANAGER

Dear Exact Name of Person: (or Dear Sir or Madam if answering a blind ad.)

Can you use an assertive and knowledgeable professional who offers outstanding supervisory and motivational abilities along with a strong background in all aspects of providing logistical support?

While proudly serving my country in the U.S. Army, I gained extensive experience in the areas of budgeting, accountability, and record keeping and earned a reputation for technical inventory management "know how." I have consistently been evaluated as "one who sets the standards" in technical knowledge, leadership, and professionalism.

The majority of my work experience has been in the supply field. I further enhanced my reputation during the War on Terror by establishing a supply point, training employees, and ensuring personnel were adequately supplied despite the problems associated with operating in a remote and inhospitable environment.

I hope you will welcome my call soon to arrange a brief meeting at your convenience to discuss your current and future needs and how I might serve them. Thank you in advance for your time.

Sincerely yours,

Richard Andrews

Alternate last paragraph:
I hope you will call or write soon to suggest a time convenient for us to meet and discuss your current and future needs and how I might serve them. Thank you in advance for your time.

RICHARD ANDREWS

1110½ Hay Street, Fayetteville, NC 28305   •   preppub@aol.com   •   (910) 483-6611

OBJECTIVE

To apply my "expert" knowledge of all aspects of supply and logistical support to an organization that can use my experience in budgeting, accounting for multimillion-dollar inventories, and supervising/training employees.

EXPERIENCE

Excelled in managing supply operations, U.S. Army:

SENIOR SUPPLY OPERATIONS MANAGER. Ft. Wainwright, AK (2005-present). Advanced to become the chief supply specialist for a 450-person organization with control over the receipt, storage, and disbursement of a $250 million inventory of parts and equipment for the free world's only armored airborne unit.
- Monitored the distribution of thousands of dollars worth of expendable supplies as well as major equipment and repair parts.
- Served as the technical advisor to other organizations.

SUPPLY CONSULTANT. Iraq (2004-05). Was known for my reliability and dedication to ensuring personnel were adequately supplied despite the drawbacks and hazards of the War on Terror.
- Established a functioning and well organized supply point.
- Inventoried and returned to the U.S. with 100% of unused supplies. Continued my record of accident-free operations through my insistence on safety in the workplace.
- Received the Meritorious Service Medal for "exceptional achievements."
- Trained personnel to provide support in remote locations separated from the main supply operation.

BATTALION SUPPLY MANAGER. Ft. Huachuca, AZ (2000-04). Earned a reputation as a high-energy professional with superior technical knowledge and strong skills in developing and training quality employees; supervised five technicians.
- Developed a training program which led to employees achieving a 100% pass rate on skill qualifications testing and "significantly" improved scores for all personnel.
- Implemented an inspection program widely adopted as a "model." Was cited as the "supply subject matter expert" and sought out to provide assistance to sister units.

SUPPLY TECHNICIAN. Ft. Benning, GA (1991-00). Supervised three supply specialists while constantly increasing my expertise in supply operations and becoming widely recognized for my technical proficiency in controlling the receipt, storage, and disbursement of $3 million worth of property and equipment.
- Was sought out to assist other companies in preparations for major inspections and to help train supply technicians.
- Guided the operation to "unprecedented near perfect scores" on critical maintenance and supply operations inspections.

Other U.S. Army experience: Managed the chemical detection station at a nuclear weapons site in Germany and became skilled in using decontamination apparatus and chemical agent monitors.

TRAINING

Excelled in special supply operations and management training programs.

PERSONAL

Was entrusted with a **Secret** security clearance. Am known as a very demanding supervisor who is tough, but fair and concerned. Outstanding references on request.

Date

Exact Name of Person
Title or Position
Name of Company
Address
City, State, Zip

SHIPPING SUPERVISOR Dear Exact Name of Person: (or Dear Sir or Madam if answering a blind ad.)

I would appreciate an opportunity to talk with you soon about how I could contribute to your organization through my leadership experience, problem-solving skills, and versatile management abilities.

As you will see from the enclosed resume, I have excelled as a junior military officer and have been recommended for promotion ahead of my peers even at a time when the military is "downsizing." While serving my country as a Captain, I have been selected for "hotseat" jobs which tested my ability to design and implement systems/procedures used to transport both hazardous and non-hazardous materials safely, often over rugged terrain. During the War on Terror, I coordinated 126 vehicles and 161 employees involved in supplying fuel and water used for emergency support. I have also acquired expertise related to the distribution of highly volatile materials, and I have developed and managed emergency spillage plans and hazardous waste procedures.

As you will also see from my resume, I have spent some time in aviation organizations refining my expertise in inventory control, logistics, warehousing, and product distribution. In those particular organizations, just one lapse in judgement could mean "life or death" for people later on, so I became skilled in "attention to detail" while working in jobs which required me to negotiate contracts, manage multimillion-dollar assets, as well as plan and administer budgets of all sizes.

You would find me in person to be a dedicated and selfless individual who is always able to put first the needs of others and the goals of the organization. I can provide outstanding references at your request, and I will cheerfully travel and relocate as your organization's needs dictate.

I hope you will call or write me soon to suggest a time convenient for us to meet and discuss your current and future needs and how I might serve them. Thank you in advance for your time.

Sincerely yours,

Tristen Brown

TRISTEN BROWN

1110½ Hay Street, Fayetteville, NC 28305   •   preppub@aol.com   •   (910) 483-6611

OBJECTIVE

To contribute to an organization that can use a resourceful thinker and problem solver who offers expertise related to product distribution management along with a proven ability to motivate people, allocate assets in the most efficient way, and manage multiple projects in a cost-conscious and time-sensitive manner.

EDUCATION

Earned **Bachelor of Arts degree in History**, University of Missouri, St. Louis, MO, 1995.

EXPERIENCE

SHIPPING SUPERVISOR. Max Factor, St. Louis, MO (2005-present). Handle the order processing of up to $2.4 million daily including product routing, order consolidating, loading, and billing. Determine small package, Less than Truck Load (LTL), and truck load shipping arrangements in addition to selecting the appropriate carrier.
- Properly train and provide safety regulation information to 19 shipping dock employees; ensure all Good Manufacturing Practices (GMP) are closely followed.
- Monitor the shipping of hazardous materials ensuring that they are accompanied by the correct MSDS sheets and are labeled according to Code of Federal Regulation 49 (FR).

Was promoted to the rank of Captain in the U.S. Army while earning a reputation as a problem solver who can find creative new solutions for stubborn problems:
RESOURCES MANAGER. Fort Leonard Wood, MO (2005). Directed a team of four professionals providing support services such as logistics, administration, budget planning, and operational planning to 11 Reserve Component organizations.
- Have been commended for my outstanding supervisory and communication skills.
- Was recommended for rapid promotion ahead of my peers.

LOGISTICS MANAGER/INVENTORY CONTROLLER. Simmons Army Airfield, NC (2003-04). Developed the organization's 2004 budget of $1 million, which contained drastic reductions in expenditures in numerous areas, while continuously managing the purchasing, warehousing, and distribution of more than 700 supply items for an aviation regiment.
- Was personally responsible for more than $226 million in equipment and building assets; negotiated contracts for maintenance and other support; monitored all work performed.
- Reduced excess supply inventory from $1.2 million to only $61,000 in just eight months.
- Rewrote and implemented better accountability procedures for inventory control.

GENERAL MANAGER. Simmons Army Airfield, NC, and Iraq (2002-03). Was specially selected for this "plum" line management job ("company commander") considered in the military to be the "true test" of a junior military officer's management skills; was "commander" of an airborne truck company within a Corps support battalion.
- Created and implemented human resource policies which resulted in the more effective management of 180 people.
- Oversaw the safe transportation of up to 400,000 gallons of fuel daily; oversaw distribution of 450,000 gallons of water over two months with only ten vehicles.

FIRST-LINE SUPERVISOR. Germany (1999-01). For an attack helicopter company, managed 22 people while supervising the provision of more than 300,000 gallons of fuel and ten short tons of ammunition supporting 37 aircraft and 60 vehicles.

PERSONAL

Thrive on responsibility. Believe in "leadership by example" and am known for my ability to "get the most" out of the people who work with me. Received the prestigious Bronze Star medal for outstanding leadership contributions during Operation Iraqi Freedom.

Date

Exact Name of Person
Title or Position
Name of Company
Address
City, State, Zip

SPECIAL INVENTORY CLERK

Dear Exact Name of Person: (or Dear Sir or Madam if answering a blind ad.)

With the enclosed resume, I would like to make you aware of my background of experience and knowledge of logistics operations gained while serving my country in the U.S. Army.

You will see from the resume that I offer a reputation as a dedicated and self-motivated young professional who is able to take on multiple responsibilities and produce outstanding results. During my six years of military service, I became known as a detail-oriented individual with excellent organizational, team work, and automated systems operations skills.

Consistently recognized as an individual who maintained meticulous and up-to-date records of supply transactions, I was also known as someone who could be counted on to stay with the job until it was done and see that it was done correctly. Trained in the systems used by the military services for logistics management, I am thoroughly familiar with both the ULLS (Unit Level Logistics System) and the SPBS (the Standard Property Book System).

My versatile background has included providing support for diverse organizations with differing types of supply and equipment needs. I have worked in an organization in the unique Special Forces environment, a medical company which provided medical evacuation support in Europe, and a military intelligence organization with 225 employees. I have handled the requisitioning, inventory control, storage, and distribution of every class of items from office supplies, to computer systems, to vehicles, to clothing, to tents, to tools and repair parts.

If you can use a supply specialist who is recognized as a reliable and detail-oriented individual with strong personal standards, I hope you will contact me soon to suggest a time when we might meet to discuss your needs. I can assure you that I could quickly become an asset to your organization.

Sincerely,

Jim Kowalsky

JIM KOWALSKY

1110½ Hay Street, Fayetteville, NC 28305 • preppub@aol.com • (910) 483-6611

OBJECTIVE   To offer my extensive knowledge of supply operations and automated supply systems to an organization that can use a detail-oriented and thorough professional with excellent organizational skills and the ability to work with others to achieve team goals.

**EDUCATION
& TRAINING**
Attended Miami-Dade Community College, Miami, FL, 2000.
Graduated from Citrus High School, Miami, FL, 1998.
Completed U.S. Army sponsored training which included the following:
  Standard Property Book System Course, 2003
  Supply Specialist Course, 1998
Through training, became skilled in using automated systems for logistics management:
  ULLS (Unit Level Logistics System)
  SPBS (Standard Property Book System)

EXPERIENCE   *Was known for my eye for detail and ability to be aware of the location of needed supplies and equipment while serving as a Supply Specialist, U.S. Army:*
SPECIAL INVENTORY CLERK. Fort Benning, GA (2005-present). Gained skills in handling supply procedures and settling issues within the unique environment of the Special Forces community while advising and informing senior personnel of any major changes in supply status.
  • Ordered and controlled the distribution of a wide range of supplies and equipment from office supplies, to major items including computers and laptops, to personal clothing items, to tools.
  • Earned recognition for my skill in maintaining filing systems while using automated systems to keep accurate, up-to-date, and detailed inventories of supplies and equipment on hand and on order as well as of personnel and administrative records.

UNIT SUPPLY SPECIALIST. Italy (2003-05). Controlled supplies and equipment in a medical company which was an element of a medical evacuation (medevac) organization.
  • Maintained a supply room which ordered, stored, distributed, and issued items ranging from pens, pencils, and office supplies, to $1 million mission-essential vehicles.
  • Ordered and received major items such as tents, vehicles, and computer systems.

SUPPLY CLERK. Fort Knox, KY (2001-03). Ensured adequate quantities were on hand while requisitioning clothing, equipment, and tools for the 225 employees of a military intelligence organization; maintained personnel records and files.
  • Became highly skilled in supply operations and was placed in charge of the very sensitive Arms Room where the organization's weapons and ammunition were stored and issued.

Highlights of other experience: While attending high school and community college, loaded and unloaded shipments for DSL in Miami, FL, and served with the U.S. Army Reserves as a Supply Clerk: provided a 100-member organization with supply support while requisitioning clothing, tools, and equipment and providing excellent customer service.

HONORS   Received awards including two U.S. Army Achievement Medals, a National Defense Service Medal, and an award recognizing my professionalism and dedication to the success of an NBC (nuclear/biological/chemical) testing project.

PERSONAL   Am proud of my reputation as a tactful young professional who can be counted on to work on the job until it is done. Highly motivated hard worker who can provide excellent references.

Date

Exact Name of Person
Title or Position
Name of Company
Address
City, State, Zip

Dear Exact Name of Person: (or Dear Sir or Madam if answering a blind ad.)

With the enclosed resume, I would like to make you aware of my skills and abilities in inventory management and logistics as well as my superior supervisory, motivational, and decision-making skills.

As you will see from my resume, I am serving my country in the U.S. Air Force where I have been entrusted with a Secret security clearance while building a reputation as a technically proficient and knowledgeable professional. I have completed almost two years of college course work in Business Administration and Logistics Management while excelling in demanding assignments and frequent relocation due to job reassignments. I have received several medals in recognition of my professionalism and accomplishments.

My expertise in utilizing a variety of different major data information systems has allowed me to develop thorough knowledge of the systems used by the military. I have become proficient with automated systems which include the Standard Base Supply System (SBSS), Air Force Equipment Management System (AFEMS), the MICAP Asset Sourcing System (MASS), and FEDLOG. I also am familiar with the Bell and Howell Automated Document Control System as well as with Automated Stock Number User Directory (ASNUD), Logistics Tracker, and Advanced Traceability and Control (ATAC).

Throughout my military career I have been evaluated as "aggressive ... decisive .... proactive" and as an expert in the management of inventory support activities ranging from controlling multimillion-dollar inventories, to managing customer service centers and parts stores, to building teams of knowledgeable inventory control and warehousing personnel through my leadership and example. I have consistently led the way to reductions in waiting times for supplies and equipment, increases in delivery times, and in setting performance records.

If you can use an experienced and mature leader who has long been recognized as a reliable and honest individual with sound decision-making and analytical skills, I hope you will contact me soon to suggest a time when we might meet to discuss your needs. I can assure you in advance that I can provide outstanding references and could quickly become an asset to your organization.

Sincerely,

Jack Sinclair

JACK SINCLAIR

1110½ Hay Street, Fayetteville, NC 28305   •   preppub@aol.com   •   (910) 483-6611

OBJECTIVE

To offer inventory management and logistics expertise to an organization that can benefit from the application of my superior supervisory, motivational, and decision-making skills.

EDUCATION & TRAINING

Completed almost two years of course work in **Business Administration and Logistics Management**, Community College of the Air Force.
Received training in leadership and supervisory development, U.S. Air Force.

SPECIAL KNOWLEDGE

Offer expert knowledge of systems and operations including: Standard Base Supply System (SBSS), Air Force Equipment Management System (AFEMS), MICAP Asset Sourcing System (MASS), Bell & Howell Automated Document Control System, FEDLOG, Automated Stock Number User Directory (ASNUD), Advanced Traceability & Control (ATAC), and Logistics Tracker; Windows XP, Microsoft Access, Excel, and Word.

EXPERIENCE

Have advanced on the basis of my inventory management know-how and expertise in supervising and training personnel in the U.S. Air Force:
SUPERVISOR FOR MOBILITY AND LOGISTICS SUPPORT. Pope AFB, NC (2005-present). Supervise six people; manage and control a $7.5 million inventory of 6,740 items of chemical warfare and mobility equipment for a 2,300-person organization which must be ready to respond on extremely short notice to worldwide crises.

SUPPLY OPERATIONS CUSTOMER SUPPORT SUPERVISOR. Pope AFB, NC (2004-05). Cited as a professional who set the pace and showed others how to provide timely and accurate service, supervised 13 subordinates while becoming known as the resident expert on equipment management for 555 items and asset accounts worth $600 million.
*   Revised training for equipment custodians which integrated AFEMS familiarization.

LOGISTICAL SUPPORT SUPERVISOR. Afghanistan (2003-04). Cited for my "aggressive" management skills which led to "remarkable success," supervised ten people in a 24-hour facility which provided logistical support for maintenance and repair of 56 aircraft.
*   Oversaw and personally researched, requisitioned, and tracked parts requests utilizing seven major data information systems to track and validate information.
*   Was credited with accomplishments which included reducing the number of delayed requisitions 30% and increasing delivery times 48 hours.

SUPERVISOR FOR CUSTOMER SUPPORT. Germany (2002-03). Established a centralized supply service point while supervising ten people, overseeing documentation of 42,000 items, and advising flight managers on issues related to a $260 million supply account.

SUPERVISOR OF DOCUMENT CONTROL. Germany (2001-02). Cited for my management skills, supervised two people while controlling access to classified documents.

AIRCRAFT LOGISTICS SUPPORT SUPERVISOR. Korea (2000-01). Achieved all-time high equipment availability rates and all-time low rates for equipment awaiting parts.

Highlights of earlier U.S. Air Force experience: Advanced while earning a reputation as a technically knowledgeable inventory specialist while controlling multimillion-dollar assets, supervising and training others, and becoming known for my research skills.

PERSONAL

Secret security clearance. Received numerous medals for my initiative and expertise.

Date

Exact Name of Person
Title or Position
Name of Company
Address
City, State, Zip

Dear Exact Name of Person: (or Dear Sir or Madam if answering a blind ad.)

Can you use an energetic and resourceful young professional who has excelled as a supervisor, manager, and instructor through a positive leadership style and adaptability?

While serving my country in the U.S. Army, I spent a great deal of my time developing, improving, and conducting training programs. In one organization I stepped into a vacancy and "tackled" the job of education specialist after discovering that the program had serious flaws in its allocation of resources and instructors as well as in the quality and thoroughness of what was being taught. I revamped the program of instruction and, when I moved to a management role, I had to train and supervise four people to handle the workload I had previously taken care of.

I was awarded numerous medals for "meritorious achievements" in a variety of jobs including controlling logistical support, supervising automated record-keeping, and working in the technical fields of data entry and telecommunications operations.

I hope you will welcome my call soon to arrange a brief meeting at your convenience to discuss your current and future needs and how I might serve them. Thank you in advance for your time.

Sincerely yours,

Corey Phillips

Alternate last paragraph:
I hope you will call or write soon to suggest a time convenient for us to meet and discuss your current and future needs and how I might serve them. Thank you in advance for your time.

COREY PHILLIPS

1110½ Hay Street, Fayetteville, NC 28305   •   preppub@aol.com   •   (910) 483-6611

OBJECTIVE

To contribute my positive and energetic leadership style, outstanding communication skills, and proven management abilities to an organization in need of an adaptable fast learner and quick thinker with experience in office administration and training program development.

EXPERIENCE

Advanced in this "track record," U.S. Army, Fort Lewis, WA:
SUPERVISOR FOR OFFICE AND TRAINING OPERATIONS. (2005-present). As the assistant to the department manager, supervised six employees while overseeing the maintenance of personnel records for 200 people, logistics support, and data processing.
- Oversaw arrangements which included scheduling and safety procedures while training and completing parachute jumps. Managed construction and repair projects at Camp Puget, a remote site which was being renovated and reactivated.

INSTRUCTOR. (2004). Worked with groups of 20 students in a leadership development course: provided instruction in basic military skills as well as leadership techniques.
- Guided students in two of three cycles to the company's highest grade point averages.

TRAINING PROGRAM MANAGER. (2003-04). Supervised a 26-person team of instructors involved in conducting 17 separate professional development courses annually.
- Ensured training was conducted safely in hazardous, and often life-threatening, courses.
- Conducted more than 20 airborne operations involving in excess of 1,000 people and suffered only three injuries, all proven to be "jumper error."
- Refined my written communication skills by preparing training plans and other materials.

OPERATIONS MANAGER and **EDUCATION SPECIALIST.** (2002-03). Rewrote and reorganized the training plans for a company involved in training engineering support personnel and also coordinated logistical support, data entry, and maintenance of student records. Gained experience using PC and became familiar with software including Adobe PageMaker, Microsoft Word, Excel, and Access.

Gained experience in operations management, U.S. Army, Fort Belvoir, VA:
SUPERVISORY TRAINING SPECIALIST. (1999-02). Was promoted to direct "special operations" training for eight subordinates.

INTELLIGENCE ANALYST and **OPERATIONS MANAGER.** (1998-99). Further refined my communication skills as the supervisor for six specialists while conducting training in "classified" subject material.

OPERATIONS CONSULTANT. U.S. Army, Italy (1995-98). Provided an executive with advice and applied my expertise in the highly specialized areas of mountain climbing and rescue operations. Trained personnel from other countries and participated in "real-world" operations including establishing rescues and running escape and evasion networks.

Highlights of other U.S. Army experience: Gained skills as a vehicle/generator mechanic.

TRAINING

Completed Ranger School, the Army's "stress test" of physical and mental limits, as well as language training, leadership, and instructional techniques.

PERSONAL

Was awarded three commendation medals, an achievement medal, and a meritorious service medal. Am known for my ability to improvise and "get the job done" despite shortages.

Date

Exact Name of Person
Title or Position
Name of Company
Address
City, State, Zip

SUPERVISORY LOGISTICS MANAGEMENT SPECIALIST

Dear Exact Name of Person: (or Dear Sir or Madam if answering a blind ad.)

I would appreciate an opportunity to talk with you soon about how I could contribute to your organization through my demonstrated expertise in planning and managing complex, large-scale projects with an emphasis on transportation, maintenance management, and logistics management.

As you will see from my enclosed resume, I am excelling in managerial roles with the North Carolina Army National Guard for which I have been providing my versatile expertise within the related fields of automated systems applications, fielding of new equipment, policy making, budgetary control, and transportation. I have played a key role in the agency's union contract negotiations, hazardous material awareness campaign, and maintenance management operations.

Among the accomplishments of which I am most proud was a project during which I spent more than a year planning and successfully coordinating with European customs officials and supporting trucking companies to move 13,000 people and 7,200 pieces of equipment from the U.S. to Italy, for a two-week training exercise. After the exercise was completed, I coordinated the details of getting all personnel and equipment back to the appropriate destination by a combination of road, rail, air, bus, and barge. In a more recent job as superintendent of a maintenance facility, I guided 103 employees in operations which eliminated a 7,000-man hour backlog of work within eighteen months.

I am confident that, through my experiences as a military officer, I have developed a strong base of knowledge which will be easily transferable to other organizations in need of a strong leader who is adept in building results-oriented teams. If you can use an articulate professional who meets challenges head on, please contact me to coordinate a meeting to discuss your needs. I can assure you in advance that I could rapidly become an asset to your organization.

Sincerely,

Terence Kaiser

TERENCE KAISER

1110½ Hay Street, Fayetteville, NC 28305 • preppub@aol.com • (910) 483-6611

OBJECTIVE

To offer management expertise to an organization which can benefit from my knowledge in transportation, maintenance, and logistics management including exceptional skills in coordinating, planning, and carrying out complex large-scale projects as a military officer.

EDUCATION & TRAINING

Bachelor of Business Administration (BBA), North Carolina State University, Raleigh, NC, 1991.

Completed programs for military executives including the graduate-level Command and General Staff College as well as courses in logistics management and automated systems.

EXPERIENCE

I have excelled in executive roles with the North Carolina Army National Guard:
SUPERVISORY LOGISTICS MANAGEMENT SPECIALIST. Rocky Mount, NC (2005-present). Provide logistics guidance and support at the state level to include plans, policy, transportation, automation, property management, and logistics financial management; manage a $481,000 Government Services Administration (GSA) lease vehicle budget.
- Acted as management representative during union contract negotiations.

TRANSPORTATION SUPPORT MANAGER. Rocky Mount, NC (2003-04). Planned and directed preparations, maintenance support, and the movement of personnel and equipment.
- Served as point-of-contact with the Department of Transportation (DOT) while arranging troop movements and establishing guidelines and restrictions for each individual project.
- Provided technical guidance for shipping of hazardous materials.
- Designed and implemented records upgrade program for 96 separate units.

MAINTENANCE FACILITY SUPERINTENDENT. Fort Bragg, NC (2000-03). Managed up to 180 people including foremen and direct support/general support and depot-level maintenance technicians, as well as production controllers and clerical personnel.
- Established a regional rebuild maintenance center for the eastern half of the nation.
- Managed quality control functions including developing standards, conducting spot checks, and reviewing completed work and reports to ensure standards were met.
- Developed and managed safety and HAZMAT awareness programs.

LOGISTICS MANAGEMENT OFFICER. Fort Bragg, NC (1998-00). Managed a state-level logistics program in which seven three-person computer teams controlled in excess of $413 million worth of equipment; fielded new equipment and disposed of obsolete systems.

ADMINISTRATIVE SERVICES LIAISON. Wilson, NC (1996-98). Acted as liaison between headquarters operations and the managers of seven 200-person units which included medical; missile, vehicle, and heavy truck maintenance; and transportation personnel.

TRANSPORTATION MANAGER. Charlotte, NC (1992-96). Officially described as creative, flexible, and always in control; developed guidance, policies, and plans for transportation services by ship, road, air, and rail.

Highlights of earlier experience: Advanced in the logistics support and transportation field as an Army officer after earlier success as an Assistant Production Foreman in charge of up to 50 people and $1 million in production a week for a company in Georgia.

PERSONAL

Volunteer with the Boy Scouts. President and founder of 400-member environmental association. On Board of Directors, American Lung Association. Hold Secret security clearance.

Date

Exact Name of Person
Title or Position
Name of Company
Address
City, State, Zip

Dear Exact Name of Person: (or Dear Sir or Madam if answering a blind ad.)

With the enclosed resume, I would like to make you aware of my background as an experienced supply operations manager who offers a reputation as a knowledgeable professional with a talent for team building and initiative.

As you will see, throughout my career in the U.S. Army I was placed in leadership roles where I continually excelled through my ability to guide, lead, and motivate others. I consistently led my units to accomplishments which resulted in high scores in inspections of supply operations and recognition as top-notch supply support facilities.

In my final military assignment at Fort Bliss, TX, I was evaluated by one senior executive as "the best of 65" managers and supervisors under his leadership. I was credited with transforming a substandard, poorly functioning supply center into the best of its kind in the parent organization within my first nine months in the unit. One example of my efforts in this job was when I took the initiative to identify excess and underutilized property. A total of more than 1,900 items valued in excess of $4.5 million were identified and reallocated. As a result of my efforts, I led the unit to recognition with a Department of the Army "Supply Excellence Award" and to receive "no faults or deficiencies" in a high-level inspection.

Prior to this assignment I was Supervisory Information Analyst for a national training center where I operated a unique multimillion-dollar data collection computer facility. Promoted to this leadership role after only eight months as a Supply Observer/ Controller, I was evaluated as a multifunctional and thoroughly knowledgeable logistician who was familiar with all aspects of supply, transportation, and maintenance.

The recipient of numerous medals and honors in recognition of my professionalism and accomplishments, I have applied my time management and organizational skills while completing 57 semester hours of college credit and, at the same time, meeting the demands of a military career with its frequent relocations and temporary duty assignments. Accustomed to intense, stressful conditions as well as rapidly changing priorities and situations, I served during the War on Terror and on peacekeeping missions in Kuwait.

If you can use an experienced supply operations manager, I hope you will contact me to suggest a time when we might meet to discuss your needs. I can assure you in advance that I could rapidly become an asset to your organization.

Sincerely,

John Rodriguez

JOHN RODRIGUEZ

1110½ Hay Street, Fayetteville, NC 28305 • preppub@aol.com • (910) 483-6611

OBJECTIVE

To offer a distinguished history of accomplishments in supply operations management to an organization that can use a well-rounded and through professional who is known for possessing a positive attitude and a talent for building teams and encouraging growth.

EDUCATION & TRAINING

Completed 57 semester hours of general studies college courses, Central Michigan University. Excelled in military training programs including advanced supply management and leadership courses as well as how to instruct personnel in hazardous cargo handling.

EXPERIENCE

Built a track record of success while earning a reputation as an exceptional and dedicated professional with a talent for team building and vision, U.S. Army:

SUPPLY ADVISOR AND MANAGER. Fort Bliss, TX (2005-present). Described as the "best of the 65" supervisors and managers, provide enthusiastic leadership while managing $42.5 million worth of property and supporting five regional operations centers with signal communications support.

- Provided the leadership which allowed the section to win the highest-level "Supply Excellence Award," awarded by the Chief of Staff of the Army; led the section to be recognized for no errors or discrepancies in a major review of logistics support, and transformed the section from substandard into the best of its kind in only nine months.
- On my own initiative, identified excess and underutilized property valued at $4.5 million and reallocated more than 1,900 items, resulting in a considerable cost savings.

SUPERVISORY INFORMATION ANALYST. Fort Snelling, MN (2001-04). Evaluated as a "multifunctional logistician, knowledgeable in all aspects of supply, transportation, and maintenance," operated a unique multimillion-dollar data collection computer facility at the national Joint Readiness Training Center (JRTC); managed 10 civilian and military professionals. Trained personnel who achieved impressive results under stressful conditions.

- Recorded and analyzed information used in preparing after-action reviews and reports for user units to take back to their home bases for study after completing training cycles.
- Provided training management support for 49 senior supervisors and managers.
- Selected as Unit Armorer, controlled a $212,000 inventory of sensitive items including weapons and ammunition; received exemplary ratings during all inspections.

SUPPLY OPERATIONS SUPERVISOR. Fort Bragg, NC (1998-00). Selected ahead of my peers to supervise and train 28 supply specialists, managed the receipt, preparation, and issuance of supplies and equipment while controlling a $5 million property inventory.

SUPERVISORY SUPPLY SPECIALIST. Italy (1995-98). Oversaw the performance and training of five subordinates in four career specialties as well as the maintenance and operation of one tactical vehicle while also controlling the procurement, receipt, storage, issuing, and accountability of approximately $1.2 million worth of equipment and supplies.

- Handled the details of turning in equipment and furniture when the unit was deactivated and physically closed down as well as upon its return from various missions.

Highlights of earlier experience: Was consistently evaluated as a knowledgeable professional with sound judgment, perseverance, dedication, and enthusiasm who set and enforced high standards while advancing as a specialist in supply operations.

PERSONAL

Will relocate according to employer needs and requirements. Awarded the Bronze Star, Meritorious Service, three U.S. Army Commendation, and two Army Achievement Medals.

Date

Exact Name of Person
Title or Position
Name of Company
Address
City, State, Zip

SUPPLY MANAGER

Dear Exact Name of Person: (or Dear Sir or Madam if answering a blind ad.)

With the enclosed resume, I would like to make you aware of my interest in exploring employment opportunities with your organization and introduce you to my extensive experience related to supply and inventory control, logistics and transportation management, and automated systems operation.

While serving my country with distinction in the U.S. Army, I held a NATO Secret security clearance and was specially selected for positions worldwide which required a strong problem solver and resourceful leader. In my most recent position, I managed the provision of all types of supplies, and I received a prestigious medal for my supply expertise during a special project.

In prior positions, I gained experience in managing supplies of all types in various kinds of organizations. For example, in a telecommunications organization I served as the supply chief for a signal organization in Europe and I maintained perfect control of $33 million in assets. In another position, I supervised 36 employees and acted as Quality Control Inspector for numerous lower-level operations. Early in my career I excelled in a position as a Property Manager controlling an inventory of residential housing, commercial building, and vehicles. I have also worked in aviation supply, and I once established "from scratch" a model supply operation serving the needs of 23 aircraft. During major projects, I have served as liaison with the Environmental Protection Agency (EPA) and as a Contract Representative with defense contractors.

During my military service I became known for my patient style in training inexperienced young supply technicians, and I take pride in the fact that many soldiers I trained have become outstanding supply managers. In one formal performance evaluation I was described as a "skillful manager with untiring endurance who always takes the initiative to achieve excellence." I offer experience in utilizing various customized database applications and software programs for purchasing and inventory control.

If my background and skills interest you, I hope you will contact me to suggest a time when we could meet in person to discuss your needs. I can provide outstanding references. Thank you in advance for your time.

Yours sincerely,

Gabriel McCoy

GABRIEL McCOY

1110½ Hay Street, Fayetteville, NC 28305 • preppub@aol.com • (910) 483-6611

OBJECTIVE   To benefit an organization that can benefit from my seven years of experience in purchasing, inventory control, shipping and receiving, warehousing, and automated logistics management.

EDUCATION   Completed college courses in supply management, records and information management, computer applications, personnel supervision, bookkeeping, and management.
Extensive U.S. Army training in logistics, materials, handling, and automated logistics.

LICENSE   Operate forklifts of 10K and below; certified in CPR; have an accident-free track record.

CLEARANCE   Held NATO Secret security clearance.

COMPUTERS   Proficient with automated systems for inventory control and transportation; have used automated systems including ULLS and SARSS.

EXPERIENCE   *Was promoted in the following track record by the U.S. Army:*
SUPPLY MANAGER. Fort Hood, TX (2005-present). Received a prestigious medal for my expert leadership during a special project known as "Action Storm 2006" while managing worldwide signal support to the post; controlled supplies and equipment valued at $29 million while managing the provision of all types of supplies including perishable items, hazardous materials, fuel, clothing, vehicles, and office supplies.
  • Was praised in writing for "unparalleled self reliance and resourcefulness."

SUPPLY MANAGER, TELECOMMUNICATIONS. Korea (2002-04). Was specially selected to serve as the supply chief for a signal organization that provided command and control communications for Korea; controlled $33 million in assets.
  • Described in writing as a "skillful manager with untiring endurance who always takes the initiative to achieve excellence."

SUPPLY MANAGER. Fort Jackson, SC (2001-02). Trained and supervised two other employees while overseeing $30 million in assets.
  • Emphasis on safety resulted in 100% accident free workplace; devised a new plan that led to better property management and inventory control with major cost-saving benefits.

SUPPLY ACCOUNTING MANAGER & QUALITY CONTROL INSPECTOR. Italy (1999-01). Supervised 36 employees and maintained document registers controlling supplies for five separate companies; was evaluated as "patient in training inexperienced soldiers in supply procedures."
  • Conducted quality control inspections of numerous lower-level supply operations.
  • Served as EPA/Contract Representative during special major training projects.

Other experience:
Supply Supervisor. Managed one person and flawlessly accounted for $10 million in supplies for laundry, transportation, property disposal, preparation of maps and sketches, other areas.
Property Manager. Controlled residential housing, commercial buildings, and vehicles.
Supply Clerk. Controlled a 300-line-item inventory; managed the provision of repair parts.
Aviation Supply Clerk. Ordered, tracked, and received aviation parts; established "from scratch" a model supply operation servicing 23 UH-1H aircraft.

PERSONAL   Proven ability to manage multimillion-dollar inventory and related logistics responsibilities.

Date

Exact Name of Person
Title or Position
Name of Company
Address
City, State, Zip

Dear Exact Name of Person: (or Dear Sir or Madam if answering a blind ad.)

With the enclosed resume, I would like to make you aware of my background as a versatile and experienced professional with a history of success in areas which include computer operations, logistics and supply, production control, and employee training and supervision.

As you will see, I am completing requirements for my bachelor's degree in Computer Science which I expect to receive this winter. I am proud of my accomplishment in completing this course of study while simultaneously meeting the demands of a career in the U.S. Army. In my current military assignment as a Technical Inspector at Fort Drum, NY, I ensure the airworthiness of aircraft utilized by the 10th Mountain Division, which is required to relocate anywhere in the world on extremely short notice in response to crisis situations.

Throughout my years of military service, I have been singled out for jobs which required the ability to quickly make sound decisions, and I have continuously maximized resources while exceeding expected standards and performance guidelines. I have been responsible for certifying multimillion-dollar aircraft for flight service, training and supervising employees who have been highly productive and successful in their own careers, and applying technical computer knowledge in innovative ways which have further increased efficiency and productivity.

I am confident that I offer a combination of technical, managerial, and supervisory skills and a level of knowledge which will allow me to quickly achieve outstanding results in anything I attempt. Known for my energy and enthusiasm, I am a creative and talented professional with a strong desire to make a difference in whatever setting and environment I find myself.

I hope you will contact me to suggest a time when we might meet to discuss your needs. I can assure you in advance that I could rapidly become an asset to your organization.

Sincerely,

Donald Pratt

DONALD PRATT

1110½ Hay Street, Fayetteville, NC 28305 • preppub@aol.com • (910) 483-6611

OBJECTIVE

To offer a versatile background emphasizing computer operations, logistics, inventory control, production control, and security to an organization that can benefit from my experience as a supervisor and manager with a reputation for creativity.

EDUCATION & TRAINING

Will receive a **B.S. in Computer Science**, Jefferson Community College, Watertown, NY, winter 2006.

Selected for extensive training, including courses for security managers and computer operations and applications as well as technical courses in aircraft repair and maintenance, professional leadership development, equal opportunity practices, and Airborne School.

COMPUTER SKILLS & CLEARANCE

Am highly computer literate and offer skills related to the following:

Word   PowerPoint   Excel   Access

Was entrusted with a Top Secret security clearance.

EXPERIENCE

Earned a reputation as a focused and goal-oriented professional, U.S. Army:

TECHNICAL INSPECTOR. Fort Drum, NY (2004-present). Officially cited for my in-depth knowledge of aviation maintenance and logistics issues, conduct technical inspections on 24 helicopters while also providing training, guidance, and supervision.

- Transformed a substandard quality control section into one which sets the example.
- Received the NATO Medal for Service for my contributions during operations in Afghanistan and Iraq, 2004 and 2006.

SUPERVISOR FOR AVIATION MAINTENANCE AND SUPPLY. Fort Drum, NY (2002-03). Made numerous important contributions while coordinating supply, maintenance, and readiness issues for units throughout the 10th Mountain Division.

- Received a letter of commendation from a three-star general for my expertise demonstrated as the Security Manager for the corps headquarters and for personally revitalizing the physical security program so that it received "commendable" ratings.
- Developed a database for managing aircraft maintenance histories which greatly increased the reliability of information about the organization's 968 assigned aircraft.
- Created and presented effective training on physical security and ADP operations.

MAINTENANCE SUPERVISOR. Fort Drum, NY (2001-02). Provided oversight for a $6 million annual operating budget and ensured the quality and timeliness of all phases of support for a fleet of 104 aircraft while also reviewing daily/monthly status reports, coordinating supply up to the wholesale level, and recommending procedural changes.

MAINTENANCE SUPERVISOR. Italy (1998-01). Cited as directly responsible for a high level of achievement and productivity; collected and processed maintenance data on 123 aircraft while controlling flight safety information and support for four divisions.

- Selected to oversee a project during which new equipment and automation assets were integrated into use; achieved a smooth transition.

TECHNICAL INSPECTOR. Korea (1996-97). Cited for my ability to quickly master technical information, made determinations on aircraft serviceability and safety.

PERSONAL

Am known for my enthusiastic style of leadership and reputation for unwavering moral and ethical standards. Was honored with numerous Meritorious Service, Commendation, and Achievement Medals in recognition of my contributions and professionalism.

Date

Exact Name of Person
Title or Position
Name of Company
Address
City, State, Zip

TRAFFIC MANAGER   Dear Exact Name of Person: (or Dear Sir or Madam if answering a blind ad.)

With the enclosed resume, I would like to make you aware of my background as an articulate professional with a strong background in transportation and traffic management, personnel management and staff development, planning and program management, and safety.

As you will see from my resume, I have earned an Associate of Arts degree in Logistics Management with emphasis on Traffic Management. My knowledge has been supplemented by numerous military training courses in the areas of leadership and management, hazardous materials transportation, as well as quality assurance and safety.

Throughout my military experience, I have excelled in all areas of transportation, and I currently serve as the sole advisor to the Director of Logistics on all technical issues related to the movement of materials and personnel. I offer comprehensive knowledge of a wide range of policies, principles, and practices related to traffic management along with in-depth experience related to Department of Transportation as well as local, state, and other federal regulations related to transportation. My highly developed supervisory, planning, project management, and staff development skills would quickly make me a valuable asset to your company.

If you can use an experienced transportation professional whose unique abilities have been proven in challenging environments, I hope you will welcome my call soon when I try to arrange a brief meeting to discuss your goals and how my background might serve your needs. I can provide outstanding references at the appropriate time.

Sincerely,

Brian Greer

Alternate Last Paragraph:
I hope you will write or call me soon to suggest a time when we might meet to discuss your needs and goals and how my background might serve them. I can provide outstanding references at the appropriate time.

BRIAN GREER

1110½ Hay Street, Fayetteville, NC 28305   •   preppub@aol.com   •   (910) 483-6611

OBJECTIVE

To contribute to an organization that can benefit from an experienced transportation professional with exceptional communication, planning, and time management skills who offers a background in operations management, training, and hazardous materials handling.

EDUCATION

Associate of Arts in Logistics Management with emphasis on Traffic Management, Community College of the Air Force, Maxwell AFB, 2006.
Completed numerous technical and leadership courses as part of my military training, including the Non-Commissioned Officers Academy and Senior Non-Commissioned Officers Academy, as well as courses in Transportation of Hazardous Materials, Quality Awareness Team Tools and Techniques, Traffic Management, and Command Freight Training.

COMPUTERS

Am highly computer literate and offer knowledge of many of the most popular operating systems and software, including proprietary systems; systems operated include: Windows XP; Microsoft Word & Excel; UPS WorldShip; SABRE Reservation System; Cargo Movement Operations System (CMOS); WorldSpan Reservation System.

LICENSES

Hold a South Carolina Commercial Driver's License with HAZMAT, Passenger Carrying, and Double Trailer Endorsements.

EXPERIENCE

TRAFFIC MANAGER. U.S. Air Force, various locations (2002-present). Have been selected for promotion ahead of my peers and advanced to positions of increasing responsibilities while providing expert planning, coordination, and traffic control of military and civilian personnel and equipment culminating in assignment at the Columbia, SC, airport.
- Serve as the sole advisor to the Director of Logistics on technical transportation issues.

Supervision, Staff Development, and Training:
- Provide supervision and training for up to 20 personnel; write periodic performance appraisals for junior managers and monthly counseling statements for all employees.
- Perform a variety of human resource functions, including implementation of the Equal Employment Opportunity (EEO) program, merit promotions, and incentive awards.

Planning and Program Management:
- Plan and develop budgetary and financial data supporting traffic management functions; manage the operational budget for the movement of commercial cargo and personnel.
- Authored the office Operating Instructions for the 154th Airlift Wing, a set of detailed guidelines by which personnel with little or no transportation experience could operate the office in my absence with no interruption in service delivery to the customer.
- By utilizing a variety of innovative means to obtain the least expensive air fares and air cargo rates possible, consistently save the government in excess of $250,000 annually.

Hazardous Materials and Safety:
- With a strong emphasis on "safety first," consistently enforce all regulations concerning safety issues; personnel under my supervision have zero time lost due to accidents.
- As a result of my extensive training in the shipping and storage of hazardous cargo, my unit has received the highest possible readiness ratings on all inspections.

AFFILIATIONS

Served on the Worship Committee and Fellowship Committee as well as chairing the Building and Grounds Committee for Carolina Presbyterian Church, Columbia, SC.

PERSONAL

Hold a Secret clearance. Received numerous awards for my exemplary performance, including the Air Force Commendation Medal, the Air Force Achievement Medal, and several certificates of appreciation. Excellent personal and professional references on request.

Exact Name of Person
Title or Position
Name of Company
Address (number and street)
Address (city, state, and zip)

**TRANSPORTATION
MANAGER**

Dear Exact Name of Person: (or Sir or Madam if answering a blind ad.)

With the enclosed resume, I would like to express my interest in exploring employment opportunities with your organization.

As you will see from my resume, I served my country with distinction in the U.S. Army, and I was the recipient of numerous medals and awards in recognition of exemplary performance and leadership.

During my military service, I earned widespread respect as a supervisor. Performance evaluations commended me in writing as "a dynamic, multifunctional manager" and I was praised for having "a great ability to always turn the weakness of others into strengths." One of my greatest pleasures was training employees and instilling in them the desire to be achievers. Because of my ability to work well with others, I am confident that I could be effective in dealing with the general public.

Because my career field was in the motor transportation field, I have become experienced in many different functional areas including inventory control and personnel supervision. I am skilled at inventory support and logistics, and I have prepared many soldiers for deployment to and from Afghanistan and Iraq. I managed hundreds of personnel and have trained personnel to become excellent problem solvers and troubleshooters, and I was praised in writing for molding maintenance crews into solid teams. One performance evaluation noted that I exhibited a management style in which I "developed employees by challenging their abilities and stimulating their initiative."

I am eager to contribute to the goals of your organization, and I hope you will contact me to suggest a time when we might discuss your needs. I can provide outstanding references at the appropriate time.

Sincerely,

Constantine Aviculus

CONSTANTINE AVICULUS

1110½ Hay Street, Fayetteville, NC 28305 • preppub@aol.com • (910) 483-6611

OBJECTIVE
I want to contribute to an organization that can use a strong leader and experienced manager with a desire to contribute to the goals of an ambitious organization.

EDUCATION
Completed two years of college courses from North Central Institute, Clarksville, TN.

EXPERIENCE
Excelled in a track record of promotion while serving in the U.S. Army:
TRANSPORTATION MANAGER ("First Sergeant"). U.S. Army, Ft. Dix, NY (2002-06). For the largest Direct Support Supply Company, managed 119 employees and assisted the commander in controlling $48 million in equipment. Prepared the unit to deploy to Afghanistan in support of Operation Enduring Freedom. On my own initiative, developed a new program that greatly enhanced the combat readiness of the entire unit.
- **Safety and training management:** Planned, coordinated, and implemented more than 80 training projects; emphasized safety with the result that there were no accidents.
- **Outstanding evaluation:** Was evaluated in writing as "a dynamic, multifunctional manager who is sought out for his extraordinary abilities."

TRANSPORTATION MANAGER ("Motor Sergeant"). U.S. Army, Ft.Hood, TX (2000-02). Was described as "working countless overtime hours" preparing for a major inspection of this Direct Support Supply Company where I was responsible for administrative control, maintenance operations, work load distribution, scheduled and unscheduled maintenance, quality control, and distribution of more than 200 items of Quartermaster-unique equipment. Managed four managers and seven junior employees; accounted for $14 million in tools.
- **Training and deployment management:** Trained 53 employees in the company-level maintenance training program. Cross-trained 12 employees in three different fields. Directed preparations for deployment and redeployment to Iraq and Afghanistan.
- **Outstanding evaluations:** On a formal performance evaluation, was praised for "a great ability to always turn the weakness of others into strengths."

DIRECTORATE MAINTENANCE MANAGER. U.S. Army, Ft. Bragg, NC (1997-2000). Was specially selected for a key maintenance management position in the Airborne and Special Operations Test Directorate where I managed maintenance, operation, and safety of a fleet of 47 vehicles valued at $12 million. Implemented the driver training and licensing program for all assigned personnel.
- **Supporting the fielding of new equipment:** Provided rapid and recovery support during major test events. My rapid and responsive maintenance support was described as "the key to the successful testing." Supported over 20 airborne heavy drop operations.
- **Employee motivation and development:** Was commended for "pushing soldiers and superiors alike to achieve high standards."

Highlights of other experience:
MOTOR ASSETS MANAGER. U.S. Army, Korea. Managed 15 employees while controlling $2 million in tools and equipment. Inherited a dysfunctional motor pool operation and rapidly brought every area into compliance with DA and Division standards; received the Commanding General's Award for superior maintenance support during a major inspection.
SENIOR WHEELED VEHICLE MECHANIC. Managed six managers and 19 employees in an artillery airborne battalion, and controlled $1 million in equipment.
MOTOR SERGEANT. Maintained 25 vehicles and managed five employees.

PERSONAL
Outstanding references on request. Known for my strong personal initiative and integrity.

Date

Exact Name of Person
Exact Title
Exact Name of Company
Address
City, State, Zip

Dear Exact Name of Person (or Dear Sir or Madam if answering a blind ad):

With the enclosed resume, I would like to make you aware of my interest in exploring employment opportunities with your organization.

As you will see from my resume, I have served my country in the U.S. Army while handling some of our military's most challenging logistics problems. Because of my reputation as a resourceful problem solver and strong leader, I was once selected for a position that involved managing support operations for a 1,700-person rapid deployment organization. I am skilled at arranging transportation by air, rail, sea, or land for all classes of supplies including hazardous materials and weapons.

In my current position as Transportation Operations Manager, I control $45 million in assets and equipment while managing more than 2,000 projects annually. My emphasis on safety has provided outstanding results during accident-free training activities and vehicular operations. I am skilled at managing people. For the past 12 years, I have routinely managed between 50-150 employees as I led them in serving the logistics and support needs of thousands of customers.

If you can use a proven leader with unquestioned integrity along with experience in managing logistics and transportation activities worldwide, I hope you will contact me to suggest a time when we might discuss your needs.

Yours sincerely,

Armando Mercado

ARMANDO MERCADO

1110½ Hay Street, Fayetteville, NC 28305 • preppub@aol.com • (910) 483-6611

OBJECTIVE

To benefit an organization that can use a logistics management specialist with experience in evaluating logistics readiness related to supply, food service, maintenance, transportation, and other areas while determining requirements for money, manpower, material, and services.

EDUCATION

Earned more than 111 college credits toward B.S. in Business Administration, Columbus State University, Columbus Technical Community College, and University of Turabo.
Leadership training: Extensive leadership and management training including the 1st Sergeant Course, Battle Staff Noncommissioned Officers Course, Transportation NCO Advanced Course (ANCOC), Transportation Basic NCO Course (BNCOC), Hazardous Cargo Instructor Course, and Primary Leadership Development Course (PLDC).
Logistics training: Training related to logistics included Air Movement Operations, Airlift Operations, Defense Packaging, and Hazardous Material Transportation Courses.

EXPERIENCE

Excelled in a fast-track career with the U.S. Army while developing resourceful solutions to logistical and distribution problems worldwide:
Nov 2004-2006: **TRANSPORTATION OPERATIONS MANAGER.** Ft. Hood, TX. As the Acting Command Sergeant Major, trained and supervised 30 employees while planning and coordinating the transportation worldwide of personnel and cargo by air, rail, vehicle, and sea. Directed the training of 1400 employees in nuclear, biological, and chemical awareness.
- **Project management:** Coordinated more than 2,000 projects annually which included organizing the transportation of soldiers to Iraq; developing and implementing training such as training for deployment and convoy operations; and directing the planning of supply lists and logistics for transporting the supplies.

Aug 2002-Nov 2004: **SUPPORT OPERATIONS CHIEF.** Ft. Benning, GA. Was selected for this position over eight other highly qualified Master Sergeants. Managed support operations provided to a rapid deployment organization with 1,700 employees; planned and coordinated Combat Service Support to thousands of soldiers in the 3rd Infantry Division. Trained and directed a staff section of 66 employees, which provides combat service support for all automated and maintenance systems (CSSMO) related to transportation, field services, maintenance, logistics operations, and supply.
- **Personnel training and supervision:** Conducted training for the leaders of soldiers deploying to Iraq in support of Operation Iraqi Freedom (OIF).
- **Emphasis on safety and quality:** Was praised for my emphasis on safety and quality control during numerous accident-free training activities.

Feb 1995-Jul 2002: **OPERATIONS MANAGER.** Ft. Benning, GA. Trained and directed 119 employees in a support organization that provided supplies including water, clothing, ammunition, food, and weapons. Controlled $48 million in equipment including weapons and nuclear, biological, and chemical (NBC) materials. On my own initiative, significantly improved every aspect of the supply program, and led the supply program to outstanding results on multiple inspections and audits.
- **Personnel training:** In the belief that individual readiness is the key to preparing an entire company to be combat ready, I developed and implemented numerous training programs that improved employee performance.

PERSONAL

Self-starter with strong personal initiative. Excellent references upon request.

Date

Exact Name of Person
Title or Position
Name of Company
Address
City, State, Zip

WAREHOUSE MANAGER   Dear Exact Name of Person: (or Dear Sir or Madam if answering a blind ad.)

With the enclosed resume, I would like to make you aware of my background as an experienced logistics and transportation manager whose excellent supervisory, staff development, and organizational skills have been proven in challenging situations requiring a quick-thinking problem solver.

Currently I am excelling as Warehouse Manager for a prominent food service distributor. I oversee the operation of a food service facility which includes a 168,000-square foot cold storage area and which ships more than $3 million worth of merchandise annually. While supervising the warehouse staff, on my own initiative I recommended and designed a blast cell for the freezer that allowed meats to be frozen almost instantly, saving the company thousands of dollars per year. I also managed the redesign and improvements to the freezer rack system, installing a rear door and reconfiguring the interior shelving so that merchandise could be displayed more effectively. In a previous position, I served as Production Supervisor, managing 12 personnel as well as providing them with training in the operation of various production machines and equipment.

Earlier, while serving as a Transportation Supervisor with the U.S. Army at Fort Benning, GA, I excelled in both logistics and support operations and transportation management. In recognition of my leadership skills, I was promoted ahead of my peers and advanced to positions of increasing responsibility in which I trained and managed as many as 27 personnel. I have completed a number of professional leadership development and logistics training courses as part of my military training, and I have recently completed a forklift certification refresher course. I feel that my knowledge and practical management experience would make me a valuable addition to your operation.

If you can use a motivated, hard-working professional who offers a track record of success in transportation and logistics management, I hope you will contact me to suggest a time when we might discuss your needs. I assure you in advance that I have an excellent reputation and would quickly become an asset to your organization.

Sincerely,

Jeremy Faircloth

JEREMY FAIRCLOTH

1110½ Hay Street, Fayetteville, NC 28305   •   preppub@aol.com   •   (910) 483-6611

OBJECTIVE To contribute to an organization that can use an experienced logistics manager with excellent supervisory and staff development skills as well as an extensive background in shipping, receiving, transportation, and distribution.

EDUCATION & TRAINING Completed a number of professional development and training programs as part of my military training, including courses in leadership development, transportation, and forklift operation. Graduated from Columbus Senior High School, Columbus, GA, 1988.

CERTIFICATIONS Certified Forklift Operator, renewed, 2006.

EXPERIENCE *With Southern Fresh Foods, have advanced in the following "track record" of increasing responsibilities for this regional food service distributor:*
2005-present: **WAREHOUSE MANAGER.** Columbus, GA. Responsible for the operation of this large warehouse which ships over $3 million worth of inventory annually; manage a cold-storage area of 168,000 square feet.
- Supervise three employees; write employee schedules and make daily task assignments.
- Interview and hire all new warehouse personnel; provide training in shipping and receiving practices as well as policies and procedures specific to Southern Fresh Foods.
- Ensure that lot numbers are assigned and all merchandise received is slotted into the appropriate physical location in the warehouse.
- Oversee and participate in the picking, packing, and loading of all outbound shipments, verifying that all merchandise is pulled accurately and matches shipping manifests.
- Managed the redesign and implementation of improvements to the freezer rack system at Southern Fresh Food; by installing a rear door and reconfiguring the display racks, labor hours were reduced and merchandise was displayed more effectively.

1998-04: **PRODUCTION SUPERVISOR.** Columbus, GA. Oversaw all operational areas of this busy manufacturing facility, managed all employees while monitoring daily production to ensure that all objectives were met.
- Supervised up to 12 personnel, providing leadership and training on the operation of various production machines as well as in manufacturing policies and procedures.
- Managed the assembly, inspection, maintenance, and repair of all production equipment.
- Through my initiative, overall production for the facility increased by 15 percent.

Highlights of earlier experience:
WAREHOUSE SUPERVISOR. Georgia Manufacturing, Inc., Columbus, GA (1994-98). Responsible for overseeing all aspects of production for this local manufacturing company, including supervision and training, quality control, shipping, and receiving.
- Provided supervisory oversight and training to a staff of 13 personnel.
- Ensured that production quotas and quality assurance objectives were achieved.
- Directed the packing and loading of finished product onto outbound trailers.

TRANSPORTATION SUPERVISOR. U.S. Army, Fort Benning, GA (1988-94). Excelled in a variety of transportation and logistics positions while serving my country in the U.S. Army; was promoted ahead of my peers and advanced to positions of increasing responsibility.
- Supervised and trained as many as 27 personnel, including six junior managers in areas related to shipping and receiving, operation of loading equipment, logistics and support procedures, transportation scheduling, and vehicle dispatching.

PERSONAL Excellent personal and professional references are available upon request.

Date

Exact Name of Person
Title or Position
Name of Company
Address
City, State, Zip

WAREHOUSE
MANAGER

Dear Exact Name of Person: (or Dear Sir or Madam if answering a blind ad.)

I would appreciate an opportunity to talk with you soon about how I could contribute to your organization through my expertise related to logistics, inventory control, and warehousing.

As you will see from my resume, I have acquired expert skills in warehouse management while being promoted to increasingly more responsible jobs in the U.S. Air Force. Most recently I took over the management of a warehouse which was inefficient and disorganized. I conducted an inventory of this multimillion-dollar operation and saved $250,000 right away by correcting errors in over 600 line items. Through combining my creativity with my technical expertise, I expanded warehouse space by 20% and saved 15% in requisition costs.

In my previous job I was handpicked from among 20 candidates for a job which involved designing a new, state-of-the-art warehouse for more 55,000 line items. After designing the new warehouse, which was cited as the "best ever seen" by fire inspectors, I directed the efficient relocation of one million items from the old to the new warehouse. New storage procedures I implemented resulted in 100% accountability of all stored stock and, through devising a new filing system and checklists, we reduced excess manhours by 10%.

I am even proud of my accomplishments in the "building-block" jobs of my career, including delivery driver, bench stock clerk, and warehouseman. In those jobs, I earned a reputation as a safety-conscious professional with an unblemished safety record in operating all the equipment and vehicles involved in the warehouse/supply field.

I hope you will welcome my call soon to arrange a brief meeting at your convenience to discuss your current and future needs and how I might serve them. Thank you in advance for your time.

Sincerely yours,

Lance Whitfield

Alternate last paragraph:
I hope you will call or write me soon to suggest a time convenient for us to meet and discuss your current and future needs and how I might serve them. Thank you in advance for your time.

LANCE WHITFIELD

1110½ Hay Street, Fayetteville, NC 28305   •   preppub@aol.com   •   (910) 483-6611

OBJECTIVE

To benefit an organization that can use an innovative problem solver and logistics expert knowledgeable about all aspects of inventory management including shipping, receiving, and warehousing as well as automated systems, personnel supervision, and budgeting.

EXPERIENCE

WAREHOUSE MANAGER. U.S. Air Force, Charleston AFB, SC (2005-present). Took over a warehouse with a multimillion-dollar inventory and immediately made changes that improved efficiency while decreasing costs; managed three people.
- Conducted an inventory; identified errors on 600 line items that reduced excess inventory by $250,000. Developed new receiving procedures that ensured 100% accountability of store assets. Expanded warehouse space by 20% by rewarehousing techniques; reduced requisition costs 15%.

WAREHOUSE SUPERVISOR. U.S. Air Force, Base Supply Warehouse, Germany (2003-05). Was handpicked over 19 other logistics experts to provide leadership in designing a new, state-of-the-art 112,000 sq. ft. warehouse which allowed the location, at a moment's notice, of more than 55,000 items worth $3.5 million; managed nine people.
- Relocated more than one million products in 3,000 line items from the old to the new warehouse with no disruption of customer service and perfect accountability; coordinated the movement of sensitive and classified materials.
- Reduced excess manhours by 10% by implementing a new filing system and checklists.
- Designed a warehouse which fire inspectors said was "the best ever seen."
- Developed a user-friendly warehouse refusal checklist that allowed new recruits to resolve potential warehouse refusals.
- Perfected the procedures for producing and processing error-free shipment documents.

PROPERTY DISPATCH SUPERVISOR. U.S. Air Force, Base Supply Warehouse, Germany (2002-03). Supervised ten people while managing the utilization of over 5,000 pieces of property, including 30 vehicles, with a perfect safety record.
- Creatively overcame a labor shortage by implementing a new personnel utilization plan.

TRAINING MANAGER. U.S. Air Force, Pope AFB, NC (1998-02). Was noted as being a "stronghold of character" while excelling in conducting briefings, planning and conducting training, and providing guidance to more than 100 people daily.
- Became known for my contagious enthusiasm and for my capacity for hard work.

WAREHOUSEMAN. U.S. Air Force, Base Supply, Hill AFB, UT (1997-98). Handled the prompt and accurate receipt, storage, and distribution of 12,000 highly specialized "war readiness" items valued at over $115 million.
- Ensured correct shelf life of all items; prepared items for worldwide distribution.
- Became proficient in warehousing and transporting hazardous materials.

EDUCATION

Completed extensive college course work in logistics management, Community College of the Air Force, Maxwell AFB, AL, 1997-05.
Completed extensive training sponsored by the Air Force in advanced warehousing techniques, automated inventory control systems, personnel supervision, and management.

PERSONAL

Am known for my supervisory skills, leadership qualities, strong initiative, and communication skills as well as my ability to learn quickly and rapidly master new systems.

Date

Exact Name of Person
Title or Position
Name of Company
Address
City, State, Zip

Dear Exact Name of Person: (or Dear Sir or Madam if answering a blind ad.)

With the enclosed resume, I would like to make you aware of my interest in exploring employment opportunities with your organization and introduce you to my versatile skills.

I offer experience in all aspects of office operations and possess strong computer skills. Proficient with Word and Excel, I have utilized automated systems for purchasing as well as for tracking parts and supplies. In my current job, I have taken the initiative to enter all inventory assets into a Microsoft Excel program for the first time in the organization's history.

As you will see from my resume, I have served my country with distinction while serving in the Air Force. I spent three years in Germany, where I worked as part of a professional supply team ordering all items for a military community of 1,000 employees. I became known for my aggressive research skills and analytical abilities and, on my own initiative, I made many significant contributions to customer satisfaction by assuring the availability of items in demand by customers. In 2006, I assisted in preparing and processing requisitions for 25,000 requisitions valued at over $17 million, and I was responsible for 2,039 line items. I once played a key role in reducing from 780 to 262 the average number of items overdue by 180 days.

Although I was strongly encouraged to remain in military service and assured of continued advancement ahead of my peers, I made the decision to enter the civilian work force. I am certain I could make contributions to an organization that can use a dedicated and hard-working individual with strong problem-solving skills and analytical abilities. I enjoy taking on stubborn problems and figuring out solutions that increase productivity and boost customer satisfaction.

If you can use a congenial young professional known for attention to detail and a strong customer service focus, I hope you will contact me to suggest a time when we might meet to discuss your needs. I can provide excellent references.

Yours sincerely,

Angelique Lincoln

ANGELIQUE LINCOLN

1110½ Hay Street, Fayetteville, NC 28305 • preppub@aol.com • (910) 483-6611

OBJECTIVE To offer strong computer and office administration skills to an organization that can use a dedicated young professional with experience in customer service, supply, inventory control, and database management along with a reputation for meticulous attention to detail.

EDUCATION **Supply, inventory control, and purchasing:** Extensive training related to supply management sponsored by the U.S. Air Force, 2002-06.
- Trained in researching parts and availability as well as ordering and purchasing.

Computer operations: Extensive formal and on-the-job training related to computers..
- Skilled with Word, Excel, and automated systems for supply management and logistics tracking (Standard Base Supply System—SBSS and Supply Interface System—SIFS).

EXPERIENCE **WAREHOUSE RECORDS TECHNICIAN.** U.S. Air Force, Elmendorf AFB, AK (2006-present). Upon taking on this new assignment at one of the Air Force's busiest airlift hubs, have made significant contributions to efficiency and productivity.
- On my own initiative, took on the responsibility of entering all warehouse assets into a Microsoft Excel program for the first time in the history of this facility.
- Maintain up-to-date information about items available in an extensive inventory.

SUPPLY TECHNICIAN. U.S. Air Force, Ramstein AB, Germany (2002-05). During my three years at this Air Force base, was asked to handle steadily more complex responsibilities, and was frequently selected to train and manage German civilians working in the supply area. For a military community with approximately 1,000 employees, was a valued member of the supply team which ordered all items needed including clothing, aviation parts, and hazardous materials as well as perishable and nonperishable supplies.
- Controlled the requisition and status processing of 2,039 line items.
- Assisted in coordinating supplies needed for more than 600 organizations with a huge volume of requested items; worked diligently in an environment in which, at any one time, there were 14,000 items due in and 10,000 items due out related to worldwide sources; became skilled in working with tight deadlines and complex supply needs.
- In 2005, assisted in preparing and processing 25,000 requisitions valued at over $17 million for stateside sources of supply; processed status updates in order to provide timely customer information and customer service.

Accomplishments:
- On my own initiative, completed a rigorous research project which validated more than 100 item records previously recorded as obsolete; researched status of in-demand items and restored incorrectly coded items to an "available" status. This greatly boosted customer satisfaction.
- Played a key role in reducing from 780 to 262 the average number of items monthly which were overdue by 180 days.
- Was commended for outstanding analytical and research skills; constantly worked in a very dedicated fashion to assure that stock codes and status records were correct.
- On a formal performance evaluation, was commended for "utilizing innovative procedures in identifying and processing over 3,000 misrouted status inputs;" assured the accuracy of supply status reporting for over 7,000 customer requirements.
- Was cited for contributing to cumulative sales of $18.4 million and a low backlogged status. Became known for my aggressive research and follow-up on delinquent requests.

PERSONAL Held Secret security clearance. Can provide excellent references upon request. Efficiently operate nearly all types of office equipment. Am tenacious and persistent in solving problems.

Date

Exact Name of Person
Title or Position
Name of Company
Address
City, State, Zip

Dear Exact Name of Person: (or Dear Sir or Madam if answering a blind ad.)

With the enclosed resume, I would like to make you aware of my experience as a versatile and articulate young manager with exceptional sales and customer service skills.

Although I have advanced rapidly in the distribution management field, I have decided to transfer my skills and abilities into an area in which I can utilize my communication and problem-solving skills for a company where I would have more customer contact.

You will notice from my resume that I excelled in a previous job as a Head Sales Representative with a beverage distribution service. While maintaining and growing established accounts as well as developing new business, I always exceeded my sales quotas and won numerous awards for achievements in monthly sales, opening new accounts, and other areas.

I am a natural leader and offer a proven ability to excel at any task I take on. When I started with Target, I was quickly entrusted with additional duties as a Team Leader. My natural leadership and my ability to motivate employees soon resulted in a promotion to Break Pack and Pick & Put Manager at a new distribution center, where I built "from scratch" a team that achieved the highest productivity and quality of any shift in the plant within six months of start up. Exceptional performance in this position earned me advancement to positions of increased responsibility.

If you can use an experienced professional whose supervisory and organizational skills have been proven in a variety of challenging environments, I look forward to hearing from you to suggest a time when we might meet to discuss your needs. I can assure you in advance that I have an outstanding reputation and would rapidly become an asset to your company.

Sincerely,

Archie Mantel

ARCHIE MANTEL

1110½ Hay Street, Fayetteville, NC 28305   •   preppub@aol.com   •   (910) 483-6611

OBJECTIVE

To benefit an organization that can use an experienced management professional with exceptional sales, customer service, supervisory, motivational, and organizational abilities.

EXPERIENCE

WAREHOUSE SUPERVISOR. National Company Storage, Richmond, VA (2006-present). While managing 35 people, am responsible for prioritizing main staff orders and checking billing statements while manifesting an average of 20 receiving trucks and 15 shipping trucks daily.

With Target Distribution Centers, advanced in a "track record" of promotion:
2004-05: **RECEIVING MANAGER.** Richmond, VA. Oversaw the receiving department for this 1.2 million square-foot regional distribution center which received more than $2 million of inventory daily.
- Managed up to 80 associates, directing the work flow to ensure that all shipments in the loading docks were emptied quickly and merchandise unloaded, were moved off the floor, and slotted in the appropriate physical location in the warehouse.
- Interviewed and hired new receiving personnel; provided classroom and hands-on skills training to as many as 40 associates at a time as well as training for all associates.
- Monitored the work of all receiving associates to ensure that standards were met or exceeded: maintained a minimum of 99.75% accuracy on freight receiving and unloaded 95% of all trailers in up to 103 loading docks within 24 hours.
- Performed analysis of previous year's data and current trends in order to develop accurate forecasts of required man hours; developed monthly schedules.
- Inspected the physical operation of the warehouse both visually and by computer, identifying, troubleshooting, and resolving problems before delays occurred.

2003-04: **REPLENISHMENT STOCK RECEIVING (RSR)** and **ORDER FILLING MANAGER.** Richmond, VA. Supervised 40 employees in a department that served as the interface between shipping and receiving; pulled merchandise that had been received and moved it to reserve bins and order-filling slots to be shipped out.
- Interviewed, hired, and trained new personnel, conducted classroom instruction and on-hands training for as many as 40 new associates at once.
- Ensured that all freight received was properly placed within the correct conveyor system modules; provided increased quality assurance and efficiency in order filling.

2001-03: **BREAK PACK** and **PICK & PUT MANAGER.** Raleigh, NC. Promoted to this position from a job as an RSR Associate, was handpicked to build "from scratch" and manage a team of Break Pack/Pick & Put Associates for a new weekend shift.
- Supervised as many as 20 associates per shift, breaking down case lots of merchandise in order to fill and pack store orders for individual quantities; processed orders .
- Was solely responsible for the interviewing, hiring, and training of my entire staff.
- Within six months of start-up, achieved the highest percentage of production and quality of any shift in the facility.

SALES REPRESENTATIVE. Harris Wholesalers, Raleigh, NC (1998-00). Started as a Sales Representative and was promoted to Head Sales Representative for a company which distributed Budweiser and other beverages as well as a variety of snacks and foods.
- Maintained established accounts; prospected for new accounts.
- Always exceeded my quota of weekly sales calls; introduced new products to existing accounts. Won numerous awards including awards for most new sales generated for one month and for most new accounts opened monthly.

PERSONAL

Excellent personal and professional references are available upon request.

You may already realize that applying for a federal government position requires some patience and persistence in order to complete rather tedious forms and get them in on time. Depending on what type of federal job you are seeking, you may need to prepare an application such as the SF 171 or OF 612, or you may need to use a Federal Resume, sometimes called a "Resumix," to apply for a federal job. But that may not be the only paperwork you need.

Many Position Vacancy Announcements or job bulletins for a specific job also tell you that, in order to be considered for the job you want, you must also demonstrate certain knowledge, skills, or abilities. In other words, you need to also submit written narrative statements which microscopically focus on your particular knowledge, skill, or ability in a certain area. The next few pages are filled with examples of excellent Federal Resumes and KSAs. If you wish to see many other examples of KSAs, you may look for another book published by PREP: "Real KSAs--Knowledge, Skills & Abilities--for Government Jobs."

Although you will be able to use the Federal Resume you prepare in order to apply for all sorts of jobs in the federal government, the KSAs you write are particular to a specific job and you may be able to use the KSAs you write only one time. If you get into the Civil Service system, however, you will discover that many KSAs tend to appear on lots of different job announcement bulletins. For example, "Ability to communicate orally and in writing" is a frequently requested KSA. This means that you would be able to use and re-use this KSA for any job bulletin which requests you to give evidence of your ability in this area.

What does "Screen Out" mean? If you see that a KSA is requested and the words "Screen out" are mentioned beside the KSA, this means that this KSA is of vital importance in "getting you in the door." If the individuals who review your application feel that your screen-out KSA does not establish your strengths in this area, you will not be considered as a candidate for the job. You need to make sure that any screen-out KSA is especially well-written and comprehensive.

How long can a KSA be? A job vacancy announcement bulletin may specify a length for the KSAs it requests. Sometimes KSAs can be 1-2 pages long each, but sometimes you are asked to submit several KSAs within a maximum of two pages. Remember that the purpose of a KSA is to microscopically examine your level of competence in a specific area, so you need to be extremely detailed and comprehensive. Give examples and details wherever possible. For example, your written communication skills might appear more credible if you provide the details of the kinds of reports and paperwork you prepared.

KSAs are extremely important in "getting you in the door" for a federal government job. If you are working under a tight deadline in preparing your paperwork for a federal government position, don't spend all your time preparing the Federal Resume if you also have KSAs to do. Create "blockbuster" KSAs as well!

FEDERAL RESUME OR RESUMIX

OLIVER A. JERRY
SSN: 000-00-0000
Address: 1110 1/2 Hay Street, Fayetteville, NC 28305
Home: (910) 483-6611
Work: (910) 483-6611
Email: preppub@aol.com

Highest permanent play plan or grade held: grade, month/year from ___ to month/year
Position, Title, Series, Grade: Accounting Technician, GS-09
Announcement Number: DN-00-000

ACCOUNTING & SUPPLY TECHNICIAN

Here you will see an example of a four-page federal resume.

Don't forget to highlight your accomplishments on your Federal Resume. Note the phrases in bold at the end of each job on the opposite page.

EXPERIENCE

ACCOUNTING and SUPPLY TECHNICIAN. Cherry Bekaert & Holland, LLP, 1860 Hannover Square, Warren, MI 56845, Charles Adams, Supervisor, phone: (333) 333-3333, hours worked: 45-50, (2004-present). Excelling in handling diverse responsibilities, have been credited with making changes which have significantly improved operating procedures while supervising three people including accounting clerks and office staff for a business with five separate plant locations.

- Streamlined operations in the accounting department and implemented changes which reduced the time needed to complete support activities; for instance, payroll processing which had taken three days is now completed in one.
- Apply knowledge in database creation to establish a new system for tracking equipment purchases and status of computers, printers, vehicles, and other equipment.
- Prepare payroll for up to 36 Cherry Bekaert employees in the company's five plants.
- Manage Workmen's Compensation claims and yearly audits, preparation of forms for OSHA, and monthly approval of employee health insurance; prepare daily bank deposits; post payroll and accounts payable check numbers; issue and then post manual checks; prepare the petty cash sheet; process state and federal tax payments.
- Verify data pertaining to the general ledger, accounts payable, and accounts receivable.

ACCOUNTS PAYABLE AND PAYROLL TECHNICIAN. Pechmann-Ellis & Associates, 2583 Ravenhill Circle, Warren, MI 56845, Charles Adams, Supervisor, phone: (444) 444-4444, hours worked: 45-50, (2001-04). After my retirement from the U.S. Army, was recruited by this commercial construction company to handle accounts payable for multimillion-dollar projects and to process payroll for 200 employees.

- Assisted in purchasing support for large projects; prepared weekly and monthly reports for project managers and supervisors.

Experience gained in the US Army:
BATTALION PROPERTY ACCOUNTING TECHNICIAN. U.S. Army, 37th Finance Division, Fort Rucker, AL, 77646. Supervisor: MAJ Edgar Nixon, (555) 555-5555, hours per week: 40, (1998-01). As a Property Book Officer and senior logistician for a logistics battalion, was commended in writing for "excellent performance in superbly

performing all assigned missions" while directing management and accountability procedures for supplies, property and equipment worth over $105 million. Worked closely with the subordinate companies to assure smooth transfers of excess equipment out of the battalion. Identified over $750,000 of excess items for turn-in with 63%+ redistributed throughout the corps. Acquired shortage items and force modernization equipment. Expertly utilized both manual and automated property accounting procedures, including VLOS and TAQlS. Exercised staff supervision of the battalion logistics low-density program. Supervised one NCO and one soldier. Ensured all M35A2 cargo trucks were turned in through supply channels. Executed the M4 carbine fielding to the battalion. Achieved "zero defects" in hand-controlled inventory. **This battalion's supply and property accountability ranked among the best at Fort Rucker. Provided the leadership for a drive to reduce excess property and became the "go-to" manager for all companies in the battalion seeking guidance in reducing excess property.**

PROPERTY BOOK OFFICER. U.S. Army, 151st Finance Division, FA Bn, Stuttgart, Germany, APO, AE 564, Supervisor: MAJ David N. Butler, (666) 666-6666, hours per week: 40, (1996-98). Supervised 11 people as Property Book Officer for a Finance Division in Stuttgart. During this time, played a key role in the operation of the Battalion's Finance office in Germany for 2 years, and maintained accountability of one Battalion fuel point, maintaining formal property book records through the use of the Standard Property Book System. Redesigned (SPBS) property valued at $2.1 billion. Provided technical expertise to the chain of command on logistical and budget policies and procedures. Ensured the battalion maintained a rating consistent with its Authorized Level of Organization. **My performance was rated as "absolutely outstanding" in this position Maintained 100% accountability of the organization's property. On my own initiative, developed training and orientation procedures which ensured smooth transition when new personnel assumed control of property. Provided leadership in fielding new modernized equipment including SINCGARS radios, data transfer devices, squad automatic weapons, and radio meters. Was described in writing as "without a doubt the subject matter expert on property management."**

PROPERTY BOOK OFFICER. U.S. Army, 43rd Intelligence Brigade, Fort Riley, KS 46323-5442. Supervisor: SSG Larry Norris, (555) 555-5555, hours per week: 40, (1993-96). Responsible for all administrative matters pertaining to the Property Book of the Intelligence Brigade, a 1,000-man independent combat team. Maintained organizational hand receipts for eight companies and one battery, including associated shortage annexes and documents supporting files in excess of $70 million. Supervised two enlisted personnel to ensure cyclic and sensitive item inventories were properly conducted and hand receipts reassigned in a timely manner. In this position, constructed a property accounting system using the Standard Property Book System (SPBS-R). In May 1994 during Operation Mission Relief, ensured the brigade's supply requirements were met, coordinating support for two other bases in Fort Campbell, KY, Fort Myer, VA, and Fort Wainwright, AK. **Yielded a zero deficit accounting record for all equipment on hand. Also oversaw the transfer of well over 100 railcars of equipment from inactivating intelligence units into the command and the fielding of new equipment. In a formal performance evaluation, was described thusly: "his knowledge, long-range vision, and desire to conduct all property and supply transactions properly have had a significant impact on the battalion."**

BATTALION PROPERTY BOOK TECHNICIAN. US Army, B-253rd Intelligence Division, Fort Hood, TX, 87646, Supervisor: SFC Scott Grenald, (666) 666-6666, hours per week: 40, (1990-93). Property Book Officer for this Intelligence division. Once assigned to the unit, maintained organizational and installation hand receipts for five batteries to include associated shortage annexes and document supporting files in excess of $50 million. Managed

How do you use this federal resume? Often you are asked to put your federal resume online at sites such as www.cpol.mil. But we don't recommend that you sit down at the computer and "shoot from the hip" when putting your resume online. We advise you to write, edit, rewrite, proof, use spell check and word count tools, and finalize your resume on paper before you sit down at a computer to put your resume online. **Then** you can (with confidence) paste your outstanding resume into the online Resumix and other online systems. Often you are asked to obey a word limit, which in some instances is 16,000 characters.

excess property by coordinating and monitoring turn-in and lateral transfer directives. Monitored training programs and supervised 11 enlisted personnel. Directed and supervised the fielding of several Force Modernization items of equipment including SINCGARS radios, M40 protective masks, M16A2 rifles, and Mobile Subscriber Equipment (MSE). **Developed a plan for the turn-in or transfer of excess equipment in the battalion totaling 27 LIN items. Maintained 100% property accountability for two separate books.**

PROPERTY BOOK TECHNICIAN. HHC-535, Artillery Brigade, APO AE 13856, Supervisor: MAJ Nathan Jennings, (777) 777-7777, hours per week: 40, (1988-90). Brigade Budget Officer/Supply Technician responsible for monitoring and advising the brigade commander, battalion commanders, and the brigade S4 on the status of budget operations and expenditures. Assisted four battalion property book officers in maintaining property book accountability and providing technical advice and assistance. As the HHC Brigade Property Book Officer, responsible for the accountability of $9 million worth of equipment, property, and supplies. Ensured proper codes and fund restrictions were placed on unit requisitions to ensure the brigade would receive proper credit, resulting in over $585,000 of funds reimbursed. Instrumental in the development of the brigade's FY budget. Monitored the budget accounts for the brigade and tracked the battalion's budget expenditures and recording procedures. Ensured excess property was identified, redistributed when possible, or disposed of in accordance with standard regulations. Communicated with outside agencies to obtain essential equipment that was critically short within the Army supply system. **Ensured all classes of supply were obtained to sustain a field artillery brigade consisting of 5 battalions, 3,000 soldiers, 90 155mm howitzers, 18 rocket launchers, and over 960 wheeled vehicles for 6 months in the Panama and during combat operations against Panamanian forces.**

Excelled in a "track record" of promotions with the US Army at Fort Polk, LA:
1986-88: **DIVISION PROPERTY BOOK TEAM CHIEF.** HHC, 67th Artillery, Fort Polk, LA 76307, Supervisor: SSG James A. Hennegan, (888) 888-8888, hours per week: 40. As Property Book Team Chief for Property Book Teams One and Two, provided property accountability for the 1st and 2nd Brigades. Managed over $89 million of assets for the 82d Signal Bn, 307 Engineer Bn, and 618th Engineer Company. Ensured all authorized property was on hand or on requisition. Verified CBS-X asset reporting, unit readiness output, and ensured all records, forms, and printouts were accurate. Responsible for installation and training of a new automated cross-leveling/redistribution program which resulted in saving the Division hundreds of thousands of dollars. **From Jan to Jul, served as the Government Accountable Officer (GAO) in Korea prior to being Team Chief for two Property Book teams consisting of 40 units. As GAO, brought all measures of supply performance above DA standards.**

1984-86: **SUPPLY TECHNICIAN.** 7th Division Infantry, Supervisor: SGT Harold G. Nicholls, (999) 999-9999, hours worked: 40. Maintained organization hand receipts for 19 units, to include associated shortage annexes and supporting documentation files. Provided an audit trail for all supply transactions, and ensured that cyclic and sensitive item inventories were properly conducted and hand receipts signed. Verified CBS-X asset reporting; established and monitored training programs and supervised four enlisted personnel. Utilized state-of-the art equipment to manage $4.6 million worth of deployable equipment of the 1/504th Parachute Infantry Regiment and the 73d Signal Battalion. Personally cited by GAO auditors and given praiseworthy comments by the Brigade Commander for the timely support and management of supplies and equipment in Honduras.

1982-84: **SUPPLY TECHNICIAN.** HHS, 321st Logistics, Supervisor: SGT Wesley K. Combs, phone unknown. Hours worked: 40. Was team chief in charge of maintaining organization and installation of hand receipts for 23 units, including associated shortage annexes and supporting documentation files. Managed excess property by coordinating and monitoring turn-in and lateral transfer directives. Verified equipment on-hand asset reporting, unit readiness output, and ensured all cards, form, and printouts were accurate. Established and monitored training programs and supervised team operations consisting of three enlisted personnel.

EDUCATION

Bachelor of Science Degree in Accounting, University of Alabama, Ft. Stewart campus GA, 2000.

Associate of Science degree in Business Administration, Central Texas College, Killeen, TX, 1993.

SPECIALIZED TRAINING, LICENSES, & CERTIFICATES

Military courses include: Unit Level Logistics System Operator Course, 2001; Property Accounting Technician, 1999; Depot Inventory Reconciliation, 1998; Physical Inventory Management, 1998; Standard Property Book System, 1998; General Supply Technician, 1997; Warrant Officer Entry Course, 1997; NCO Officer Logistics Course, 1996; Supply NCO Advanced Course, 1996; Division Logistics Course, 1995; Unit and Organizational Supply, 1995, and Organizational Maintenance of Radio Field Equipment, 1994.

AWARDS

Humanitarian Service Medal, Noncommissioned Officer's Professional Development Ribbon, Army Service Medal, Overseas Service Ribbon (2nd award), Germany Liberation Medal, Legion of Merit, Bronze Star Medal, Meritorious Service Medal, Army Commendation Medal (2nd award), Army Achievement Medal (3rd award), Army Good Conduct Medal (4th award), National Defense Service Medal (2nd award), European Service Medal with 3 Bronze Service Star.

FEDERAL RESUME OR RESUMIX

VICTOR A. NEILSON
1110 ½ Hay Street
Fayetteville, NC 28305
Home: (910) 483-6611
Cell: (910) 483-6611
E-mail: preppub@aol.com

SSN: 123-45-6789
Date of birth: 01/01/1973
Country of Citizenship: United States
Veteran's Preference: 5%

CUSTOMER SERVICE REPRESENTATIVE & EQUIPMENT COORDINATOR

EXPERIENCE

May 2005-present: **EQUIPMENT COORDINATOR & CUSTOMER SERVICE REPRESENTATIVE.** PRP, Inc., 1110½ Hay Street, Dallas, TX 28305. $48,000 per annum. Supervisor: Corey Bailey, 910-483-6611. Am a key member of the management team of a company which leases critical industrial equipment including power generators, temperature control equipment, and air compressors to customer organizations which include chemical plants, manufacturing plants, building contractors, military organizations, and other customers. Perform major functions including the following:

- **Quality Assurance:** Perform analysis/investigations to ensure proper maintenance of power generators, temperature control equipment, and air compressors. Assure that leased equipment is in quality operating condition prior to delivery to customers. When leased equipment is returned, check material for evidence of carelessness or misuse of equipment or property. Determine liability for property that is damaged, lost, or destroyed. Conduct and document safety and environmental inspections. Coordinate all labor for normal or emergency repair of equipment.

- **Customer Service:** Coordinate with customers. Manage delivery schedules of leased equipment.

- **Logistics Management:** Coordinate the logistics involved in providing customers with leased equipment. Organize transportation of equipment via commercial carriers and expertly prepare and review all paperwork and documentation to assure completeness for future audits.

- **Contract Negotiation:** Negotiate contracts with customers for leased equipment. Negotiate key details of leases including price, delivery, customer support services, and other issues.

- **Experience with Military Contracting:** Coordinate with military contracting representatives and have become knowledgeable of the process of responding to solicitations as well as providing quality assurance information to contract specialists.

Oct 2001-Apr 2005: **CUSTOMER SERVICE REPRESENTATIVE & CONTRACT SPECIALIST.** United Rentals, 1110½ Hay Street, Dallas, TX 28305. $40,000 per annum. Supervisor: Chris Turner, Phone 910-483-6611. Prospected for new accounts while servicing existing customers. Coordinated with all levels of management in various industries including manufacturing and construction. Negotiated long-term and short-term leases for major pieces of construction equipment. Was handpicked to train new customer service representatives.

Aug 1999-Oct 2001: **EQUIPMENT COORDINATOR & CONTRACT SPECIALIST.** John Equipment, 1110½ Hay Street, Dallas, TX 28305. $30,000. Supervisor: Richard Stone, Phone 910-483-6611. For a $6 million fleet of construction equipment, prepared and maintained rental/lease agreements and handled collections as needed. Edited and filed rental agreement reports, customer reports, and equipment reports for business operations.

Dec 1997-Jul 1999: **ENGINEERING WORK-STUDY.** Smith Memorial Hospital, 1110½ Hay Street, Dallas, TX 28305. Supervisor: Al Morris, Phone 910-483-6611. While completing requirements for my Bachelor of Business Administration degree, excelled in a work-study program with the Smith Memorial Hospital during which I repaired and maintained all mechanical hospital equipment. Worked without supervision while repairing and maintaining ceiling tile, sinks, and drains throughout the hospital. Also worked in the X-ray room, where I prepared and maintained records for customers and agency use while interacting with all levels of hospital personnel.

Sept 1995-Nov 1997: **POWER GENERATION EQUIPMENT REPAIR SUPERVISOR.** Dallas Army National Guard, Detachment, 125th Engineer BN, 1110½ Hay Street, Dallas, TX 28305. Rank: E-5. Supervisor: Chief Warrant Officer Caleb Lonestar, Phone 910-483-6611. As a proud member of the National Guard, maintained and repaired diesel generator systems and vehicles throughout the unit. Handled extensive responsibility for quality assurance as I inspected and repaired all equipment in order to assure 100% serviceability. Became highly experienced in inspecting and operating all types of vehicles ranging from quarter-ton trucks, to five-ton cargo trucks, to forklifts. Trained, supervised, and counseled junior employees in equipment operation and military matters. As a supervisor, was responsible for maintaining safety in all phases of maintenance and equipment movement.
- **Equipment operation:** Gained experience in operating heavy equipment including bulldozers. Gained experience in operating and maintaining M1A1 Abrams tanks as well as numerous types of wheeled and track vehicles.

Sept 1992-Sept 1995: **GENERATOR REPAIR SPECIALIST & QUALITY ASSURANCE TECHNICIAN.** U.S. Army, Fort Hood, TX 28305. Rank E-4. Supervisors: Multiple. Phone unknown. On active duty with the U.S. Army, maintained 40 generator systems while continuously performing quality assurance inspections. Inspected paperwork to ensure that correct repair and maintenance procedures were followed.

COMPUTER EXPERTISE

Experienced in utilizing custom software programs for procurement, supply management, logistics management, and accounting management.
Skilled in utilizing Microsoft Word and the MS Office including Excel and PowerPoint.
Completed computer training in Windows and Word.

EDUCATION & TRAINING

Completed the **Bachelor of Business Administration (B.B.A.) degree,** Southern Methodist University, Dallas, TX, 2000.
Graduated from Primary Leadership Development Course, Reserve Component Noncommissioned Officers Course, Fort Hood, 1997.
Graduated from the Ordnance Center and School, Power Generation Equipment Repairer Course, Fort Bragg, NC, 1993. Completed training in these and other areas:

Arc Welder Repair	Gas Engine Repair	Circuit Board Repair
Exciter and Exciter Regulator Repair	Ignition Systems	Starter Motor Repair
Liquid Cooling	Fuel Circuits	Battery Charging

Completed Basic Training, U.S. Army Training Center, Fort Benning, GA, 1992.

HONORS

Certificates of Achievement; Army Commendation Medal; numerous letters of commendation.

FEDERAL RESUME OR RESUMIX

OSCAR S. THELLMAN
SSN: 123-45-6789
1110 1/2 Hay Street
Fayetteville, NC 28305
Home: (910) 483-6611
Work: (910) 483-6611
E-mail: preppub@aol.com

Vacancy Announcement Number:
Country of Citizenship: U.S.
Veterans' Preference:

LOGISTICIAN **EDUCATION**

B.A., History and a minor in Political Science, University of Kentucky, Lexington, KY, 1995.
- Was voted to the office of Junior Class Vice President.
- Financed my college education through employment with JC Penney department store.
- Held membership in Kappa Phi Theta fraternity and was elected Scholarship Chairman: devised an educational study program which resulted in improving the fraternity's average GPA and was adopted by the Honors Society for implementation campus-wide.
- In my freshman year, played on intramural flag football, softball, and soccer teams.
- Was captain of the University of Kentucky's Soccer Team during my junior and senior years.
- Was member of the Political Debate Club.
- In community service, participated in building houses with the Multicultural Community Development organization.

Graduated from W. J. Morgan High School, Lexington Kentucky, 1990.
- Played on the school basketball and rugby teams.

Skill Summary: Developing and implementing training programs; analyzing and planning operations within tight time constraints; exceptional written and verbal communication skills; mentally and physically tough; well-organized and focused; highly proficient both technically and tactically; detail oriented.

Foreign Language: Speak French and Italian.

Foreign Area Knowledge: Very well versed in world events and an avid reader of international publications covering world news. As the son of a U.S. Army Lieutenant Colonel, traveled extensively worldwide and lived in Italy from fifth-ninth grades.

Foreign Travel: Italy, France, and Kosovo.

EXPERIENCE

Jan 2004-present. Full-time. **LOGISTICIAN.** $42,000.00 per year, U.S. Army, HHC, 3-147th Chemical Battalion, Fort Rucker, AL, MAJ William Sullivan, (777) 777-7777. As Senior Logistician, supervise ten supply and logistical professionals while ensuring the more than 350 soldiers in five chemical companies are fully supplied in case of war.
- Act as the Budget Officer with control of in excess of $475,000 including holding an JPOA credit card used to make purchases outside the normal military supply channels.
- As the battalion's movement officer, plan logistics support for units from other states participating in joint exercises such as the large-

scale event Operation Anaconda. Handled planning for unit movements overseas to Afghanistan and Iraq.
- Prepare budget spreadsheets and cost estimates for a unit which is currently preparing to relocate to Fort Hood, TX with all personnel and equipment. Am overseeing all aspects of planning logistical support for this large and detailed project.
- On my own initiative, designed a new spreadsheet in Excel which transformed a budget management system lacking in adequate controls into a successful and cost-effective one.

Sep 2000 to Jan 2004. Full time. **CHEMICAL OFFICER.** $35,000.00 per year, U.S. Army, 2-229th Chemical Battalion, Fort Monroe, VA, SSG Benson K. Kinnard, (666) 666-6666. As the advisor to the battalion commander on NBC (Nuclear/Biological/Chemical) operations, supervised five NBC technicians as an S-3 action officer planning and conducting evaluations of individual unit NBC training and operations.
- Coached and mentored personnel to a prestigious honor as the "NBC Room of the Quarter" which meant being selected over 42 other departments in 14 battalions.
- Prepared and presented reports and briefings to the Commanding General of the Chemical Battalion, including Unit Status Reports (USR), Commander's Readiness Conference (CRC), and Quarterly Training Briefs (QTB).
- Qualified as a tactical operations center officer and handled this managerial responsibility during exercises and deployments in a battalion with a no-notice worldwide mission.
- Officially evaluated a **"an exceptional officer—bright, articulate, and mature,"** was cited for having joined this unit during a period when the operations tempo was high, quickly integrating myself into operations and becoming a positive force toward unit effectiveness.
- On my own initiative, revitalized the inspection program and implemented changes in training and operational procedures which included ordering new masks and protective suits.

Mar 1997 to Sep 2000. Full time. **STUDENT. Executive Development Program**, $30,000.00, Officer Basic Course, U.S. Army Chemical School, Fort Riley, KS, SFC Theodore G. Macon, (888) 888-8888. Earned high ratings in the areas of oral communication, written communication, and in contributing to the quality of group work.

Mar 1995 to Mar 1997. Part-time. **ASSISTANT PLATOON LEADER.** $6,000.00 per year, US Army, 72nd Air Defense Artillery, Fort Bliss, TX, Michael Tresvant (999) 999-9999. While attending college full-time, assisted the platoon leader and platoon sergeant in a unit with as many as 40 people.
- Provided leadership while accounting for more than $500,000 worth of property.
- Planned and carried out group and individual training.

HONORS & AWARDS	Recognized for my exemplary performance with two Good Conduct Medals, Army Achievement Medals, and a Service Ribbon, National Defense, Reserve Component.

MILITARY TRAINING

Air Movement Operations	Loadmaster Operations
Chemical Battalion Corps Budget Officer Course	Chemical Officer Basic Course
Infantry Advanced and Basic Individual Training	Hazardous Material Handlers Course

FIREARMS An Expert Marksman, am proficient with most U.S. small arms.

OTHER INFORMATION Hold a Secret security clearance.
Familiar with many popular computer operating systems and software, including full proficiency with Windows XP; Microsoft Word, Excel, Access, PowerPoint, and Outlook.

FEDERAL RESUME OR RESUMIX

JOACHIM IGNATIUS

1110 1/2 Hay Street, Fayetteville, NC 28303

preppub@aol.com

Home: 910-483-6611

LOGISTICS CHIEF

OBJECTIVE	To benefit an organization that can use a strong leader and articulate communicator with skills related to program management, project management, financial management, and personnel management.
EDUCATION	**M.S., Engineering Management,** University of Oklahoma, 2001. Excelled academically with a 3.875 GPA. **B.S., Civil Engineering,** United States Military Academy, West Point, NY, 1996. Graduated with a 3.007 GPA. Valedictorian of Southern High School, Southern, MO, 1992. **Highlights of professional training as a military officer:** Graduated from the Engineer Captain's Career Course—designed to refine leadership and managerial skills; Airborne School; Air Assault School; Sapper School; Ranger School.
COMPUTERS	Proficient with Word, Excel, and PowerPoint. Knowledge of numerous database programs.
EXPERIENCE	**ASSISTANT PROFESSOR OF MILITARY SCIENCE.** University of Ohio, Toledo, OH (2005-present). As a civilian instructor at this urban university, teach leadership skills to 20 third-year cadets who are preparing to become U.S. Army officers. Also oversee all training and operations for an ROTC organization of 100 cadets. Have used my West Point education, combat experience in Iraq, and background as an officer while grooming some of America's future military leaders.

Excelled while advancing to Captain, U.S. Army:

PROGRAM MANAGER ("Staff Officer"). Iraq and Germany (2004-2005). Tracked $250 million in construction projects and personally managed projects valued at more than $35 million as I supported all Iraqi Security Force reconstruction projects in North-Central Iraq. Interacted with Iraqi government officials, the U.S. Department of State, and Army units to identify, define, fund, contract, and construct projects for these organizations: the Iraqi Army, Department of Border Enforcement, Iraqi Police Service, the Facilities Protection Service, and the regional Iraqi Joint Coordination Centers. Projects included fire stations, courthouses, prisons, and border forts.

- **Quality control:** Took over the management of numerous projects that were forgotten or stalled. Established a system for determining project status, built effective relationships with project officers, and brought projects in on time and within budget. Instituted new methods of selecting employees which respected cultural differences; this improved the stability of the workforce at a time when high unit turnover and frequent terrorist attacks were destabilizing our progress in accomplishing goals.
- **From a performance evaluation:** "Joachim brought order and discipline to our system for allocating funding for new construction and standardized how we measure requirements and track progress. His contributions to the mission in Iraq were enormous."

GENERAL MANAGER ("Company Commander"). 9th Engineer Battalion, Iraq and Germany (2003-04). Led a 94-person mechanized combat engineer company while overseeing $20 million in assets that included a fleet of tracked and wheeled vehicles. The company was selected as "the best in the U.S. Army Europe" and the second best Army wide in the annual Engineer Competition. Was evaluated in writing as "a phenomenal leader with exemplary planning and coordination skills."

- **Leadership:** Commanded 94 soldiers in a mechanized combat engineer company during the two-week assault and occupation of Fallujah ("Operation Clean House"). Implemented initiatives that denied the enemy a supply source for Improvised Explosive Devices (IEDs). Engineered safer traffic control patterns.
- **Training management:** Developed and trained the only Iraqi Bomb Disposal Company in Baghdad. Emphasized junior leader development, and was recognized for making significant contributions in clearing ordnance and improving security through my relentless emphasis on training, preventative maintenance, and safety.
- **From a performance evaluation:** "He is at his finest in the field leading soldiers. A tough leader whose caring leadership, demanding standards, and exceptional competence resulted in a cohesive, well trained organization."

PROGRAM MANAGER & PROJECT MANAGER ("Assistant Brigade Engineer"). Afghanistan and Germany (2001-03). While stationed in Germany, deployed to Afghanistan for nine months, where I planned engineer operations, oversaw terrain analysis teams, coordinated de-mining efforts of Non-Governmental Organizations (NGOs), and acted as Officer in Charge of the Mine Action Center. Routinely interacted with United Nations civil authorities and NATO multi-national officers.

- **Personal initiative and problem solving:** While in Afghanistan, identified a deficiency in military search operations and devised a plan which utilized the Polish Army's training techniques to train four U.S. officers and 40 soldiers in skills related to personal, vehicle, route, venue, and building searches. Published an article describing this innovative training approach.
- **From a performance evaluation:** "He has a true gift for being able to quickly analyze, synthesize, and articulate complex plans. Versatile and agile, he can bounce between combat engineering subjects, terrain visualization products, peacekeeping operations, and mine action center duties without missing a beat."

ENGINEER & PROJECT MANAGER ("Assistant Brigade Engineer"). Ft. Drum, NY (2000-2001). For a combat engineer company, was involved in planning engineering projects and developing training plans. Deployed to Bosnia-Herzegovina where I directed engineering support projects and established the company's maintenance program.

SUPPORT SERVICES MANAGER ("Executive Officer"). Ft. Drum, NY (1999-2000). Planned and organized all resources required to train a 94-person company, and coordinated maintenance for a fleet of vehicles. Managed engineering projects and synchronized logistical requirements. Was in charge of planning and directing the deployment and redeployment of 94 people and multimillion-dollar assets to Bosnia.

GENERAL MANAGER ("Platoon Leader") & ENGINEER. Ft. Drum, NY (1997-99). In two separate management positions, led a 31-person combat support engineer platoon and a 27-person combat engineer platoon. Controlled a $3.5 million inventory of heavy construction equipment. Designed and managed construction projects including a parking lot and a major road upgrade.

PERSONAL   Highly intuitive problem solver with a commitment to safety and quality assurance. Recipient of numerous medals, badges, and other honors including the Bronze Star.

FEDERAL RESUME OR RESUMIX

MARVIN WILLIAMS
1110 1/2 Hay Street
Fayetteville, NC 28303
e-mail: preppub@aol.com
Home: (910) 483-6611

OBJECTIVE

I want to contribute to an organization that can use a strong leader and resourceful problem solver whose distinguished experience as a military officer includes project management, personnel supervision, strategic planning, and computer operations management.

LOGISTICS MANAGER

LANGUAGE, COMPUTERS, & CLEARANCE

Basic conversational skills in modern Arabic
Proficient with Word, PowerPoint, and Excel; WordPerfect; and Access
Top Secret/SCI security clearance, valid until 2009

EDUCATION

Master's degree in Aviation Business Administration (MBA), Embry Riddle Aeronautical University, Daytona, FL, 2003. Excelled academically with a 3.54 GPA.

- In this highly technical degree, was exposed to Critical Path Scheduling and financial analysis principles. Developed skills related to defining and implementing overall scheduling infrastructure including software selection and implementation, and gained knowledge related to computer hardware standards and network storage.
- Was extensively educated in principles related to continuous process improvement and quality assurance.

Bachelor of General Studies, Lamar University, Beaumont, TX, 1996.

Military training: As a military officer, completed the Individual Terrorism Awareness Course, Psychological Operations Officer Course, Middle East Studies, Joint Psychological Operations Course, Aviation Officers Advanced Course, Advanced Influence Course, Aircraft Survivability Equipment/Electronic Warfare, Combat Lifesaver Course, Marine Corps Combat Aidsman Course, Arabic Language, the World and Middle East Regional Studies Course, and the Jumpmaster Course.

EXPERIENCE

Advanced to the rank of Captain while serving with distinction in the U.S. Army:
DETACHMENT COMMANDER & PROJECT MANAGER. Ft. Benning, GA, and Iraq (2003-present). Controlled half a million dollars in equipment while supervising a headquarters team as well as three psychological teams with eight mid-managers and four junior employees. Planned and implemented information campaigns that contributed to smooth elections and crowd control. Demonstrated my ability to manage multiple simultaneous projects in fast-paced and constantly changing conditions.

- During the elections in Iraq, commanded the detachment which ensured the largest voter turnout of any city in Iraq with over 83% of the population.
- Established a recruiting and information plan that allowed the detachment to play a key role in recruiting, hiring, and training more than 800 new Iraqi police. Trained Iraqi security forces..

- Directed humanitarian assistance at three sites that provided aid to over 240,000 people.
- Established the first radio station in Iraq, and then performed the groundwork for the station to be turned over to the local contractor. Conducted town meetings with citizens to provide information.
- Received the prestigious Bronze Star Medal for exceptionally meritorious service during Operation Iraqi Freedom and for my contributions to the Global War on Terrorism while conducting activities during some of the heaviest fighting in Operation Iraqi Freedom.

ASSISTANT OPERATIONS MANAGER. Ft. Irwin, CA (2002-03). For an organization which trained 2,500 Special Operations soldiers annually, managed a wide range of support operations while developing course products for training Psychological Operations Officers.
- Was praised in writing as "an outstanding officer with a remarkable ability to grasp to complexities of Psychological Operations and an ability to translate concepts into tasks which lead to tangible and high quality results."

COMMANDER & CONTRACTOR LIAISON. Ft. Bragg, NC (2000-02). Was handpicked for this vital executive position. Served as one of only three Commanders in the U.S. training military aviators prior to deployment. Managed activities of 117 employees, and maintained equipment availability for a fleet of 45 vehicles and related equipment valued at $110 million. On a formal performance evaluation, was commended for "exceptional technical competence in maintenance and supply."
- Maintained an equipment operational readiness rate of over 93%. Worked closely with Raytheon and Sierra Industries to ensure that the Aircraft Survivability Equipment Trainer IV (the ASET IV system) was maintained to the highest possible readiness. Trained ASET IV operators on how to better troubleshoot the system to improve readiness. On my own initiative, identified and communicated methods of fielding better generators for the systems and identified a more reliable parts replacement systems that reduced turnaround time and downtime.
- Coordinated with Raytheon and STRICOM to identify and purchase $3.2 million in parts for ASET IV in order to establish a prescribed parts list (PLL) and improve efficiency. Coordinated with Spectrum Management NTC and China Lake in order to identify issues related to operating ASET IV in compliance with FCC and FAA.
- Trained aviation battalions, and was described as "tactically and technically a master of his trade." Earned widespread praise for my ability to plan, organize, and train soldiers in environments where I had little to no supervision. Established new employee support programs that improved morale, and led my team to compete successfully in numerous competitions.

EXECUTIVE OFFICER. Ft. Hood, TX (1999-00) Assisted the chief executive officer in training, administration, and supervision of 81 employees while overseeing maintenance and accountability of a fleet of vehicles, radio systems, and weapons systems valued at $42 million. Devised and managed a highly rated maintenance program which resulted in four successful inspections with "no faults" noted. Became known for my commitment to excellence and strong leadership. Was evaluated as "a superb trainer and administrator."

MID-LEVEL MANAGER ("PLATOON LEADER"). Ft. Bragg, NC and Korea (1997-99). Excelled in three different positions as a Platoon Leader. In one assignment, managed $6.5 million in equipment in an airborne Avenger/Stinger platoon with 18 soldiers. In another assignment, managed a 28-person Bradley Fighting Vehicle platoon in Korea, where I controlled more than $12 million in assets including trucks, vehicles, and related equipment.

PERSONAL   Received numerous medals, certificates, and ribbons for exemplary performance.

FEDERAL RESUME OR RESUMIX

DIMITRI CANAAN

1110 Hay Street, Fayetteville, NC 28303

work e-mail: preppub@aol.com

Home: (910) 483-6611

MATERIAL EXAMINER & LOGISTICS MANAGER

OBJECTIVE I want to contribute to an organization that can use a supply and logistics professional who offers expertise related to logistics administrative management along with experience in developing programs and operational guidance for the conduct of logistics liaison assistance activities.

EDUCATION **Associate degree in General Education,** Sampson Technical Community College (FTCC), Sanford, NC, 1999. Diploma in Electrical/Electronic Technology, FTCC, 1999. Certification in Automotive Mechanics, FTCC, 1986. High School Diploma from John F. Kennedy High School, Fairhaven, NY, 1974.

Professional training:

Certified ULLS-S4 Automated, FTCC, 2004. Graduate of the Defense Logistic Agency ABCs of Demilitarization Defense Supply Center, Columbus, OH, 2003. Graduate of the Army Chief of Staff Resource Management Staff Budget Officers Course, Fort Bragg, NC, 1994. Graduate of the Advance Noncommissioned Officer Candidate Course, U.S. Army Quartermaster School, Ft. Lee, VA, 1988. Graduate of the Standard Property Book System-Redesigned, U.S. Army Quartermaster School, Ft. Lee, VA, 1987. Graduate of the Unit Organizational Supply Specialist Armorer Course, U.S. Army Quartermaster School, Ft. Lee, VA, 1974.

Certifications:

Certified Forklift Operator and certified in Material Handling Equipment, rated up to 50,000 pounds. Certified ULLS-S4 Automation.

EXPERIENCE **MATERIAL EXAMINER & LOGISTICS MANAGER.** Defense Logistic Agency Defense Reutilization and Marketing Service (DRMS), Ft. Hood, TX (2001-present). Have excelled in a broad range of supply and logistics activities.

- **Supply management:** Receive materials from military and civilian Department of Defense activities and receiving agencies for disposal. Prepare the DD1348 Turn-In Document and assure correct documentation of the stock number, nomenclature, quantity, unit of issue, disposal authority code, demilitarization, and condition code.
- **Hazardous waste management:** Ensure compliance with local, state, and federal laws regarding hazardous and universal waste and hazardous waste handling, solid waste and recycling management, land disposal restrictions, and medical waste.
- **Quality assurance and inspections:** Inspect usable property for dents, broken and missing parts, and corrosion. Make decisions about acceptability. Downgrade property to scrap as appropriate, and identify scrap by visual, spark, chemical, magnetic, and other test methods. Reject items not properly identified.
- **Warehousing and property management:** After offloading property, determine special handling requirements for hazardous

materials, precious metals security, and demilitarization, and assign appropriate classification instructions for warehousing. Identify and segregate precious metals. Segregate the storage of property requiring demilitarization.

- **Transportation and logistics:** Coordinate shipment of items to various Army depots for demilitarization. Ensure that property dangerous to public health and safety is properly identified, certified, and tagged. Inspect trucks for appropriate weight and ensure that forms and tickets are signed. Expert in completing paperwork for security clearances. Have processed more than 100 security clearances. Re-palletize and relocate property as necessary. Drive up to five-ton stake and platform trucks, ½ ton pickups, and operate a variety of forklift trucks varying from 2,000-15,000 pounds up to 168 inches. Ensure proper handling to eliminate damage to cargo.
- **Safety management:** Ensure the adherence to safe work practices, and ensure that mechanical problems are fixed prior to operation.
- **Database maintenance:** After performing property inventories, enter information into the Defense Reutilization and Marketing Service Automated Information System (DAISY) database.

Honors and awards:
- Received the Joint Meritorious Unit Award, January 2006, for providing continuous logistics support to the nation's war fighters. Provided superior support to Operations Noble Eagle and Enduring Freedom while providing support to operations in the Balkans. Worked as part of team that provided 100% of the bulk fuel, troop support commodities, consumable repair parts, distribution, logistics information, disposal operations, and humanitarian support in hostile and austere environments.
- Recipient of two Meritorious Service Medals, five Army Commendation Medals, and eleven Army Achievement Medals.

INVENTORY MANAGER & FIELD MANAGER. U.S. Army, Ft. Dix, NJ (1995-00). Excelled as a senior logistics and supply consultant while providing advice and technical assistance to Ft. Bragg supported units and receiving agencies. Provided oversight for the handling, operation, and maintenance of all warehousing and material equipment at the Ft. Bragg issue site. Improved the audit trail of equipment issued to receiving units by managing the Warehouse Receipt Tracking System and was able to streamline the storage/locations of items at the fielding site. Ensured the smooth fielding of over 36 million dollars worth of systems to Fort Bragg Units. Was the Impact Credit Card Holder.

ASSET CONTROL MANAGER. U.S. Army, Ft. Bragg, NC (1989-95). Supervised assets assigned to a tactical Airborne Infantry and Military Police unit while acting as Fleet Manager for 70 military and civilian vehicles. Acted as Budget Manager of the unit's funds. Conducted inspections of subordinate units and provided technical advice. Was praised in writing as a "logistics warrior who upheld the highest tradition of excellence in support." Was the Impact Credit Card Holder. Was instrumental in the accountability of millions of dollars worth MTOE Equipment and Personal Inventories upon return from Desert Storm and Desert Shield Operations.

SUPPLY SERGEANT & LOGISTICS MANAGER. U.S. Army, Camp Casey, Korea (1983-88). Directed the supply and re-supply of the HHC 46th Support Group while maintaining a manual property book system. Managed the supply and re-supply operations of a tactical Armor and Antitank unit. Became proficient with the standard property book system (SPBS). Provided technical assistance related to equipment recordkeeping and parts supply. Became skilled in working with Prescribed Load Lists (PLLs).

PERSONAL   Outstanding references. Offer proven problem-solving ability. Work well under pressure.

FEDERAL RESUME OR RESUMIX

Emiline Worthington
1110 1/2 Hay Street
Fayetteville, NC 28305
Home Phone: 910-483-6611
Cell: 910-483-6611
Work: 910-483-6611
Work e-mail: preppub@aol.com

SSN: 000-00-0000
Date of birth: March 18. 1980
Country of Citizenship: United States
Veteran's Preference: 10 point compensable

MEDICAL SUPPLY MANAGER

12/11/2000 to present. PATIENT **ADMINISTRATION CLERK**. Ft. Hood Army Medical Center Patient Administration Division, Ft. Hood, TX 88310. 40 hours per week. GS-0303-GS4. Supervisor: Mrs. Gray Tikeley, 807-907-2279. Began in this position in 12/11/2000 and continued until 10/01/2003, at which time I was called back to active duty when my National Guard unit was reactivated and mobilized for service in Iraq. In January 2005, returned to my position with the Army Medical Center. Have earned respect for my outstanding customer service and patient relations skills as I handle multiple tasks as a receptionist, recordkeeping specialist, and clerk in a busy medical clinic providing a variety of medical specialties. Have become very knowledgeable of medical equipment, medical forms, and medical terminology. Kept accountability of records while inputting data into the CHCS software.

Office automation: Operate a computer and provide office automation support. Apply my training related to the CHCS software.

Medical recordkeeping: Assemble and maintain records in strict compliance with federal and military regulations. Maintain patient records and file results of lab tests, X-rays, EKGs, and other tests.

Written communication: Compile data for a variety of reports, and ensure correct grammar, spelling, and format. Prepare releases of information for patients.

Customer service and patient relations: Have been commended for my outgoing personality and cheerful disposition as I serve patients and work resourcefully to solve their problems.

10/01/2003 to 11/03/2004. **AUTOMATED LOGISTICS SPECIALIST.** The Army National Guard, HHC 230 SPT BN, 700 U.S. Hwy, 117 S., Goldsboro, NC 27533. 40 hours per week. Rank: SPC E-4. Supervisor: Sgt. Willie Smith, 919-272-7081. During my employment with Army Medical Center from 2000-present, was recalled to active duty for 15 months when my National Guard unit was mobilized for deployment to Iraq in support of Operation Iraqi Freedom. Worked as a Supply Clerk and Motor Pool Clerk, and resolved numerous problems related to transportation problems and fleet management issues. Kept control of publications relating to motor pool procedures. Supervised two soldiers in the absence of the supervisor.

09/10/1997 to 04/30/2000. **SUPPLY TECHNICIAN.** Cascade Diecasting, Raleigh, NC 28306. 40 hours per week. Supervisor:

Mr. Derick Marion, 336-000-0000. Utilized a computer in order to create shipping supply documents. Was responsible for hand receipts while also maintaining records and accounting for property book items. Maintained working files related to parts ordered and received. Compiled weekly inventory reports while maintaining records, performing purchasing, monitoring orders, and controlling inventory. Advanced to handle Item Manager functions as I was involved in requisitioning, receiving, and issuing supplies and equipment. Inspected equipment for serviceability.

10/15/1994 to 09/18/1995. **WAREHOUSE CLERK.** TRF Map Depot, Ft. Bragg, NC 28310. 40 hours per week. Clerk WG-4. Supervisor: Mr. Walter Ball, 910-396-4474. Received a Top Secret security clearance while working at this facility which maintained and stored maps for various units on the Ft. Bragg installation. Received U.S. government mail, and loaded/unloaded mail in proper outgoing locations.

11/12/1986 to 07/01/1994. **MATERIEL STORAGE AND HANDLING SPECIALIST.** U.S. Army, 824th Quartermaster Company (Air Drop Support), Building A6292 Pratt Street, Ft. Bragg, NC 28307. After completing Basic Training at Ft. Dix, NJ, and Advanced Individualized Training (AIT) at Ft. Lee, VA, assumed my first position in the materiel storage and handling field. Became skilled in issuing and receiving parts for vehicles, and provided outstanding customer service to all units within a battalion. Became an inhouse expert on hazardous materials (HAZMAT) procedures.

- From 1991-1994, with the C/123rd Support BN, performed Item Manager functions related to the documentation and fiscal control of non-expendable items by requisitioning, receiving, and issuing equipment such as vehicle parts. Utilized an automated property control program and applied my clerical skills in performing complex transactions.
- Edited requests for non-expendable supplies and equipment including regular, special, and high-value items. Operated word processing equipment to prepare a variety of material including correspondence, forms, reports, and other documents. Ensured proper accountability through appropriate coding. Compiled and provided budgetary data used by supervisors in forecasting and in justifying funding requests. Worked in a warehouse which contained Class IX parts, and also worked in the supply room. Became skilled in maintaining 100% accuracy of hand receipts. Utilized SAMS, SARS, and ULLS software. Was honorably discharged in 1994 as an E-4 promotable.
- From 1990-91, deployed to Saudi Arabia with the 49th Quartermaster Company, where I was involved in supply administration.

CLEARANCE | Held a Top Secret security clearance while working at TRF Map Depot, Ft. Bragg, NC.

EDUCATION | Completed one year of college course work in Early Childhood Education, Wake Technical Community College, Raleigh, NC. GPA 3.0.
Completed Primary Leadership Development Course, U.S. Army, 1993.
Graduated from Elon Senior High School, Elon, NC, 1985.

TRAINING | **Medical terminology and medical equipment training:** Trained in Composite Health Care Systems (CHCS), Womack Army Medical Center, Ft. Bragg, NC, 2000. Extensive on-the-job training related to medical terminology and medical equipment at Womack Army Medical Center, 2000-present.
Computer training: Microsoft training, 1998. Trained in the QAD system, 1997. Completed one week of training related to Enable, 1992. On-the-job training from 1991-94 related to SAMS, SARS, and ULLS computer programs used in the supply and logistics field.
Supply, logistics, and materials management training: Advanced Individualized training as a Materiel Storage and Handling Specialist, Ft. Lee, VA, 1987. Learned materiel storage handling procedures. Completed Hazardous Cargo Procedures Training, 1992.

FEDERAL RESUME OR RESUMIX

RUSSELL N. HERMANN
1110 1/2 Hay Street
Fayetteville, NC 28305
Work: (910) 483-6611
Home: (910) 483-6611
E-mail: preppub@aol.com
SSN: 000-00-0000

Country of Citizenship: U.S.
Vacancy Position:
Vacancy Announcement Number:

SUPPLY MANAGER

Notice the words in bold at the end of each job. Don't forget to mention your accomplishments and achievements!

EXPERIENCE

SUPPLY MANAGER.
Start and End Dates: Aug 2003-present. **Hours worked per week:** 40+. **Current Salary:** $37,000 **Employer's Name and Address:** Lowe's, 4933 Haynes Avenue, St. Louis, MO 56778. **Supervisor's Name and Phone Number:** Phillip Gaston, 777-777-7777. Manage $15 million in home repair equipment and supplies while prudently utilizing an Lowe's company credit card for purchases. Utilize the automated system known as to monitor spending. Manage a financial database using the ORACLE system to record purchasing transactions. Advise the General Manager on all matters related to supply while supervising, training, and counseling four junior employees. **Was praised in writing for "providing critical budgeting support for 2006 fiscal year."**

SUPPLY & WAREHOUSE SUPERVISOR.
Start and End Dates: Sep 2001-Aug 2003. **Hours worked per week:** 40+. **Salary:** $24,600. **Employer's Name and Address:** Home Depot, Warehouse Division, 63 17th Street, Parkville, MO 54335. **Supervisor's Name and Phone Number:** Andrew Malone, 666-666-6666. Was promoted to this position after working as a bookkeeper during my first year with Home Depot. Managed over $12.5 million in equipment distributed to numerous chains throughout the U.S. Trained, motivated, and supervised four employees while advising the Warehouse General Manager on all supply operations matters. **On my own initiative, developed a program that reduced fraud, waste, and abuse. Resourcefully integrated the use of illustrations, exhibits, and charts into the training process which I used for junior employees.**

Other military experience:
SUPPLY MANAGER (SUPPLY SERGEANT).
Start and End Dates: Dec 1999-Sep 2001. **Hours worked per week:** 40+. **Salary:** SSG. **Employer's Name and Address:** US Army, 7/89th Supply and Services Brigade, Fort Leonard Wood, MO 58556. **Supervisor's Name and Phone Number:** Matthew Clemmons, 555-555-5555. Accounted for $18 million in equipment, installation property, and furnishings while managing, training, and motivating two employees. Purchased and managed the receiving and distribution of class I, II, III, and V supplies which included hazardous materials, perishable items, office equipment and computers, and other materials.

Was the resident expert on all logistical matters and advised the organization's CEO. **Was commended in writing for providing flawless logistical support during the company's field training exercises, and was praised as "a key player who promotes harmony and team work." On my own initiative, improved the organization's efficiency by cross training numerous individual in supply functions. Was praised for "maintaining one of the best arms rooms in the Army."**

SUPPLY & TRANSPORTATION MANAGER (SUPPLY & TRANSPORTATION NCO).
Start and End Dates: Oct 1996-Dec 1999. **Hours worked per week:** 40+. **Salary:** SSG. **Employer's Name and Address:** US Army, 17th Support Battalion, Fort Hood, TX. **Supervisor's Name and Phone Number:** Jonathan Baker, 444-444-4444. Was handpicked to serve as the Supply and Transportation Manager for the Maintenance and Operations Coordination Center located at the Vandenberg Air Force Base in California. Managed over $650,000 in equipment while providing rigorous oversight for maintenance and inventory control in three different organizations. Became knowledgeable of both the Materials and Manufacturing Directorate and routinely utilized both information sources. **On a formal evaluation, was evaluated as "an exemplary soldier who presents a professional image and standard for all to follow."**

SUPPLY & TRANSPORTATION NCO.
Start and End Dates: Mar 1989-Oct 1996. **Hours worked per week:** 40+. **Salary:** SGT. **Employer's Name and Address:** US Army, Combat Training Center, Fort Buchanan, Puerto Rico, APO AP 04586-1894. **Supervisor's Name and Phone Number:** Samuel Rhodes, 333-333-3333. Excelled in managing the supply and transportation function for a dual service/ multi-national computer-assisted exercise training center. Thoroughly trained more than 180 armed forces and civilian contractors on military supply accountability procedures. **Was described in writing as "totally focused on customer satisfaction" and earned praise for my ability to take charge of daily situations and analyze customer needs.**

UNIT SUPPLY SPECIALIST.
Start and End Dates: Jul 1985-Mar 1989. **Hours worked per week:** 40+. **Salary:** SPC. **Employer's Name and Address:** US Army, 17th Support Battalion, Fort Hood, TX 77851. **Supervisor's Name and Phone Number:** Ellis Jackson, 111-111-1111. Performed maintenance adjustments and diagnostic certification and verification testing of assemblies and sub assemblies of LANCE, SHILLELAGH, TOW AND DRAGON weapon systems. Worked within a Supply Management Section and was commended for my attention to detail in flawlessly processing more than 745 requisitions. **Was singled out for rapid promotion ahead of my peers into supervisory roles because of my strong personal initiative and leadership.**

EDUCATION & SPECIALIZED TRAINING

Received an **Associate in Arts,** Columbia College, Columbia, MO, June 2000.
Received Certificates of Training from numerous courses including these:
* MS PowerPoint Course, 2005
* Standard Property Book System Course, 2001
* AIT Supply Services Training, 2001
* Defense Hazardous Materials Handling, 2000
* Justice and Pre-Law, Columbia College, 2000

CLEARANCE

Secret Security Clearance

LANGUAGE

Proficiently read, write, and speak Spanish. Studied Farsi.

COMPUTERS

Strong working knowledge of software including Word, Excel, and PowerPoint.

FEDERAL RESUME OR RESUMIX

ZORAIDA MADERA

1110 ½ Hay Street
Fayetteville, NC 28305
Phone: (910) 483-6611
Fax: (910) 483-2439
Email: preppub@aol.com
SSN: 012-34-5678

Country of Citizenship: U.S.
Vacancy Position:
Vacancy Announcement Number:

SUPPLY MANAGER (SUPPLY SERGEANT)	**EXPERIENCE**	**SUPPLY MANAGER (SUPPLY SERGEANT).** Start and End Dates: May 2005-present. Hours worked per week: 40+. Current Salary: SSG. Employer's Name and Address: AR-PERSCOM W/DY 434th Transportation Co., Fort Bragg, NC. Supervisor's Name and Phone Number: Michael Hoover, (910) 483-6611. Managed $20 million in equipment while prudently utilizing an IMPAC credit card for supplies and equipment. Utilized the automated system known as Unit Level Logistics Systems (ULLS-S4). Advised the organization's commander on all matters related to supply and logistics while supervising, training, and counseling four junior employees. **Was praised in writing for "providing critical logistical support for Readiness Training Command 2006."**

SUPPLY MANAGER (SUPPLY SERGEANT). Start and End Dates: May 2003-April 2004. Hours worked per week: 40+. Salary: SSG. Employer's Name and Address: 434th Transportation Company, Fort Bragg, NC. Supervisor's Name and Phone Number: Oliver Twitchell, (910) 483-6611. Managed over $30 million in equipment which belonged to a transportation company. Managed the organization's IMPAC credit card for supplies and equipment. Maintained property under the Standard Property Book System (SPBS). Trained, motivated, and supervised four employees while advising the organization's CEO on all logistical matters. On my own initiative, developed a program that reduced fraud, waste, and abuse. **Resourcefully integrated the use of illustrations, exhibits, and charts into the training process which I developed for junior employees.**

SUPPLY MANAGER (SUPPLY SERGEANT). Start and End Dates: July 2001-Apr 2003. Hours worked per week: 40+. Salary: SSG. Employer's Name and Address: 17th Transportation Company, Fort Campbell, KY. Supervisor's Name and Phone Number: Richard Mitchell, (910) 483-6611. Accounted for $26 million in equipment, installation property, and furnishings while managing, training, and motivating two employees. Purchased and managed the receiving and distribution of class I, II, III, and V supplies which included hazardous materials, perishable items, office equipment and computers, and other materials. Was the resident expert on all logistical matters and advised the organization's CEO. Was commended in writing for providing flawless logistical support during the company's field training exercises, and was praised as "a key player who promotes harmony and team work." **On my own initiative, improved the organization's efficiency by cross training numerous individual in supply functions. Was praised for "maintaining one of the best arms rooms in the Army."**

SUPPLY & TRANSPORTATION MANAGER (SUPPLY & TRANSPORTATION NCO). Start and End Dates: Nov 2000-June 2001. Hours worked per week: 40+. Salary: SGT. Employer's Name and Address: Preparation Center, Fort Campbell, KY. Supervisor's Name and Phone Number: John Johnston, (910) 483-6611. Was handpicked to serve as the Supply and Transportation Manager for a combined USAREUR and US Air Forces in Europe (USAFE) simulation center. Managed over $800,000 in equipment while providing rigorous oversight for maintenance and inventory control in three different organizations. **Became knowledgeable of both the Army and the Air Force Supply Systems since I routinely utilized both systems. On a formal evaluation, was evaluated as "an exemplary soldier who presents a professional image and standard for all to follow."**

SUPPLY & TRANSPORTATION NCO. Start and End Dates: July 1997-October 2000. Hours worked per week: 40+. Salary: SGT. Employer's Name and Address: Preparation Center, Fort Campbell, KY. Supervisor's Name and Phone Number: John Johnston, (910) 483-6611. Excelled in managing the supply and transportation function for a dual service/ multi-national computer-assisted exercise training center. Thoroughly trained more than 250 Army, Air Force, and civilian contractors on Army supply accountability procedures. **Was described in writing as "totally focused on customer satisfaction" and earned praise for my ability to take charge of daily situations and analyze customer needs.**

UNIT SUPPLY SPECIALIST. Start and End Dates: April 1994-May 1996. Hours worked per week: 40+. Salary: SPC. Employer's Name and Address: Camp Zama, Japan. Supervisor's Name and Phone Number: Adam Easton, (910) 483-6611. Received both the Army Commendation Medal and the Army Achievement Medal while serving as a Supply Specialist for the Equipment Maintenance Branch. Worked within a Supply Management Section and was commended for my attention to detail in flawlessly processing more than 900 requisitions. **Was singled out for rapid promotion ahead of my peers into supervisory roles because of my strong personal initiative and leadership.**

EDUCATION & TRAINING	Received an **Associate in Arts**, Central Michigan University, May 1993. Received Certificates of Training from numerous courses including these: • Operator Training for Unit Level Logistics Systems-S4 (ULLS-S4), 2004. • MS PowerPoint Course, 2004. • Standard Property Book System Course, 2004. • Active Guard Reserve Entry Training, 2003. • Defense Hazardous Materials Handling. 2003. • Physical Security Officer Training Program, 2004 and 2003. • IMPAC Purchase Card Training, 2003. • Unit Alcohol Drug Coordinator and Breathalyzer Operator Certification, 2002.
CLEARANCE	Secret Security Clearance and an Entrance National Agency Check (ENTNAC).
LANGUAGE	Proficiently read, write, and speak Spanish.
COMPUTERS	Strong working knowledge of software including Microsoft Word, Excel, PowerPoint.
HONORS	Recipient of numerous awards including the Air Force Organizational Excellence Award and the Army Superior Unit Award. Named NCO OF THE QUARTER, 2004 and 1997.

EXAMPLE OF A KSA

PAIGE L. FORBES

SSN: 000-00-0000

SUPPLY CLERK, GS-05 ANNOUNCEMENT #XYZ123

**SUPPLY CLERK,
GS-05
Announcement #XYZ123
KSA #1**

KSA #1: Ability to communicate orally.

Overview of my work experience: In the jobs described below, I have received a **Certificate of Outstanding Performance** each and every year from 2003-present. I have been cited each year for **performing all duties in an outstanding manner.** I have been commended on numerous occasions for my outstanding oral communication skills as well as for excellent problem-solving, negotiating, and decision-making skills. Through my ability to communicate tactfully and graciously, to explain complex technical issues, and to train and motivate other employees, I have earned a reputation as an outstanding communicator in every aspect of my job.

In my current position as Supply Clerk, NF-2, I communicate with customers, vendors, and others in the process of performing my job. After I review, analyze, and prepare a wide variety of documentation and paperwork, I communicate orally with vendors, customers, and employees. I communicate orally with new or junior employees while training them to utilize a variety of data systems and using personal computers, I operate a computer with Microsoft Word Software, Time Management Labor System software, and Microsoft Office software to include Word, Excel, PowerPoint, and Access. One of my responsibilities is to maintain the internal supply budget on Excel software and prepare flyers for the MWR Auction on PowerPoint. Furthermore, I maintain and prepare all NAF time cards using the Time Management Labor System software. In addition, I maintain the annual budget for Supply & Warehouse and the Recycling Section, and I use the internal software (NAF Financial Management Budget System). My knowledge of computer programs enables me to type all performance appraisals for all employees within the section, to type memoranda for the Chief, Technical Services Branch, to maintain and print all NAF time cards, to maintain annual budget for Supply and Warehouse and Recycling Section and Forward to Budget Office. I have operated computers with Microsoft Word software to maintain the NAF property book, adding property when received, deleting property whoever it is turned in or missing.

Notice how often the communication KSA comes up.

In my position as Personnel Clerk, I communicated orally with potential employees after receiving applications and briefed them about positions available. I communicated extensively through telephone conversations with Activity Managers to coordinate pickup of referrals and selection of new employees. I also telephoned applicants when they were accepted for the position.

Knowledge and Training related to this KSA:
- In 2005 I took a Microsoft Office course at Galveston Technical Community College. This course enabled me to use Word, Excel, PowerPoint, and Access to type a variety of material and documents for the Supply and Warehouse Section.
- In 2001 I took 116 hours of IBM Operations at Western Texas Technical College.
- In 2000 I took a NAF Financial Management Budget System Course at Fort Hood, TX. This course gave me the knowledge, skills and ability to maintain the NAF budget for Supply and Warehouse, and the Recycling Section.

PAIGE L. FORBES

SSN: 000-00-0000

SUPPLY CLERK, GS-05 ANNOUNCEMENT #XYZ123

KSA #2: Ability to communicate in writing.

Overview of my work experience: In the jobs described below, I have received a **Certificate of Outstanding Performance** each and every year from 2003-present and have been cited each year for **performing all duties in an outstanding manner.** I have been commended on numerous occasions for my ability to communicate in writing in a concise, articulate, and effective manner. I have earned a reputation as an excellent writer.

In my current position as Supply Clerk, NF-2, I communicate extensively in writing in the process of reviewing, analyzing, and preparing a wide variety of documentation and paperwork while assuring that paperwork is always within guidelines established by regulatory authorities and other authorities. In creating documents for written communication and transmission, I maintain, update, and utilize a variety of data systems and using personal computers. I operate a computer with Time Management Labor System software and Microsoft Office software to include Word, Excel, PowerPoint, and Access. I communicate in writing by composing and typing all correspondence for Supply and Warehouse Section. While communicating in writing, I demonstrate my outstanding knowledge of English grammar and my mastery of spelling. One of my responsibilities is to communicate in writing as I present my analysis of the supply budget on Excel software and as I prepare flyers for the MWR Auction on PowerPoint. Furthermore, I maintain and prepare all NAF time cards using the Time Management Labor System software. In addition, I maintain the annual budget for Supply & Warehouse and the Recycling Section and I use the internal software (NAF Financial Management Budget System). My writing skills combined with my knowledge of computer programs enables me to write and edit all performance appraisals for all employees within the section; to type memoranda for the Chief, Technical Services Branch; to maintain and print all NAF time cards, and to maintain written correspondence related to the annual budget for Supply and Warehouse and Recycling Section and Forward to Budget Office.

Sometimes the "oral" and "in writing" skills are joined in one KSA; sometimes they are separate as they are here.

Knowledge and Training related to this KSA:

- In 2005 I took a Microsoft Office course at Galveston Technical Community College. This course enabled me to use Word, Excel, PowerPoint, and Access to type a variety of material and documents for the Supply and Warehouse Section.
- In 2001 I took 116 hours of IBM Operations at Western Texas Technical College. This refined my knowledge, skills, and abilities in operating a computer.
- In 2000 I took a NAF Financial Management Budget System Course at Fort Hood, TX. This course gave me the knowledge, skills and ability to maintain the NAF budget for Supply and Warehouse, and the Recycling Section.
- In 1999 I took 33 hours of word processing with Word at Galveston Technical Community College. This enabled me to type documents and material using Word.

EXAMPLES OF KSAs

CURTIS L. STRICKLAND

SSN: 000-00-0000

SUPPLY SPECIALIST, GS-06/07 ANNOUNCEMENT #XYZ123

KSA 1. Ability to perform SARSS-1 catalog research and file management functions.

In my present position as General Supply Specialist (since 5/2002) for a major civilian contracting firm, I am the interface between the ULLS-A/G (Unit Level Logistics System Air/Ground) and the SARSS-1 system for my unit and am the "resident expert" in solving problems between the systems.

- Establish and maintain an accurate, detailed, and current log sheet for all SARSS-generated Supply Status Reports (SSRs)
- Ensure that logsheets for SARSS-generated SSRs include all of the following information:
    - SSR voucher number
    - Determination of whether or not causative research is required
    - Number of line items listed on the SSR
    - Total and adjusted gains to date
    - Total and adjusted losses to date
    - Total and adjusted dollar value to date
    - Date submitted for review or approval and date returned
- Establish, update, and maintain and SSR suspense file for all SSRs currently in progress, adding all documentation to the file as research is conducted.
- Ensure that the access roster to the SSR suspense file is strictly maintained to maximize document control.

While serving as an Operations NCO (1996-2002) at MMC level, I functioned as Training NCO. Conducted both hands-on and formal classroom instruction for hundreds of people on the operation of the SARSS-1 system, which encompassed input-output, daily/monthly transactions, document history inquiries, and current trends and problems with the system.

Education and training:

Bachelor of Arts in Business Administration, Morgan State University, Baltimore, MD, 2002. Completed extensive training which included course work completed at the U.S. Army Quartermaster School:

Commissary Management
Senior Supply/Services Sergeant
Supply NCO Advanced Course
DSU/GSU Mechanized Stock Control
Division Logistics Systems
Unit and Organizational Supply Basic Course
Basic Supply NCO Course
Aircraft Repair Parts Specialist
Stock Control and Accounting Specialist

Additional course work included NCO Logistics Program, TRANE/Bryant Decentralized Automated Service Support System, and the U.S. Army Basic Leadership Course.

KSA 2. Provide technical advice on SARSS-1 procedures in compliance with regulatory requirements.

In my present position as General Supply Specialist (since 5/2002) for a major civilian contracting firm, I am the interface between the ULLS-A/G (Unit Level Logistics System Air/Ground) and the SARSS-1 system for my unit and am the "resident expert" in solving problems between the systems.

- Establish and maintain an accurate, detailed, and current log sheet for all SARSS-generated Supply Status Reports (SSRs)
- Ensure that logsheets for SARSS-generated SSRs include all of the following information:
  - SSR voucher number
  - Determination of whether or not causative research is required (
  - Number of line items listed on the SSR
  - Total and adjusted gains to date
  - Total and adjusted losses to date
  - Total and adjusted dollar value to date
  - Date submitted for review or approval and date returned
- Establish, update, and maintain and SSR suspense file for all SSRs currently in progress, adding all documentation to the file as research is conducted.
- Ensure that the access roster to the SSR suspense file is strictly maintained to maximize document control.

While serving as an Operations NCO (1996-2002) at MMC level, I functioned as Training NCO. Conducted both hands-on and formal classroom instruction for hundreds of people on the operation of the SARSS-1 system, which encompassed input-output, daily/monthly transactions, document history inquiries, and current trends and problems with the system.

Education and training:

Bachelor of Arts in Business Administration, Morgan State University, Baltimore, MD, 2002. Completed extensive training which included course work completed at the U.S. Army Quartermaster School:

Commissary Management
Senior Supply/Services Sergeant
Supply NCO Advanced Course
DSU/GSU Mechanized Stock Control
Division Logistics Systems
Unit and Organizational Supply Basic Course
Basic Supply NCO Course
Aircraft Repair Parts Specialist
Stock Control and Accounting Specialist

Additional course work included NCO Logistics Program, TRANE/Bryant Decentralized Automated Service Support System, and the U.S. Army Basic Leadership Course.

EXAMPLES OF KSAs

KENNETH S. MOSLEY

SSN: 000-00-0000

SUPPLY SUPERVISOR, GS-07/11 ANNOUNCEMENT #XYZ123

KSA #1: Knowledge of Impact of DLA Logistical Support to Military Services Readiness.

With more than 18 years in the military, I have extensive knowledge of the importance of effective logistical support operations to the readiness of military services. DLA Logistics Support Programs are responsible for providing military operations with the materiel necessary for them to function at a high state of readiness. I have held logistics management positions where I oversaw logistics support for day-to-day operations as well as for troop movements and deployments, and I was often handpicked as a consultant for special projects.

In my current position as a Supervisory General Supply Specialist since 06/05, I apply my knowledge of the impact of DLA logistical support while managing, directing, and implementing supply and services functions to military organizations throughout the U.S. and the Middle East. Supervising 95 members of a multinational workforce, I manage activities which include subsistence requisitioning, transportation, storage, accountability, and the preparation of materials for storage, transportation, and utilization. In addition to planning and directing various financial management and operational programs for the Supply and Services Division, I provide logistical support diverse facilities. These include the Central Issue Facility, laundry, Installation Property Book Office, Self Service Supply Center, graves registration, retail fuel operations, and organizational property book operations.

While serving as Supply/Maintenance Management Officer for the 14th Support Battalion from 12/03-05/05, I was entrusted with a project for which I planned, organized, and directed the closeout of an Army Area Supply Depot for Class II, III (P), VII, and IX supplies during a down-sizing. **A main objective was to complete the downsizing without compromising the level of service or the combat readiness of customer organizations.** To accomplish this I transferred all on-hand stock to another supply point and set up a Central Receiving Point which in still in operation. I developed the internal and external Standard Operating Procedures as well as the structure for the transportation network which supported the operation. Prepared and presented briefings to general-level officers and gained their direct approval for my plan of action. **Despite the complexity of the project, supply support continued without interruption, combat readiness was not compromised, and more than 25 positions were phased out at a savings of $1.3 million annually.**

As a Supervisory Inventory Management Specialist, from 04/00 until 11/03, I directed day-to-day operations in a Commodity Management Branch that supported military operations throughout the region. I supervised 20 Item Managers to ensure that they maintained, adjusted, and established requisition objectives, retention levels, maintenance work requests, and the proper disposition of serviceable and unserviceable assets.

Due to my extensive knowledge of logistical support, I was handpicked as a Branch Chief for a Material Management Center in Afghanistan from 6/95-03/00. While supervising 20 employees, I directed and approved local purchase activities for procurement of perishable and semi-perishable food products in support of the U.S. military presence in Bosnia. I was selected for this position on the basis of my reputation for expertise in analyzing, managing, coordinating, and procuring any type of product including subsistence.

I was selected because of my thorough understanding of supply management logistical support functions for what was essentially a top-level consulting/staff position as a Storage Specialist in a Defense Logistics Agency Stockpile Depot (8/94 to 5/95). I analyzed the effectiveness of existing supply, procurement, transportation, cataloguing, provisioning, storage, and distribution procedures. Conducted formal and informal management studies to evaluate overall performance of systems and to identify improvements.

While serving as Support Supply Technician and Accountable Officer, I oversaw logistics management, supervision, and coordination for all sections of the largest non-divisional Class II, III, IV, and VII supply point in Hawaii from 5/91-7/94. In an operation which exceeded $75 million annually in supplies, I oversaw activities ranging from personnel supervision, to procurement, to the management of the receipt, storage, and issuance of supplies to supported customers. I obtained required supplies through standard military procedures as well as from local sources.

Education and Training Related to this KSA:
In addition to earning my Bachelor of Arts degree from Eastern Michigan University in Ypsilanti (2002) and an Associate of Arts degree from Henry Ford Community College (7/01), have also attended the following colleges and universities: Brigham Young University, Laie, Hawaii, 1999, nine semester hours; McNeese State University, Lake Charles, LA, 1997, nine semester hours; Military training programs I completed included the following:

The Contracting Officer Representative Course and a Management and Leadership workshop, US Army Quartermaster School

Introduction to Management in Logistics and Introduction to Defense Financial Management correspondence courses

Tactical Army Combat Service Support computer System/Standard Army Retail Supply System-1 (TACCS/SARSS-1) Supervisors Workshops

Logistics Applications Automated Marking and Symbols (LOGMARS)

Decentralized Automated Service Support Systems (DAS-3)

Direct Support Unit Standard Supply System (DS-4) Management Course

Division Logistics Property Book Management Course

KSA #2: Knowledge of Supply Management Logistical Support Functions such as Supply, Procurement, Transportation, Cataloguing, Provisioning, Storage, and Distribution.

In my current position as a Supervisory General Supply Specialist since 6/05, I apply my knowledge of supply management logistical support functions while managing, directing, and implementing supply and services functions throughout the U.S. and the Middle East. With approximately 95 members of a multinational workforce under my supervision, I manage a wide range of activities which include subsistence requisitioning, transportation, storage, accountability, and the preparation of materials for storage, transportation, and utilization. While planning and directing financial management and operational programs for the Supply and Services Division, I oversee logistical support functions such as supply, procurement, transportation, cataloguing, provisioning, storage, and distribution. I oversee these activities in areas as diverse as the Central Issue Facility, laundry, Installation Property Book Office, Self Service Supply Center, graves registration, retail fuel operations, and organizational property book operations.

From 04/00 until 05/05 as a Supervisory Inventory Management Specialist, directed day-to-day operations in a Commodity Management Branch. Supervised 20 Item Managers and applied my knowledge while seeing that they maintained, adjusted, and established requisition objectives, retention levels, maintenance work requests, and the proper disposition of serviceable and unserviceable assets.

On the basis of my knowledge of logistical support functions, I was handpicked as a Branch Chief for a Material Management Center in Afghanistan from 6/95-03/00, supervising as many as 20 employees while directing and approving local purchase activities related to procuring perishable and semi-perishable food products. I was selected because of my reputation for expertise in analyzing, managing, coordinating, and procuring any type of product including subsistence. I continuously directed, coordinated, and evaluated the findings of management studies which had been designed to evaluate performance and identify system improvements.

Due to my extensive knowledge of supply management logistical support functions, I was selected for what was essentially a top-level consulting/staff position as a Storage Specialist in a Defense Logistics Agency Stockpile Depot (8/94 to 5/95). I analyzed the effectiveness of existing supply, procurement, transportation, cataloguing, provisioning, storage, and distribution procedures, conducting formal and informal management studies to evaluate overall performance of systems and to identify improvements. By troubleshooting problems with existing systems and suggesting solutions I was able to increase the level and quality of assistance available to customers and effect more efficient service delivery.

On another occasion, from April 1991-November 1992 I took over as Supply Management Officer at a time when the operation was plagued with chronic backlogs of maintenance jobs, with some jobs more than 90 days late. The backlogs, as well as serious malfunctions and shortages in the supply system which caused stockouts and downtime, were having a strong negative impact on military services readiness and causing extreme customer dissatisfaction. I planned and directed assigned missions of Area V retail supply, supervising and guiding the work of 125 warehouse personnel, including eight supply managers and four maintenance managers. To deal with this situation, I analyzed supply pipeline problems, production schedules, shop stock levels, and the excess repair parts program in order to develop more effective methods of managing these areas. Prioritized various projects, including requirements determination, maintenance operations, forecasting, procurement, and financial management. Delegated tasks to the supervisor who was most capable of quickly and effectively dealing with a given situation. Maintained open lines of communication between my office and personnel at all levels. Provided "leadership by example" and conducted myself in a reasonable and consistent manner, ensuring that all employees were treated fairly by all levels of management. Gained the trust and respect of warehouse, maintenance and support personnel. I improved the profitability of Area V retail supply activities while reducing stockouts and inventory carrying costs, as well as increasing customer satisfaction and service delivery. By cutting costs while increasing overall efficiency, was able to obtain the maximum benefit from available human, physical, and financial resources.

Education and Training Related to this KSA:

In addition to earning my Bachelor of Arts degree from Eastern Michigan University in Ypsilanti (2002) and an Associate of Arts degree from Henry Ford Community College (7/01), have also attended the following colleges and universities: Brigham Young University, Laie, Hawaii, 1999, nine semester hours; McNeese State University, Lake Charles, LA, 1997, nine semester hours; Military training programs I completed included the following:

The Contracting Officer Representative Course and a Management and Leadership
   workshop, US Army Quartermaster School
Introduction to Management in Logistics and Introduction to Defense Financial
   Management correspondence courses
Tactical Army Combat Service Support computer System/Standard Army Retail
   Supply System-1 (TACCS/SARSS-1) Supervisors Workshops
Logistics Applications Automated Marking and Symbols (LOGMARS)
Decentralized Automated Service Support Systems (DAS-3)
Direct Support Unit Standard Supply System (DS-4) Management Course
Division Logistics Property Book Management Course

KENNETH S. MOSLEY

SSN: 000-00-0000

SUPPLY SUPERVISOR, GS-07/11 ANNOUNCEMENT #XYZ123

KSA #3: Knowledge of DoD Major Supply Program Goals, Objectives, Work Processes, and Administrative Operations.

Throughout my extensive career in military and civilian logistics support, I was frequently placed in "hot-seat" management jobs in charge of logistics management and was often handpicked to act as a consultant for special projects. In these roles, I have consistently demonstrated my knowledge of DoD major supply program goals, and objectives, as well as of work processes and administrative operations.

From February 2001 to August 2001, I was asked to assume leadership of the Armament & Combat Vehicle Division for the Middle Eastern Materiel Management Center at a time when this center was experiencing low morale, lagging productivity, and unacceptable customer support levels. I was selected for this position because of my reputation as an effective leader and innovative problem-solver. As Chief of the Armament and Combat Vehicle Division, (GS-10), I established free and open lines of communication among Management Center command staff, local Bosnian National employees, and U.S. military personnel. While emphasizing a Total Quality Approach to management, I established a dialog which enabled me to develop a team approach to problem analysis and problem solving. Through retraining of existing staff; providing fair, consistent supervision; and the implementation of a viable awards program, I improved productivity throughout the organization. I designed and implemented procedures to reward to excellent performers while offering firm but tactful counseling for marginal performance. Utilized group activities such as Division meetings, Division picnics, and other in-house promotions to foster a team atmosphere and strengthened the bond between co-workers. Within a few weeks, I had quickly gained the respect of Division personnel and improved the morale and productivity of Management Center employees. Productivity nearly doubled, customer satisfaction soared, and the general attitude of the Center's staff reflected a confident, competent, and professional work force. The 13 Bosnian managers, master sergeant, and two Bosnian junior employees I managed significantly improved their ability to efficiently handle the requisitioning, redistribution, and excess turn-in of assets valued at more than $425,000.

On another occasion, from April 1991-November 1992, took over as Supply Management Officer at a time when the operation was plagued with chronic backlogs of maintenance jobs, with some jobs more than 90 days late, as well as serious malfunctions and shortages in the supply system causing stockouts, downtime, and extreme customer dissatisfaction. As Supply Management Officer, planned and directed assigned missions of Area V retail supply, supervising and guiding the work of 125 warehouse personnel, including eight supply managers and four maintenance managers. Analyzed supply pipeline problems, production schedules, shop stock levels, and excess repair parts program in order to develop more effective methods of managing these areas. Prioritized various projects, including requirements determination, maintenance operations, forecasting, procurement, and financial management. Delegated tasks to the supervisor who was most capable of quickly and effectively dealing with a given situation. Maintained open lines of communication between my office and personnel at all levels. Gained the trust and respect of warehouse, maintenance and support personnel.

Improved the profitability of Area V retail supply activities while reducing stockouts, decreasing inventory carrying costs, and boosting customer satisfaction. Reduced costs while increasing overall efficiency, obtaining the maximum benefit from available human, physical, and financial resources.

As a Supply/Maintenance Management Officer for the 14th Support Battalion, I was asked to plan, organize, and direct the close-out of an Army Area Supply Depot for Class II, III (P), IV, VII, and IX supplies in a Theater downsizing initiative, without compromising the service to or Combat Readiness of existing customers. To comply with Theater downsizing initiatives, planned and executed the closure of a Major Supply Point while assuring uninterrupted service to all customers. Planned and directed all aspects of the transfer of all on-hand stocks to another Army Supply Point and set up a Central Receiving Point that is still in operation. Developed internal and external Standing Operating Procedures and organized the structure of the transportation network to support the operations in an armistice and combat environment. Planned, organized, and directed briefings for General Level Officers on my planning matrix for the project and gained direct approval to execute this plan. Assured careful planning and implementation of procedures used to transport HAZMAT materials. Resolved numerous problems and overcame multiple complexities in directing this major project under tight deadlines in such a way that Combat Readiness was not compromised. Over 25 manned positions were phased out, resulting in a $1.3 million savings per year, without negatively impacting the level of service provided to the Customers or degrading their Combat Readiness. Millions of dollars in assets were transferred safely, a new service center was opened, and an inefficient site was closed with no loss of customer service.

Education and Training Related to this KSA:
In addition to earning my Bachelor of Arts degree from Eastern Michigan University in Ypsilanti (2002) and an Associate of Arts degree from Henry Ford Community College (7/01), have also attended the following colleges and universities: Brigham Young University, Laie, Hawaii, 1999, nine semester hours; McNeese State University, Lake Charles, LA, 1997, nine semester hours; Military training programs I completed included the following:

the Contracting Officer Representative Course and a Management and Leadership workshop, US Army Quartermaster School
Introduction to Management in Logistics and Introduction to Defense Financial Management correspondence courses
Tactical Army Combat Service Support computer System/Standard Army Retail Supply System-1 (TACCS/SARSS-1) Supervisors Workshops
Logistics Applications Automated Marking and Symbols (LOGMARS)
Decentralized Automated Service Support Systems (DAS-3)
Direct Support Unit Standard Supply System (DS-4) Management Course
Division Logistics Property Book Management Course

ABOUT THE EDITOR

Anne McKinney holds an MBA from the Harvard Business School and a BA in English from the University of North Carolina at Chapel Hill. A noted public speaker, writer, and teacher, she is the senior editor for PREP's business and career imprint, which bears her name. Early titles in the Anne McKinney Career Series (now called the Real-Resumes Series) published by PREP include: *Resumes and Cover Letters That Have Worked, Resumes and Cover Letters That Have Worked for Military Professionals, Government Job Applications and Federal Resumes, Cover Letters That Blow Doors Open,* and *Letters for Special Situations.* Her career titles and how-to resume-and-cover-letter books are based on the expertise she has acquired in 25 years of working with job hunters. Her valuable career insights have appeared in publications of the "Wall Street Journal" and other prominent newspapers and magazines.

PREP Publishing Order Form

You may purchase our titles from your favorite bookseller! Or send a check, money order or your credit card number for the total amount, plus $4.00 for postage and handling, to PREP, 1110 1/2 Hay Street, Suite C, Fayetteville, NC 28305. You may also order our titles on our website at www.prep-pub.com and feel free to e-mail us at preppub@aol.com or call 910-483-6611 with your questions or concerns.

Name: _____

Address: _____

E-mail address:_____

Payment Type: ☐ Check/Money Order   ☐ Visa   ☐ MasterCard

Credit Card Number: _____ Expiration Date: _____

Put a check beside the items you are ordering:

☐ $16.95—REAL-RESUMES FOR RESTAURANT, FOOD SERVICE & HOTEL JOBS. Anne McKinney, Editor

☐ $16.95—REAL-RESUMES FOR MEDIA, NEWSPAPER, BROADCASTING & PUBLIC AFFAIRS JOBS. Anne McKinney, Editor

☐ $16.95—REAL-RESUMES FOR RETAILING, MODELING, FASHION & BEAUTY JOBS. Anne McKinney, Editor

☐ $16.95—REAL-RESUMES FOR HUMAN RESOURCES & PERSONNEL JOBS. Anne McKinney, Editor

☐ $16.95—REAL-RESUMES FOR MANUFACTURING JOBS. Anne McKinney, Editor

☐ $16.95—REAL-RESUMES FOR AVIATION & TRAVEL JOBS. Anne McKinney, Editor

☐ $16.95—REAL-RESUMES FOR POLICE, LAW ENFORCEMENT & SECURITY JOBS. Anne McKinney, Editor

☐ $16.95—REAL-RESUMES FOR SOCIAL WORK & COUNSELING JOBS. Anne McKinney, Editor

☐ $16.95—REAL-RESUMES FOR CONSTRUCTION JOBS. Anne McKinney, Editor

☐ $16.95—REAL-RESUMES FOR FINANCIAL JOBS. Anne McKinney, Editor

☐ $16.95—REAL-RESUMES FOR COMPUTER JOBS. Anne McKinney, Editor

☐ $16.95—REAL-RESUMES FOR MEDICAL JOBS. Anne McKinney, Editor

☐ $16.95—REAL-RESUMES FOR TEACHERS. Anne McKinney, Editor

☐ $16.95—REAL-RESUMES FOR CAREER CHANGERS. Anne McKinney, Editor

☐ $16.95—REAL-RESUMES FOR STUDENTS. Anne McKinney, Editor

☐ $16.95—REAL-RESUMES FOR SALES. Anne McKinney, Editor

☐ $16.95—REAL ESSAYS FOR COLLEGE AND GRAD SCHOOL. Anne McKinney, Editor

☐ $25.00—RESUMES AND COVER LETTERS THAT HAVE WORKED. McKinney, Editor

☐ $25.00—RESUMES AND COVER LETTERS THAT HAVE WORKED FOR MILITARY PROFESSIONALS. McKinney, Editor

☐ $25.00—RESUMES AND COVER LETTERS FOR MANAGERS. McKinney, Editor

☐ $25.00—GOVERNMENT JOB APPLICATIONS AND FEDERAL RESUMES: Federal Resumes, KSAs, Forms 171 and 612, and Postal Applications. McKinney, Editor

☐ $25.00—COVER LETTERS THAT BLOW DOORS OPEN. McKinney, Editor

☐ $25.00—LETTERS FOR SPECIAL SITUATIONS. McKinney, Editor

☐ $16.95—REAL-RESUMES FOR NURSING JOBS. McKinney, Editor

☐ $16.95—REAL-RESUMES FOR AUTO INDUSTRY JOBS. McKinney, Editor

☐ $24.95—REAL KSAs--KNOWLEDGE, SKILLS & ABILITIES--FOR GOVERNMENT JOBS. McKinney, Editor

☐ $24.95—REAL RESUMIX AND OTHER RESUMES FOR FEDERAL GOVERNMENT JOBS. McKinney, Editor

☐ $24.95—REAL BUSINESS PLANS AND MARKETING TOOLS ... Samples to use in your business. McKinney, Editor

☐ $16.95—REAL-RESUMES FOR ADMINISTRATIVE SUPPORT, OFFICE & SECRETARIAL JOBS. Anne McKinney, Editor

☐ $16.95—REAL-RESUMES FOR FIREFIGHTING JOBS. Anne McKinney, Editor

☐ $16.95—REAL-RESUMES FOR JOBS IN NONPROFIT ORGANIZATIONS. Anne McKinney, Editor

☐ $16.95—REAL-RESUMES FOR SPORTS INDUSTRY JOBS. Anne McKinney, Editor

☐ $16.95—REAL-RESUMES FOR LEGAL & PARALEGAL JOBS. Anne McKinney, Editor

☐ $16.95—REAL-RESUMES FOR ENGINEERING JOBS. Anne McKinney, Editor

☐ $22.95—REAL-RESUMES FOR U.S. POSTAL SERVICE JOBS. Anne McKinney, Editor

☐ $16.95—REAL-RESUMES FOR REAL ESTATE & PROPERTY MANAGEMENT JOBS. Anne McKinney, Editor

☐ $16.95—REAL-RESUMES FOR SUPPLY & LOGISTICS JOBS. Anne McKinney, Editor

_____ TOTAL ORDERED (add $4.00 for shipping and handling)